# Chevrolet Small-Block

Revised Edition

## PARTS INTERCHANGE MANUAL

Ed Staffel

I0803398

S-A DESIGN

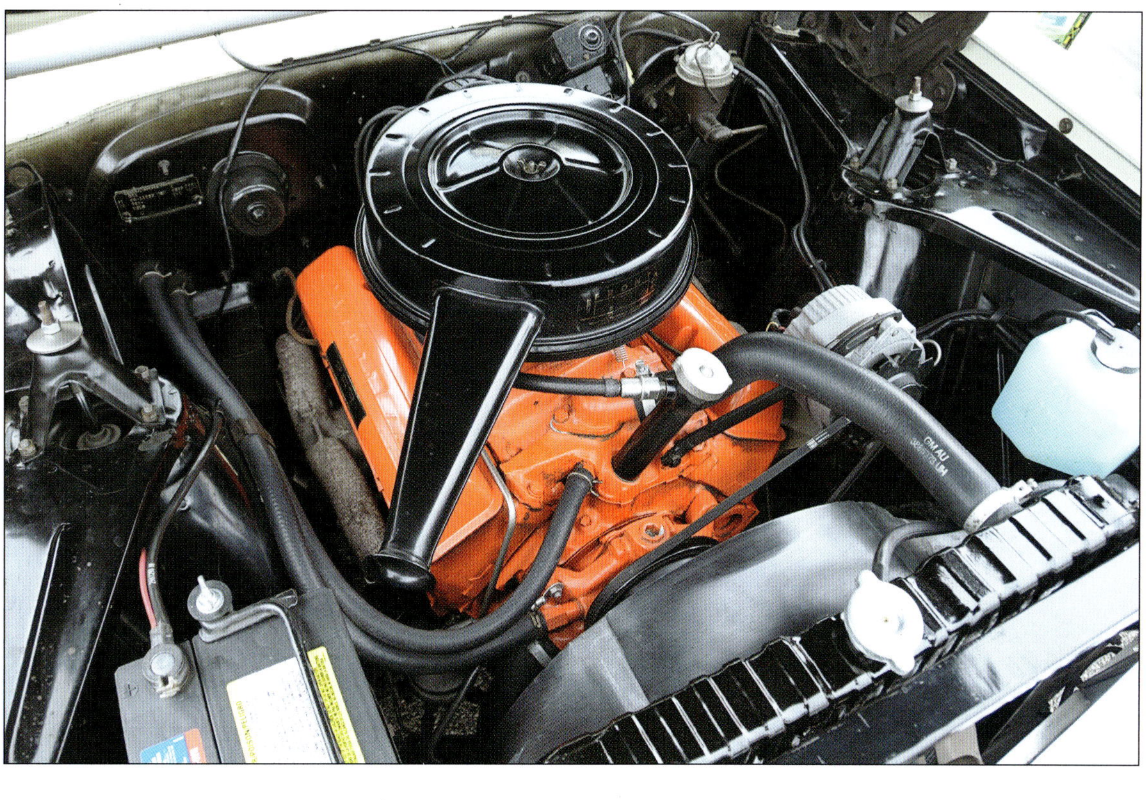

CarTech®

CarTech®

CarTech®, Inc.
6118 Main Street
North Branch, MN 55056
Phone: 651-277-1200 or 800-551-4754
Fax: 651-277-1203
www.cartechbooks.com

© 1997, 2010, and 2019 by Edward J. Staffel Jr.

All rights reserved. No part of this publication may be reproduced or utilized in any form or by any means, electronic or mechanical, including photocopying, recording, or by any information storage and retrieval system, without prior permission from the Publisher. All text, photographs, and artwork are the property of the Author unless otherwise noted or credited.

No portion of this book may be reproduced, transferred, stored, or otherwise used in any manner for purposes of training any artificial intelligence technology or system to generate text, illustrations, diagrams, charts, designs or other works or materials.

The information in this work is true and complete to the best of our knowledge. However, all information is presented without any guarantee on the part of the Author or Publisher, who also disclaim any liability incurred in connection with the use of the information and any implied warranties of merchantability or fitness for a particular purpose. Readers are responsible for taking suitable and appropriate safety measures when performing any of the operations or activities described in this work.

All trademarks, trade names, model names and numbers, and other product designations referred to herein are the property of their respective owners and are used solely for identification purposes. This work is a publication of CarTech, Inc. and has not been licensed, approved, sponsored, or endorsed by any other person or entity. The Publisher is not associated with any product, service, or vendor mentioned in this book and does not endorse the products or services of any vendor mentioned in this book.

Edit by Bob Wilson
Contributing editor Todd Ryden
Photography by Todd Ryden
Layout by Hailey Samples

ISBN 978-1-61325-498-1
Item No. SA55

Library of Congress Cataloging-in-Publication Data
Names: Staffel, Ed, author. | Ryden, Todd, author.
Title: Chevrolet small-block parts interchange manual / Ed Staffel, Todd Ryden.
Description: Revised edition. | Forest Lake, MN : CarTech, [2019]
Identifiers: LCCN 2019008842 | ISBN 9781613254981
Subjects: LCSH: Chevrolet automobile--Motors--Parts. | Chevrolet automobile--Motors--Modification--Handbooks, manuals, etc. | LCGFT: Handbooks and manuals.
Classification: LCC TL215.C5 S6998 2019 | DDC 629.25/040288--dc23
LC record available at https://lccn.loc.gov/2019008842

Written, edited, and designed in the U.S.A.
Printed in China
10 9 8 7 6 5 4 3 2

CarTech books may be purchased at a discounted rate in bulk for resale, events, corporate gifts, or educational purposes. Special editions may also be created to specification.
For details, contact Special Sales at 6118 Main Sstreet, North Branch, MN 55056 or by email at sales@cartechbooks.com.

DISTRIBUTION BY:

*Europe*
PGUK
63 Hatton Garden
London EC1N 8LE, England
Phone: 020 7061 1980 • Fax: 020 7242 3725
www.pguk.co.uk

*Australia*
Renniks Publications Ltd.
3/37-39 Green Street
Banksmeadow, NSW 2109, Australia
Phone: 2 9695 7055 • Fax: 2 9695 7355
www.renniks.com

*Canada*
Login Canada
300 Saulteaux Crescent
Winnipeg, MB, R3J 3T2 Canada
Phone: 800 665 1148 • Fax: 800 665 0103
www.lb.ca

# CONTENTS

**Acknowledgments**....4
**Introduction**....4

**Chapter 1: Cylinder Blocks**....5
- Production Cast-Iron Bare Blocks....13
- Maximum Bore-Size Limits....13
- Blocks....14
- Cast-Iron Bowtie Blocks....16
- Aluminum Bowtie Blocks....16
- Cylinder Sleeves....17
- Freeze Plugs....17
- Cam Bearings....17
- Main Caps....20
- Main Bearings....22
- Block Dowel Pins....22
- Used Engine Blocks....23

**Chapter 2: Gaskets and Fasteners**....24
- Intake Manifold Gaskets....24
- Carb Gaskets....25
- Head Gaskets....25
- Valve Cover Gaskets....27
- Oil Pan Gaskets....28
- Gasket Sealants....28
- Fasteners....30
- Main Cap Bolts and Studs....30
- Cylinder Head Bolts and Stud Kits....30

**Chapter 3: Rotating Assemblies**....32
- Two-Piece Seal Cranks....33
- One-Piece Rear Seal Cranks....33
- Used Cranks....34
- Cast Versus Forged Cranks....34
- Crank Prep....35
- Rod Bearings....36
- Pilot Bushings....38
- Vibration Dampers....38
- Flywheels and Flexplates....41
- Starters....43
- Connecting Rods....43
- Rod Bolts....47
- Piston Pins....47
- Floating Versus Pressed-On Piston Pins....47
- Rod Prep....50
- Pistons....51
- Piston Rings....55

**Chapter 4: Lubrication Systems**....58
- Oil Pans....59
- Windage Trays....62
- Oil Filters and Block Adapters....62
- Oil Coolers....64
- Oil Gauges....64

**Chapter 5: Cylinder Heads**....65
- Service Replacement Cast-Iron Heads....75
- Cast-Iron Bowtie Heads....76
- Aluminum Production Heads....76
- Aluminum Racing Heads....76
- Aftermarket Cylinder Heads....78

**Chapter 6: Valvetrain**....79
- Timing Sets....80
- Camshafts....82
- Static Compression Versus Dynamic Compression and Cam Selection....88
- Valve Lifters....90
- Hydraulic Flat Tappets....91
- Factory Production Hydraulic Roller Tappets....91
- Aftermarket Roller Tappets....91
- Vacuum Storage Tanks and Electric Vacuum Pumps....91
- Pushrods....92
- Roller Lifter Guideplates....92
- Pushrod Guideplates....92
- Rocker Arms....93
- Rocker Arm Studs and Bolts, Balls, and Nuts....94
- Valves....95
- Valve Springs....95
- Oil Seals....96
- Retainers....96
- Valve Stem Locks....96
- Valve Covers....96

**Chapter 7: Induction System**....100
- Plenums....101
- Cast-Iron Intakes....105
- Aluminum 4-Barrel Intakes....105
- Intake Manifold Gaskets....106
- Fuel Injection....106
- Carb Spacers....109
- Carb Sizes....110
- Carb Tuning....112
- Mechanical Fuel Pumps....115
- Fuels....116
- Nitrous Oxide, Superchargers, and Turbochargers....117
- Air Filters....121

**Chapter 8: Ignition Systems**....123
- Distributor Advance....123
- Stock HEI....125
- Chevrolet Performance and the Aftermarket....127
- Rev Limiters and Timing Controls....128
- Alternators....130
- Plug Wires....130
- Spark Plugs....131
- Distributor Drive Gears....131

**Chapter 9: Exhaust, Cooling, and Engine Swaps**....133
- Tube Exhaust Headers....136
- Starter Shield....136
- Water Pumps and Brackets....137
- Deep Pulleys....140
- Underdrive Pulleys....140
- Thermostats....140
- Water Temperature Senders....141
- Radiators, Fans, and Fan Shrouds....141
- Emissions....142
- Engine Swaps....142
- Engine Break-In....143

**Source Guide**....144

# Acknowledgments

I want to thank the following people who have graciously gone out of their way to help in the preparation of this book:

David Hakim at Federal-Mogul Corporation, Southfield, Michigan; Richard Rodriguez, Parts Manager at Crawford's Santa Fe Chevrolet, who patiently looked up part numbers and took an active interest in the completion of this book; Ken Casey Jr., GM/Performance Parts Specialist at Burt Chevrolet/GM Performance Parts, Englewood, Colorado; Eric Townsley and Chris, John, Michael, and Caroline at Santa Fe Auto Machine, Santa Fe, New Mexico; the crew at Super Shops in Albuquerque, New Mexico; and the Rocky Mountain Rodent Research Council, Santa Fe, New Mexico.

— Ed Staffel

I would like to thank Greg Stafford at Car Parts Machine in El Paso for letting me go through their shop in search of parts to photograph for this revised edition. Also, Steve Brule at Westech Performance in Mira Loma, California, for years of help with different projects. Kudos as well to Warren Ekery at Scoggin Dickey Performance Center in Lubbock, for his assistance with part numbers, Bill Tichenor of Holley, Bill Martens at Chevrolet Performance, Barry Kluczyk, and to the CarTech team. Thank you everyone!

— Todd Ryden, Contributing Editor

# Introduction

Most folks feel they don't need an introduction to small-block Chevy V-8 engines. So many people have grown up driving, building, or racing one, that the engine seems very familiar. The most-popular and best-designed automotive engine is still around after six decades of service. More than 60 million small-blocks have been produced and millions of words have been written about how to build them.

In the late 1980s, the small-block changed. And it did one more time in the mid-1990s. The Generation I family of motors we know so well has been joined by the Generation II branch of the family, followed by the Vortec line of motors that branched off with more changes. Over the years, interchanges between these engine generations has gotten a little more complicated.

Old ideas about what works and what doesn't need to be updated. Computer-controlled ignitions, transmissions, and various forms of electronic fuel injection were new in the 1990s, and technology continues to advance the performance that the small-block Chevy is capable of producing.

Though a small-block hasn't been bolted into a production-built Chevrolet in more than two decades, Chevrolet Performance continues to develop improved components for the SBC as well as crate engines. If fact, several small-block crates make more power than any production version did, even from the muscle car heyday! Plus, these engines deliver good idle quality, low maintenance, less noise, and better fuel economy! It is a delicate balancing act that is not easy to do. The company continues to improve the parts available for Gen I– and Gen II–based engines with new blocks, heads, roller cams, aluminum intakes, and other parts to continue to push the performance envelope that was first defined in 1955.

Meanwhile, those of you into older car restoration, racing, or rodding can still find everything you need to build a stock 250-hp cruiser small-block or a 1,200-hp turbocharged motor set on kill. Between Chevrolet Performance and a healthy, enthusiast-driven aftermarket, almost anything you could want for a small-block Chevy is available; oil pan to throttle body or flexplate to water pumps, everything is available!

This book contains information on all of the small-block motors made from 1955 through 1996. It covers Gen I, Gen II, and the Vortec small-block engines introduced in 1996 so you can identify the parts you have and the parts you need to assemble a smooth-running, great-performing powerplant.

# CYLINDER BLOCKS

Block casting numbers are found on the ledge to the rear of the number-7 cylinder on the driver's side of the small-block V-8s. The casting date of the block can usually be found on the rear of the case on the passenger's side of the block on a ledge behind the number-8 cylinder. Some block casting dates are found at the rear on the driver's side.

When you look at casting numbers and stamped numbers, in any part surface, sometimes the numbers are not as crisp and clear as they could be. Sometimes an 8 looks like a 3 or a 6. Also, individual digits in a number may be missing. The last digit may be missing or perhaps it just can't be discerned by the eye. At times, Chevrolet ground off the cast number and replaced it with a number stamped by hand. These were rare instances, but they did occur.

Casting dates are usually expressed this way: "C 18 4." In this example, the C means the month of March, 18 is the day of the month, and 4 is the last digit of the year. This last digit may mean 1964, 1974, 1984, or 1994, so you must also check the other characteristics of the block to determine in which decade and year it was made. Some parts have the decade and year cast on them; these identifiers look like this: "C 18 84."

*The block casting number "3896944" is found on a ledge at the rear of the block on the driver's side. Sometimes you really need to check the numbers, as the last three digits are tough to make out in this example. The number on this block identifies it as a 283.*

*The block casting date, which is the date the block was made, is found on a ledge at the rear of the block. This is not the date when the engine was assembled.*

Chevrolet introduced new model years in September or October of each year, so when you see a casting date of "L 16 7" for example, this indicates a casting date used in the 1968 model year because it translates into December 16, 1967. A 1968-model Camaro assembled on January 6, 1968, might contain a number of parts that were cast in December 1967. Casting dates should precede hand-stamped engine assembly dates.

The engine assembly date and which factory assembled the engine are indicated by numbers and letters that are stamped into the block when the engine is assembled and placed into a specific vehicle at the factory. These stamped letters and numbers are usually found on a ledge forward of the number-2 cylinder on the passenger-side deck of the block. These stamped symbols are visible after the motor is assembled. The stampings show the month and day of the month the engine and vehicle assembly took place. At the end of the stamped symbols, the one-, two-, or three-letter engine suffix code identifies what type of motor it is, what

*A block casting date of "L 5 6" is found at the rear of this block and translates to December 5, 1966. The "L" stands for the 12th month of the year.*

*The engine assembly date and the suffix code tell you about the original engine and vehicle in which the motor was placed. This information is usually found on a ledge on the front of the engine block on the passenger's side. "VI027DE" tells you that this engine was assembled in the Flint, Michigan, plant (F); in the 10th month (October); on the 27th day. The "DE" suffix code in that year (1968, which is found with the block casting date code at the rear of the block), indicates a 307-ci small-block and manual transmission. Many later blocks also have a portion of the VIN stamped in this same location.*

type of vehicle the motor went into, what type of transmission was originally mated to the engine, and other features. Finally, on later blocks, there are also numbers that match the last five, six, or seven digits of the Vehicle Identification Number (VIN) that has been assigned to the vehicle.

*Late-model blocks have their casting numbers on the rear ledge of the case along with the original size of the engine indicated in liters. This 350 block (5.7 liters) features a one-piece rear main seal and was obviously cast in Mexico.*

An example of a hand-stamped engine assembly date and suffix code looks like this: F0213ZE 023456, which translates into an engine assembled at the Flint (F), Michigan, factory on February 13 (the second month, 02, 13th day, 13)—years are not stated here—and a 327/250-hp engine (in 1965) with a manual transmission and A/C (ZE). The number also indicates that the car was a Chevy II that was the 23,456th vehicle assembled in the series.

All of these casting numbers and stamped numbers are consulted when someone wishes to determine if this is a numbers-matching engine and vehicle. Even more information is available on the trim tags, VIN plates, and hidden VINs and casting numbers, codes, and dates, which are found on other major powertrain components and vehicle frames. Whether the numbers match can be extremely important to someone who is buying a restored or restorable classic, and it can have an effect on the desirability, originality, and value of the vehicle. Knowledge of the correct casting numbers, date codes, suffix codes, and engine assembly code stampings help a buyer decide whether a 1965 Corvette with a 327/375-hp fuel-injected engine is an original numbers-matching car or not.

If the block has previously been decked (a machining operation to ensure the flatness of the block surface or to reduce the piston deck to block deck height to 0), these stamped letters and numbers may have been machined right off the passenger-side block deck surface and may no longer be visible. Engines that were replaced under factory warranty might use the CE suffix code or may not have any assembly or suffix code information at all. Also, criminals may have restamped the block in order to fake a more valuable or rare matching numbers block. Be careful! These days some rare vehicles with rare options have become high-dollar investments. It is possible to fake engine numbers, trim tags, VIN plates, and other documentation, all in an effort to increase the resale value of a vehicle.

Since the mid-1980s, many late-model small-blocks rated the engine size in liters (such as 4.3L, 5.0L, or 5.7L), and this number is cast into the ledge at the rear of the block on the driver side. Also, on late-model blocks, the last three digits of the block casting number are cast into each side of the block between the freeze plugs in large, easy-to-read numerals.

A number of changes to the blocks have occurred over the years. Some changes to keep in mind are: In 1955, the 265 block did not have an oil filter. The 265 also used a slightly different method of engine lubrication in 1955 and 1956. These 265 blocks feature two oil passage holes in the block at the rear cam journal to feed oil to the lifter galleries and

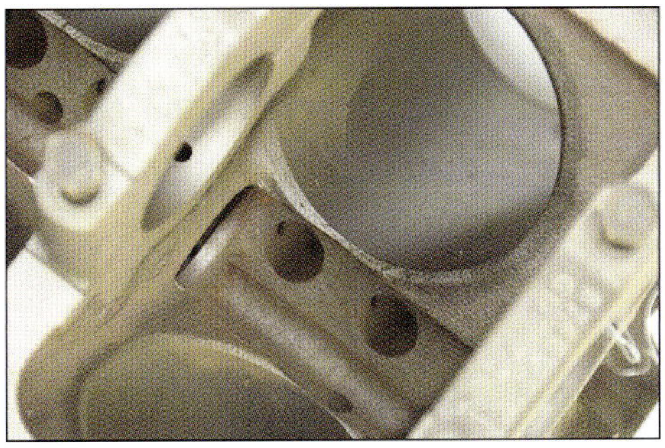

*This early 283 block from 1955 to 1961 (left) was cast without a scallop shape at the bottom of the cylinder bores. This limits the crank stroke to 3 inches. Later small-blocks have the scallops at the bottom of each cylinder barrel to allow the use of longer cranks (right).*

heads. This requires the use of a rear cam bearing that has two matching holes in the cam bearing and a camshaft that has two flats ground into the rear journal of the cam itself. If you use an incorrect rear cam bearing or use a camshaft without the two flats in the rear cam journal, oil does not circulate to the lifter galleries and won't get to the heads. This system was changed in 1957. The later blocks have an annular groove in the rear of the block itself and use a different-style rear cam bearing and rear cam journals without flats.

## Block Casting Numbers

| Casting Number | Size (ci) | Model Year | Main Bearing Cap Design | Notes |
|---|---|---|---|---|
| 140029 | 350 | 1980–1984 | 2 | |
| 330817 | 400 | 1972–1980 | 2 | |
| 355909 | 262 | 1975 | 2 | |
| 355909 | 305 | 1976–1979 | 2 | |
| 360851 | 262 | 1975–1976 | 2 | Monza V-8 |
| 361979 | 305 | 1978–1979 | 2 | |
| 366245 | 350 | 1978–1979 | 2 | |
| 366286 | – | – | 4 | Bowtie, aluminum, siamesed, straight nodular-iron main caps, two-piece seal, 4.00- to 4.150-inch bores, 0.45-inch main journals |
| 366287 | – | – | 4 | Bowtie, aluminum, siamesed, straight nodular-iron main caps, two-piece seal, 4.00- to 4.150-inch bores, 0.45-inch main journals |
| 366299 | – | – | 4 | Bowtie, aluminum, nodular-iron splayed caps, wet sump, 4.00-inch bore |
| 389257 | 302 | 1967 | 2 | |
| 393288 | 283 | 1965–1967 | 2 | |
| 460703 | 350 | 1978 | 4 | |
| 460776 | 305 | 1978–1979 | 2 | |
| 460777 | 305 | 1978–1979 | 2 | |
| 460778 | 305 | 1978–1979 | 2 or 4 | Some Canadian heavy-duty truck blocks have four-bolt main caps |
| 471511 | 267 | 1979–1982 | 2 | |
| 3556519 | 283 | 1958–1961 | 2 | |
| 3703524 | 265 | 1955 | 2 | No oil filter |
| 3720991 | 265 | 1956–1957 | 2 | |
| 3731548 | 265 | 1957 | 2 | No side motor mounts |
| 3731548 | 283 | 1957 | 2 | No side motor mounts |
| 3737739 | 283 | 1958–1964 | 2 | |
| 3756519 | 283 | 1958–1962 | 2 | |
| 3782870 | 327 | 1962–1967 | 2 | |
| 3789817 | 283 | 1962–1964 | 2 | |
| 3789817 | 327 | 1962–1967 | 2 | |
| 3789935 | 283 | 1961–1964 | 2 | |
| 3790721 | 283 | 1962–1964 | 2 | Chevy II recessed oil filter boss |
| 3790721 | 327 | 1965–1966 | 2 | Chevy II recessed oil filter boss |
| 3791362 | 327 | 1962–1967 | 2 | Chevy II recessed oil filter boss |
| 3792563 | 327 | 1965 | 2 | |
| 3792582 | 283 | 1964–1965 | 2 | |

## Block Casting Numbers *(Continued)*

| Casting Number | Size (ci) | Model Year | Main Bearing Cap Design | Notes |
|---|---|---|---|---|
| 3794226 | 283 | 1958–1963 | 2 | |
| 3794460 | 327 | 1962–1964 | 2 | |
| 3814660 | 327 | 1968–1969 | 2 | |
| 3830944 | 327 | 1963 | 2 | |
| 3834810 | 283 | 1964–1966 | 2 | |
| 3834812 | 283 | 1962–1963 | 2 | |
| 3837739 | 283 | 1958–1962 | 2 | |
| 3849852 | 283 | 1957–1966 | 2 | |
| 3849935 | 283 | 1965–1967 | 2 | |
| 3858174 | 327 | 1964–1967 | 2 | |
| 3858180 | 327 | 1964–1967 | 2 | |
| 3858618 | 350 | 1968–1976 | 2 | |
| 3862194 | 283 | 1965–1967 | 2 | Chevy II recessed oil filter boss |
| 3862812 | 283 | 1962–1964 | 2 | |
| 3892657 | 302 | 1967 | 2 | Z28 Camaro |
| 3892657 | 327 | 1967 | 2 | |
| 3892657 | 350 | 1967 | 2 | Camaro |
| 3896944 | 283 | 1967 | 2 | |
| 3896948 | 283 | 1966–1967 | 2 | |
| 3903352 | 327 | 1967 | 2 | |
| 3914636 | 307 | 1968 | 2 | |
| 3914638 | 327 | 1968 | 2 | Truck |
| 3914653 | 307 | 1968–1973 | 2 | |
| 3914660 | 327 | 1968 | 2 | |
| 3914678 | 302 | 1968 | 2 | Z28 Camaro |
| 3914678 | 327 | 1968 | 2 | |
| 3914678 | 350 | 1968 | 2 | |
| 3932371 | 307 | 1969–1973 | 2 | |
| 3932373 | 307 | 1968–1973 | 2 | |
| 3932386 | 302 | 1969 | 4 | Z28 Camaro |
| 3932386 | 327 | 1969 | 2 | |
| 3932386 | 350 | 1969 | 4 | |
| 3932388 | 350 | 1969 | 2 or 4 | |
| 3951509 | 400 | 1970–1971 | 4 | |
| 3951509 | 400 | 1974–1980 | 2 | |
| 3951511 | 400 | 1970–1973 | 4 | Some replacement blocks had two-bolt main caps |
| 3956618 | 302 | 1969 | 4 | Z28 Camaro |
| 3956618 | 327 | 1968–1969 | 2 | |
| 3956618 | 350 | 1969 | 2 or 4 | |
| 3956632 | 307 | 1969 | 2 | |
| 3959512 | 327 | 1962–1967 | 2 | Also used for some replacement blocks |
| 3970010 | 302 | 1969 | 4 | Z28 Camaro |
| 3970010 | 327 | 1969 | 2 | Trucks and industrial |
| 3970010 | 350 | 1969–1980 | 2 or 4 | |
| 3970014 | 350 | 1970–1976 | 2 or 4 | |
| 3970020 | 307 | 1970–1973 | 2 | |
| 3970024 | 307 | 1969–1973 | 2 | |
| 4715111 | 305 | 1980 | 2 | |
| 6259425 | 350 | 1969–1976 | 2 | |
| 10036033 | 350 | – | 4 | Goodwrench crate motor, two-piece rear seal, made in Mexico |
| 10051182 | – | – | 2 or 4 | Bowtie, 3.75- to 4.30-inch bores, one- or two-piece rear seal |
| 10051184 | – | – | 4 | Bowtie, 4.00- to 4.155-inch bores, one- or two-piece rear seal |
| 10054727 | 350 | 1986-up | 2 or 4 | One-piece rear seal, some made in Canada |
| 10066036 | 350 | – | 2 or 4 | Target Master/Goodwrench crate motor, two-piece rear seal, made in Mexico |

## Block Casting Numbers *(Continued)*

| Casting Number | Size (ci) | Model Year | Main Bearing Cap Design | Notes |
|---|---|---|---|---|
| 10066038 | 350 | 1994 | 4 | Goodwrench crate motor, two-piece rear seal, made in Mexico |
| 10090511 | 350 | 1990 | 2 | LT5, ZR1 Vette, 375 hp |
| 10125327 | 350 | 1992-up | 2 or 4 | Gen II LT1, reverse-flow cooling |
| 10125327 | 350 | 1996-up | 2 or 4 | Gen II LT4, reverse-flow cooling |
| 10134996 | – | – | 4 | Bowtie, aluminum, 4.125-inch bore, 2.65-inch main journals |
| 10153558 | 350 | 1991–1992 | 4 | LT5, ZR1 Vette, 375 hp |
| 10168588 | 265 | 1994–1996 | 2 | L99, Gen II, 4.3-Liter V-8, Caprice, reverse-flow cooling |
| 10199001 | 350 | 1993–1995 | 4 | LT5, ZR1 Vette, 405 hp |
| 10243878 | 305 | 1996–1998 | 2 | Vortec truck, roller cam, one-piece rear seal |
| 10243880 | 350 | 1995–2000 | 2 or 4 | Vortec truck, Gen I crate motors and "ZZ" roller cam, one-piece rear seal |
| 14010201 | 305 | 1980–1985 | 2 | |
| 14010202 | 305 | 1980–1985 | 2 | |
| 14010203 | 305 | 1980–1985 | 2 | |
| 14010207 | 350 | 1980–1985 | 2 or 4 | |
| 14010209 | 350 | 1980–1985 | 4 | |
| 14010280 | 267 | 1979–1982 | 2 | |
| 14011064 | 350 | 1983 | 4 | |
| 14011148 | 350 | 1987–1989 | — | Roller cam, one-piece rear seal |
| 14016376 | 267 | 1979–1982 | 2 | |
| 14016379 | 350 | 1977–1979 | 2 or 4 | |
| 14016381 | 305 | 1980–1984 | 2 | |
| 14016382 | 305 | 1979–1984 | 2 | |
| 14016383 | 305 | 1980–1985 | 2 | Truck |
| 14079287 | 350 | 1986–1990 | — | Truck |
| 14088526 | 350 | 1987–1989 | — | Roller cam, one-piece rear seal |
| 14088548 | 350 | 1986–1988 | 2 or 4 | |
| 14088551 | 305 | 1986–1987 | 2 | One-piece rear main seal |
| 14093627 | 305 | 1987–1991 | 2 | Roller cam, one-piece rear seal |
| 14093638 | 350 | 1987–1995 | 2 or 4 | Roller or flat tappet cam, one-piece rear seal |
| 14094766 | 305 | 1986-up | 2 | One-piece rear seal |
| 14101148 | 350 | 1987-90 | 4 | One-piece rear seal |
| 14102058 | 305 | 1987-91 | 2 | Roller cam, one-piece rear seal |
| 22551656 | – | – | 4 | Rocket block, 4.00- to 4.190-inch bores, 2.45-inch mains, splayed caps, dry sump, two-piece rear seal, 9.025-inch deck |

*The 1961 283 block also had a tower in the front of the lifter valley. This tower connected to the oil filler tube that was present in intake manifolds until 1969, when the block casting was changed and the oil fill location was moved to the valve covers.*

*This 1967 283 block shows the rear of the block, which at that time had a cast-in tower and baffle assembly mounted in the lifter gallery for a crankcase ventilation system. Block castings were changed in 1969 to remove this tower.*

*Some blocks will show a number such as "010" on the rear of the block or on the front under the timing cover. This means that 1-percent additional nickel was used in the casting process. Sometimes only a single "020" is found, meaning that 2-percent additional nickel was used.*

*If you are using a manual transmission and mechanical clutch linkage, you may need to mount a ball and stud to the block in order to use the linkage Z-bar. Make sure that the block you use has the mounting boss in the correct location for your vehicle application. This block shows two; one near the filter boss and the other just to its left. Some blocks have multiple locations; some blocks have none. If you are updating to a hydraulic clutch or an automatic transmission, you don't have to worry about this.*

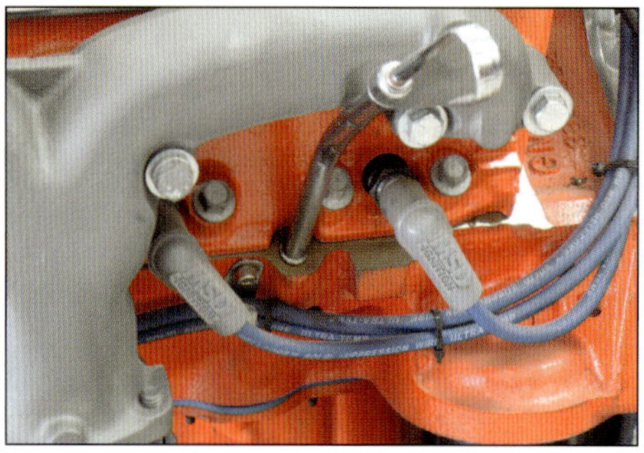

*Chevrolet changed the location of the oil dipstick on different applications. Many simply went through the oil pan rather than the block. Other blocks may be machined for one on either the driver's or passenger's side near the head mounting deck. This block shows a driver-side-mounted dipstick.*

The rear main seals of blocks used a rope seal from 1955 to 1958. During 1959 through 1985, they took a two-piece neoprene lip rear main oil seal. The circular, one-piece rear main seal was introduced in 1986 on production engines, although some replacement motors, crate engines, and Bowtie blocks still used two-piece rear main seals and matching cranks.

Front engine mounts were used in early blocks and were later replaced with side-mounted engine mounts. Some of the early blocks have no bolt bosses cast into the side of the blocks for engine mounts. If your block is from the 1950s, check it to make sure you use the correct front or side engine mounts.

The 265 and 283 blocks made from 1955 to 1961, which used 3-inch-stroke cranks, do not have any reliefs cast into the block where the block webbing meets the bottom of the cylinder barrels. The 1962-and-later 327 blocks have reliefs cast into the lower end of the block where the barrels meet the block webbing. This allowed the use of the longer 3.25-inch-stroke 327 cranks. If you have an early 265 or 283 block that does not have these reliefs, it is difficult to install a 3.25-inch or longer stroke small journal crank.

Small journal blocks made from 1955 to 1967 used 2.30-inch main bearing journals with a road draft tube boss at the rear of the lifter valley that mounted an oil separation canister in the lifter valley, which connected to the block and the road draft crankcase ventilation tube. Also, a tube cast into the front of the lifter valley mated to an oil fill tube on the front of the intake manifold. The 1969-and-later blocks eliminated the oil fill tube and the road draft tube. The oil fill tube on the front of the intake manifolds was also eliminated. Crankcase ventilation and the addition of oil were accomplished through the valve covers.

Many of the V-8 Chevy IIs made in the 1960s with 283 or 327 small-blocks have a unique block. Engine clearance in these 1962 to 1967 vehicles required that the oil filter boss on the driver's side be moved up or recessed up in the block. In 1965 to 1967, the dipstick hole in these blocks was plugged and the dipstick tube went directly into the unique Chevy II oil pan.

If you intend to use a manual transmission in your vehicle, along with mechanical clutch linkage, and if the clutch linkage Z-bar requires a block-mounted pivot ball and stud, then the block you use must have a threaded bolt boss (usually near the oil filter–mounting boss) for the pivot ball and stud. Chevrolet placed this threaded boss on the block in a number of different locations. Some blocks have no threaded bosses; some blocks have only one threaded boss; and some blocks have a variety of bosses to fit a number of engine and vehicle combinations. Make sure the block you use has a threaded boss for the pivot ball and stud where you need it. An alternative is to use an automatic transmission or to use a hydraulically operated clutch linkage assembly.

The 350 engine was introduced in the 1967 Camaro. This 1967 Camaro 350 block used a larger main journal (2.45 inches) crankshaft. Other changes were made in the block webbing and bearing saddles to increase strength and to accommodate the larger journal cranks. Other large journal blocks in different displacements were introduced in 1968-and-later model years.

From 1970 through 1980, 400 small-blocks used 2.650-inch main bearing journal crankshafts and a slightly shorter connecting rod (5.565 inches). These blocks also used siamesed cylinder barrels with

*These photos show the difference between the rear main seal designs: a two-piece seal (left) and a one-piece-seal (right).*

4.125-inch standard bores in order to fit the increased cubic-inch displacement inside the original outside dimensions of a small-block V-8 case. These 400 blocks used externally balanced vibration dampers, flywheels, and flexplates.

The oil dipstick entry location moved around over the years. The dipstick tube entry was usually through the driver's side of the block deck and then into the oil pan. However, there are blocks on which the dipstick tube enters the block on the passenger's side and then runs into the pan. On a few engine/vehicle combinations, the hole in the block that was meant for the dipstick was plugged, and the dipstick tube entered the side of the oil pan in order to clear obstructions such as the exhaust manifolds. Most interchange situations don't cause a dipstick problem as long as you use an oil pan that matches the block dipstick's mounting position—driver's side or passenger's side. If there is an obstruction that prevents dipstick entry into the block, you can replace it with a pan that allows the dipstick tube to enter directly into the side of the pan. This usually clears up any problems with stock exhaust manifolds. A few late-model Gen I blocks have a dipstick entry position on both sides of the pan rails. Take the time before you choose the parts to determine which ones you need.

The 1986-and-later production blocks switched to a one-piece rear main seal, which required other changes to crankshafts, oil pans, flywheels, flexplates, and engine block sealing surfaces, affecting the interchangeability of parts between the two-piece oil seal and one-piece oil seal motors. All production small-blocks with one-piece rear main seals are externally balanced. Some GM engines' replacement crate motors and some of the performance Bowtie blocks still use two-piece rear main seals.

PN 14088556 is a stock aluminum rear seal retainer for one-piece rear oil seals on 1986-or-later production blocks with matching oil pan, timing cover, and pan gaskets. It also uses an adapter-to-block gasket (PN 12337823) and rear crank seal (PN 10088158).

PN 10051118 is a seal adapter that allows the use of a two-piece-style crank in a one-piece seal block with a one-piece-style oil pan and pan gasket. It requires a two-piece seal, adapter gasket (PN 12337823), and one-piece oil pan gasket (PN 14088505). The Moroso (PN 38315) seal adapter allows the use of a two-piece-style crank with a one-piece oil seal–style block, and it allows the use of an early two-piece-style oil pan, timing chain cover, and pan gasket.

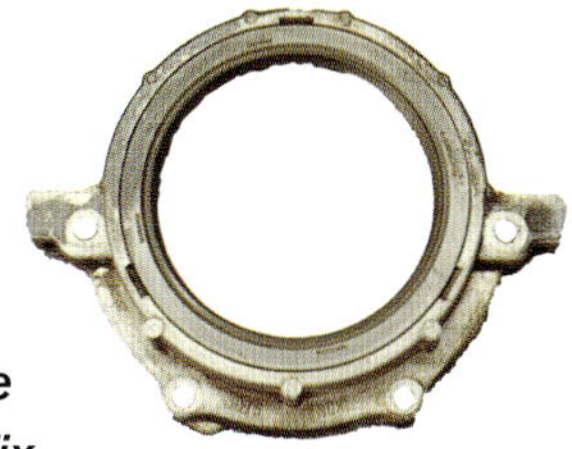

*This is the one-piece seal and mounting fixture that was used on 1986-and-later production small-blocks.*

*The 1986-on model blocks machined for roller lifters and camshafts have taller machined lifter bores and three bolt bosses in the middle of the lifter valley to hold the lifter retainer fixture that was used with production Chevy hydraulic roller lifters.*

*Some blocks, such as this 1961 283, have dual-starter bolt patterns. Most blocks only have one pattern—either straight or offset.*

*When you have your block bored, make sure the final honing is done with a torque plate bolted in place. The plate distorts the cylinder walls in a way that is similar to the block distortion when the heads are torqued down on the block. The cylinders are round when honed and this helps improve ring seal.*

*Walk into your friendly Chevrolet dealer and order PN 10105123 and you'll receive a bare, cast-iron 350 block. This is the 1986-on block with four-bolt mains, a one-piece rear seal, and clearanced for a 3.80-inch-stroker crankshaft. (Photo Courtesy Chevrolet Performance)*

The 1987-and-later Gen I blocks were produced with taller lifter bores for use with factory-installed hydraulic roller cams and roller lifters with bolt bosses in the lifter valley for a roller lifter retainer spider. Flat tappet cams and lifters can be used in these blocks. The late-model hydraulic roller lifters are taller than a hydraulic flat tappet lifter and should be used with shorter factory pushrods for production roller lifters. All Gen II production engines use hydraulic roller cams and roller lifters.

Aluminum blocks weigh approximately 90 pounds bare. Cast-iron production blocks weigh about 150 pounds. The heavier Bowtie cast-iron bare blocks weigh approximately 185 pounds due to their thicker cylinder walls and decks and reinforced block webbing.

There are significant differences between the Gen I, Gen II (introduced in 1992), and Vortec small-block V-8s (introduced in 1996).

The large-diameter flywheels and flexplates (14 inches) that were used with one-piece oil pans may not fit some early engine and vehicle applications. The crossmembers and small-diameter bellhousings were originally made to be used with a 12¾-inch flywheel or flexplate. To fit the larger flywheels and flexplates, change the bellhousing or change to the smaller-diameter ones. Keep in mind that most blocks are drilled for two different starter bolt patterns, while some blocks have only been drilled for one starter mounting position.

## Small-Block General Specifications

**Configuration:**
90-degree ohv V-8, with cast-iron or aluminum blocks and heads

**Cylinders (Front to Rear):**
Driver's side: 1-3-5-7
Passenger's side: 2-4-6-8

**Firing Order (Clockwise on Distributor):**
1-8-4-3-6-5-7-2 (Gen I, Gen II, and Vortec)
Computer controlled, no distributor

**Crankshaft:**
Gen I, II, and Vortec: Forged or cast, five main bearings, thrust on rear bearing

**Crankshaft Journal Diameter:**
1955–1968 small journal: Mains 2.30 inches, rods 2.00 inches
1967–1996 medium journal: Mains 2.45 inches, rods 2.10 inches
1970–1980 400 Crank: Mains 2.65 inches, rods 2.10 inches
1989-up LT5: Mains 2.76 inches, rods 2.10 inches

**Crank Strokes:**
Small journal: 3.0 inches and 3.25 inches
Medium journal: 3.0, 3.10, 3.25, and 3.48 inches
400 Cranks: 3.75 inches
LT5 350: 3.66 inches

**Rod Length:**
Forged steel 5.7 inches center to center
5.565-inch 400 rod
5.740-inch LT5 rod
5.940-inch Gen II 265-ci L99 V-8

**Pistons:**
Cast, hypereutectic, or forged aluminum slipper skirt design

**Lubrication:**
Full pressure oiling, wet sump
Some Bowtie blocks offered for dry sump

**Block Bores:**
3.50 to 4.126 inches

**Bore Centerlines:**
4.040 inches

**Cubic-Inch Displacements:**
262, 265, 267, 283, 302, 305, 307, 327, 350, 400

**Compression Ratios:**
8.0:1 to 11.0:1

**Induction:**
2-barrel
4-barrel
Inline 2 x 4 barrel
Crossram 2 x 4 barrel
Rochester Mechanical Fuel Injection
Throttle Body Fuel Injection (TBI)
Crossfire 2 x TBI
Tuned Port Fuel Injection (TPI)
Sequential Fuel Injection with mass airflow sensor

**Engine Weight:**
Approximately 550 pounds cast iron ■

*If you're looking for a serious block to use as the foundation for high output, the 350 Bowtie cast-iron block is a good start. This block (PN 12480047) is CNC machined with four-bolt mains, splayed caps, tall lifter bores, and is set up for a maximum bore of 4.155 inches. (Photo Courtesy Chevrolet Performance)*

## Abbreviating Casting Numbers

It is common to abbreviate the casting numbers when speaking or writing about them. Rather than using seven, eight, or nine digits, the last three digits are commonly used when making reference to them. Thus, a block with casting number 3970010 is referred to as the "010" block. A cylinder head with casting number 340292 is also called a "292" head. Chevrolet rarely used the same last three digits in a similar part, so there is little duplication or confusion. Some parts with the same casting number were used in a number of different model years and engine combinations. Look closely at the casting numbers and casting dates. Sometimes they are difficult to see and an 8 may look like a 3. Sometimes the last digit in a number is missing, or rust, corrosion, grease, or dirt may obscure the number. ■

On some of the early one-piece rear main seal production blocks, the boss for the mechanical fuel pump was cast into the block. However, the holes for the fuel pump pushrod and oil drainback were not always drilled. Check your block to see if these holes exist if you intend to use a mechanical fuel pump in your application.

Not all one-piece rear main seal blocks were set up for factory production hydraulic roller cams. Some late-model Gen I four-bolt blocks used in trucks contain the one-piece rear main seal but do not have the threaded bosses in the lifter valley that are used to bolt on the roller lifter retainer. These truck blocks used a flat tappet cam and a one-piece rear main seal.

To add to the confusion, a few one-piece rear main seal production blocks share the same block casting number but may have been drilled for either two- or four-bolt main caps. The "638" casting is one example. The only sure method of determining whether you are looking at a two- or four-bolt case is to remove the oil pan and take a look.

### Production Cast-Iron Bare Blocks

PN 10066034 is a Gen I, 4-inch-bore, bare block with four-bolt gray-iron main caps. This block uses a two-piece rear main oil seal and its bearing saddles are sized for cranks with 2.45-inch main journals, non-siamesed, 4.00- to 0.060-inch bores, a 9.025-inch deck height, and a wet-sump rear cap.

PN 10105123 delivers a bare, non-siamesed block with 4.00-inch bores, a 9.025-inch deck, 2.45-inch main journals, a wet-sump cap, four-bolt straight main caps, and a one-piece rear seal. This Gen I block has a lifter valley that is machined for use with either factory roller or flat tappets and respective cams. The block weighs 181 pounds. This Gen I block was used with all ZZ 350 HO and CC 350/300 crate motors and is machined in the lifter valley for a factory hydraulic roller cam. The block can accept up to a 3.75-inch stroke crank.

Chevy Performance also offers a 383-ci block (PN 88962516) with a 4.005-inch bore, which has also been clearanced for a 3.800-inch stroker crankshaft.

### Maximum Bore-Size Limits

There are limits beyond which a block should not be bored. In addition, replacement pistons are sized for particular bore sizes. Oversize pistons are generally available in Standard (Std.) 0.010-, 0.020-, 0.030-, 0.040-, and 0.060-inch sizes. Other sizes are available from custom piston makers, but the sizes given here are the most common.

If you are boring a block, stay within reason. As the bores are made larger, the actual thickness of the cylinder barrel wall becomes thinner, and as it gets thinner, it weakens and is subject to more distortion. Bore the block to the minimum amount needed to clean up the walls and still retain as much barrel wall thickness as possible. This helps the barrels maintain strength and resist flexing.

Bowtie blocks come with thicker barrel walls than production blocks, so even at large overbore sizes the walls are still thick enough to withstand the racing abuse these blocks no doubt see.

Also, when a block is cast, there is a remote possibility that the casting molds shifted when the molten

## Engine Assembly and Suffix Codes

When an engine is completely assembled and placed into a particular vehicle at the factory, an engine assembly date code and suffix code are stamped into the block casting. Usually, this stamped code is found on a ledge on the engine block deck located at the front of the passenger's side of the block. These codes are visible to the eye even with the motor in the vehicle, although you may have to move the alternator if it is mounted on the passenger's side to see the block ledge beneath it. These engine assembly and suffix codes can give you a great deal of information when you decode them.

The code may look like this: F0317ZM. The F stands for the Flint, Michigan, factory where it was made. The 0317 stands for the month and day of the month, in this case the third month 03, on the 17th day. Years and decades are not given in these engine assembly codes. The letters at the end, ZM, are the engine suffix code.

Various combinations of letters were used to indicate the vehicle model type, engine size, transmission type, and other things such as air-conditioning that were used on this particular vehicle when it was made. In this case, ZM was used on a 1966 Chevy II to indicate a 327 engine, a Powerglide automatic transmission, and air-conditioning.

On some blocks, parts of the VIN are also stamped onto this ledge.

These engine assembly codes, suffix codes, part casting numbers, and other features are used to determine whether a particular vehicle is an original "numbers-matching" vehicle. Numbers-matching original vehicles are sought by collectors. Keep in mind that it is possible to fake a numbers-matching vehicle in order to increase its value to collectors. This is particularly true of rare, and therefore, more-valuable vehicles that had a low-production-number part or combination of parts. Be careful!

Also, sometimes when a block is decked during a rebuild in order to ensure flatness or to reduce the deck height, the engine assembly and suffix codes can be machined right off a small-block by an inattentive machinist. ■

metal was poured in. This results in a "core shift" in the finished block. Core shift in a block can cause many problems, one of which is that cylinder walls might be very thin on one side of the cylinder and thicker on the other. Lifter bores can be off of their correct positions and cause valvetrain geometry problems.

Another possible problem with boring is that the cylinder barrels may have porous sections. In this case, as the boring bar cuts into the cylinder wall to open it up, it may hit a porous section. If that happens, bore to the next largest bore, if you can. If the porous section is too deep, the block may need a sleeve or have to be scrapped. If you are already at the maximum bore size, you should obtain another block and start over.

In addition, rust inside the water jackets or on the piston side of the cylinder walls can eat into the wall thickness and cause a problem when the block is bored. If you find a block that has been sitting around outside for a while, be cautious. It may have features you desire, the price might be low, or you might be doing someone a favor by hauling the block out of wherever it is, but rust can ruin the usefulness of any block.

Sonic testing a block before boring can determine if there is a problem with core shift, porosity, or thin cylinder walls. Now, don't get paranoid. These types of problems don't happen often, but they do occur.

### Blocks

*262:* The 262 has a standard bore of 3.671 inches and a stroke of 3.10 inches. These were thin block castings and should only be bored a maximum of 0.030 inch over, which would give a bore diameter of 3.701 inches. All of these Gen I blocks have two-bolt main caps and use 2.45-inch journal cast cranks. They were factory installed in 1975 to 1976 Novas and Monzas.

*265:* The Gen I blocks were made from 1955 to 1957 with a bore of 3.750 inches and stroke of 3 inches. They can be bored up to 0.125 inch over to a maximum bore diameter of 3.875 inches, which is the same as a standard-bore 283 block. All of these blocks have two-bolt main caps and use small journal 2.30-inch cranks. Blocks made in 1955 had no provision for an oil filter.

The Gen II 265, 4.3-liter V-8, introduced in 1994 in Caprice sedans and wagons can be safely bored 0.040 inch over. These are two-bolt blocks and use 2.45-inch main journal and 3-inch stroke cranks with a one-piece rear main seal. Don't mix this block up with the Chevy 4.3-liter V-6 or the 5.7-liter Gen II LT1 motor that was used in the Impala SS.

*The performance aftermarket offers a variety of small-block Chevy-based blocks. Dart's Special High Performance (SHP) small-block offers some great features for performance enthusiasts. (Photo Courtesy Dart)*

*Another aftermarket source for blocks and engines is World Products. This is the Motown 350 cast-iron block, which is also offered in aluminum to save about 90 pounds.*

*The bottom end of the PN 10134400 aluminum race block is all business. The block is CNC machined with cast-iron sleeves and the crank is secured with stout splayed four-bolt steel main caps. (Photo Courtesy Chevrolet Performance)*

*267:* This is another thin-cylinder-wall Gen I casting, which should only be bored a maximum of 0.030 inch over. This block has two-bolt caps and uses a 2.45-inch main journal crank. It had a 3.50-inch standard bore and 3.48-inch stroke and were made from 1979 through 1982.

*283:* Blocks originally having this displacement are a mixed bag. The blocks have a 3.875-inch standard bore and use a 3-inch stroke. The 1957 block castings can be bored a maximum of 0.060 inch over. The 1958 to 1962 blocks had thicker cylinder walls and can be bored 0.125 inch over to a maximum diameter of 4 inches. The 1963 to 1967 blocks went back to thinner cylinder barrel walls and should be limited to a 0.060-inch overbore. The 283 has two-bolt main caps and uses the small main journal 2.30-inch crankshafts.

*302:* These 4-inch standard-bore blocks can be bored 0.040 inch over. Many can go as large as 0.060 inch over, but this is cutting it thin and you may have problems. In 1967, the 302 used a small journal 2.30-inch crank with a 3-inch stroke and the block had two-bolt main caps. In 1968 and 1969, the Z28 302 used a 2.45-inch main journal crank and the block used four-bolt main caps.

*305:* These 5.0-liter Gen I motors are all medium-journal 2.45-inch blocks, and production blocks were only made with two-bolt main caps. They can be safely bored 0.040 inch, with some blocks going to 0.060 inch over. These Gen I blocks were introduced in 1976 with a 3.75-inch bore and 3.48-inch stroke. Blocks made from 1986 to 2003 have a one-piece rear main seal. A Vortec 5000 305 was introduced in 1996. Later-model blocks have been cast for use with roller cams.

*307:* Most of these 3.875-inch standard bores can be opened up 0.060 inch. I have heard of some being bored 0.125 inch over to 4 inches, but this is risky. If you need a 4-inch-bore medium-journal block, go find a good 350 core. These two-bolt blocks use a 2.45-inch main journal crank with a 3.25-inch stroke (the same stroke length as a 327). They were factory installed from 1968 until 1973.

*327:* These blocks were factory installed from 1962 through 1968 and have a 4-inch bore with a 3.25-inch stroke. They were all two-bolt blocks and the 1962 to 1967 blocks used small journal 2.30-inch crankshafts. The 1968 327 used a medium journal crank with 2.45-inch-diameter main journals. It can be safely bored 0.040 inch, with some blocks able to go up to 0.060 inch over.

*350:* The Gen I 350 first made its appearance in the 1967 Camaros. The Gen I and II cast-iron 4-inch blocks can be bored 0.040 inch over to 4.040 inches, and some blocks can go to 4.060 inches. All Gen I and II 350s used medium-journal 2.45-inch cranks with 3.48-inch strokes, and the blocks came in two- or four-bolt main cap varieties. Production blocks made from 1986-on have one-piece rear main seals. Many of the blocks made from 1987-on used roller cams.

*400:* The Gen I 400 is unique in that it has siamesed cylinder barrels. The standard bore of 4.125 inches can be increased safely to 0.040 inch over, with some blocks going to 0.060 inch over. This block came with either two- or four-bolt main caps from 1970 to 1980, and it was the only production motor to use a crankshaft with 2.65-inch main journal diameters and 3.76-inch strokes. The connecting rod length was shortened to 5.565 inches in order to fit everything in. These 400 engines were all externally balanced.

## Cast-Iron Bowtie Blocks

PN 12480174 (casting number 10051184) has siamesed cylinders, 9.025-inch deck, with a 3.980- to 4.030-inch bore range. It has four-bolt mains, 2.45-inch crank journals, wet-sump oiling and a one-piece oil seal, and tall lifter bores. This bare block is CNC-machined and weighs 196 pounds.

PN 12480047 (casting number 100511184) is a Bowtie Sportsman Block with the same specs as the above block but it features a two-piece oil seal and weighs about 8 pounds more.

If you're looking for a 350 main with a 400 bore size, Chevrolet Performance offers two Bowtie blocks to consider. Both feature siamesed cylinders with deck heights of 9.025 inches with a bore range of 4.117 to 4.755 inches. The mains are drilled at 20 degrees and accept nodular caps. The difference is in the rear main seals: PN 12480175 has a one-piece seal, while PN 12480157 features a two-piece seal. (Both blocks are based on casting number 100511184.)

PN 12480049 is a four-bolt block with 400 main and 350 bore size that has been CNC-machined to within +/-0.005-inch tolerances. It has splayed caps on the center three mains to accept four-bolts. The finished bore is 3.980 inches with a range up to 4.155 inches. The max stroke is 3.750 inches and has a wet oiling system. Another block is offered (PN 24502503) that includes steel caps rather than nodular like its sister block.

PN 24502650 was treated to a reduction in deck height (8.325 inches), so a short stroke/short rod, big bore motor was easier to build with improved high-RPM power, more direct intake port runner angles, compact size, weight reduction, and a lower center of gravity. The bore range is slightly larger at 3.980 to 4.185 inches and accepts a 283 crank journal for a max stroke of 3.250 inches. This block weighs in at a svelte 167 pounds.

## Aluminum Bowtie Blocks

As with most things cast in aluminum versus iron, the major benefit is less weight. Chevrolet Performance offers several cast-aluminum race blocks with the same features as the cast-iron blocks, but they tip the scales at 100 pounds or even less. T-356 aluminum is used and CNC machined and fit with centrifugal spun cast-iron cylinder sleeves. Each of the aluminum blocks uses a two-piece rear main seal and has enlarged cam bosses allowing for larger cam bearings if desired. The wet oiling system is designed with priority on the mains, though the block cab be converted to a dry sump system with plugs.

PN 10134400 (casting number 10134996) offers siamesed cylinders with a 9.025-inch deck height. The block is set up for steel main caps with bolts at a 20-degree angle with the crank journal size at 400. The rough finished bore is at 4.117 inches with a max of 4.135 inches. There is also a similar block offered (PN 10185075), but it has main journal sizes of a 350 with a smaller bore starting point of 3.986 inches. The bare block weighs in at 90 pounds.

PN 24502495 is a tall-deck aluminum Bowtie case with a deck height of 9.525 inches and it can be decked to 9.0 inches. Deck thickness is 1.125 inches. Four-bolt splayed 8620 alloy steel caps are used on the center three

*Additional tin or nickel is added to the cast iron in some blocks. These high-tin and -nickel blocks are very desirable. In this photo, the extra tin is noted on the rear face of this 350 block by the "010" signifying that 1 percent more tin was used to help the molten metal flow into the casting mold. The "020" indicates that 2 percent more nickel was used in this block, which helps make the cylinder barrels harder and more durable. These casting identifiers are also found on the front face of these blocks under the timing cover.*

*Buying a used small-block can be a gamble. Do you know the history of the engine? Has it been stored inside or in the open? Can you tell if a block or head is cracked? Also, you'll need to research what the engine was used in to help make sure your new replacement parts work!*

## Bowtie Casting Numbers

Casting numbers generally can be used to identify most Chevrolet parts. However, I must caution you about two casting numbers that have been used on one Bowtie block and another casting number that has been used with some aluminum Bowtie 18-degree and 15-degree heads. I bring this up because you may be looking at a used casting and should know the differences.

On cast-iron Bowtie blocks, casting number 10051184 was used to indicate a block with standard lifter bore angles, and the same block and casting numbers were used to identify the SB2 block with SB2 aluminum heads. There are also other variations between PN 24502503 and PN 12480175 (which are both based on casting number 10051184). One block uses nodular caps (PN 24502503) while the other uses steel caps. Also, the "503" uses a two-piece seal, while the other uses a one-piece seal. One casting number but two completely different pieces. ■

caps, while the front and rear caps are straight four-bolt caps. Use 2.65-inch main journal cranks and a 400-style two-piece rear main seal. It has sleeves that are semi-finished at 4.117 inches, and it can be bored to 4.135 inches. The pan rails are spread 0.800 inch and take strokes of 4.00 inches without modification, strokes of 4.125 inches with minor grinding, and a 4.25-inch stroke with major grinding and modifications.

This block uses big-block Chevy-type cam bearings (Federal-Mogul PN 1811M), and the camshaft tunnel itself is raised 0.391 inch from the standard location. This dry-sump block has priority main oiling. There is no provision for an internal oil pump. The oil filter boss has been deleted and a starter can be fitted to either side of the case. There is no provision for a mechanical fuel pump, either, because the fuel pump boss has been deleted. You need an aftermarket oil pan in order to fit the wider pan rails. Also, the camshaft should have big-block journal sizes and a longer aftermarket timing chain or belt to fit the raised cam tunnel.

### Cylinder Sleeves

So you look at your cast-iron block and find that a cylinder barrel is cracked or has a window. What now? Some folks believe that when this happens the only thing left to do is cart the bare block off to the dump or local recycling center. An alternative is to try to save the block by using a repair sleeve.

A machinist overbores the cylinder barrel and then press fits a barrel sleeve into the block. The sleeve is then bored to size. It's done all the time by competent machinists, and iron sleeves are used routinely in aluminum blocks. The question is: Is it worth the expense and bother?

If the motor is going to be used for stock or moderate street performance, then a sleeved cylinder works just fine. If the block needs more than one sleeve, you probably shouldn't bother. It's cheaper and easier to get another undamaged cast-iron block. However, if you're working with a rare, numbers-matching block for a restoration project, it may be worth replacing more than one sleeve to retain the original numbers-matching engine.

Aluminum blocks, on the other hand, have iron cylinder liners in all of the barrels. Replacement sleeves are available from Chevy Performance or the aftermarket. PN 12480004 is a standard bore steel sleeve for late-design aluminum blocks, including PN 10134400. This sleeve has a 3.980-inch bore and can go up to 4.135 inches.

### Freeze Plugs

Small-blocks use $1^5/_8$-inch-diameter freeze plugs, which are available in brass as PN 94673017. Aluminum race blocks, however, use a threaded freeze plug with an O-ring seal. Other freeze plugs are available through the aftermarket.

Some 400 small-blocks used three freeze plugs per side. Other 400s had a boss in the middle of the side of the block for the third freeze plug, but the boss was not drilled. You can use this unique freeze plug design to help identify 400 small-blocks. Other small-block displacements only had two freeze plugs per side.

### Cam Bearings

With the exception of the 1955 and 1956 265 blocks, which used a unique rear cam bearing and rear cam journal, Gen I production cases can use the following cam bearings: PN 474005 fits position number-1; PN 474006 fits in positions number-2 and number-5; and PN 474007 fits in positions

## Crate Engines—UPDATE!

Chevrolet has always offered small-block "crate motors" over the counter. That expanded tradition continues today and enables the buyer to purchase a complete or partial motor. These crate motors are all new from the oil pan to the valve covers and come with warranties. Chevrolet also realizes that a number of the currently offered late-model production engines appeal to enthusiasts who want to put these engines into earlier-model vehicles, whether they are classic hot rod coupes and trucks or to punch up the power in vehicles that never had factory-installed V-8s.

Likewise, the aftermarket performance industry has done what it can to provide engine parts that improve performance of late-model vehicles and still meet the required national, state, and local vehicle emissions standards. The following is just a sampling of what is currently available from Chevrolet Performance.

Before getting into the performance side of Chevrolet's crate engine program, there are three economical choices if you're simply looking for a quality replacement engine at a great price. PN 12681429 is a classic 350-ci engine designed to replace worn out small-blocks from 1973 to 1985. It is based on a new four-bolt block, flat tappet valvetrain, iron heads, and perimeter-style valve covers. For 1996–2002 replacements, there's the L31 Vortec 5.7L PN 12530283 (4-bolt) and PN 12530282 (2-bolt) engine with cast-iron Vortec heads. Finally, there's the 350 ci for 1985–1987 light-duty trucks as PN 12681430.

Now, let's get into the performance side of the offerings, starting with the 350/290 Base (PN 193556580). Bang for the buck starts here with a four-bolt block with aluminum pistons working with 76-cc iron heads to deliver a safe 8.0:1 compression ratio. The engine is rated at 308 hp at 5,100 rpm and 347 ft-lbs of torque at 3,900 rpm. The engine is basically a long-block but Chevy offers a Deluxe model (PN 19355659) that includes a 4-barrel intake complemented with chrome valve covers and air cleaner.

PN 19955662, the 350 HO Turn-Key engine, is topped with a set of iron Vortec heads fit with 1.94/1.50-inch valves. Compression is set at 9.0:1 and a flat tappet cam is supplied with peak power coming on at 5,100 rpm with 333 hp and 381 ft-lbs of torque. The Turn-Key crate engine comes with a 4-barrel intake, HEI distributor, a Holley carb, fuel pump, plug wires, and a complete front serpentine belt assembly including a new alternator, power steering pump, and air-conditioner compressor. A long-block package is also available as PN 19355660.

Next in the crate list is the SP350/357 that delivers 357 hp and 407 ft-lbs of torque. Based on the same block and Vortec heads as the 350 HO, the addition of a hydraulic roller cam with a little more lift and duration provides a little more kick to the output numbers. The Base model (PN 19367080) is basically a long-block; a Deluxe model (PN 19367082) is supplied with an intake, carb, HEI distributor, damper, and flexplate. To make it even easier, the Turn-Key model is supplied with even more, including the starter, carb, and a complete front accessory drive.

The next level of small-block offered by Chevrolet Performance is the SP350/385 rated at 385 hp at 5,600 rpm. The Base model (PN 19417624) is built on a four-bolt iron block foundation and features a forged-steel crankshaft, an aggressive hydraulic roller cam, and a beefed-up valvetrain. The big difference comes through the aluminum heads originally based on the proven Fast Burn design. A Deluxe version is also offered with a complete front drive as PN 19417623.

If you're looking for a high-output crate engine equipped with a reliable EFI system, the classic Ram Jet 350 is still available as PN 19417619. The EFI intake gives a nod to its heritage with a resemblance to the original Rochester mechanical fuel injection system. The EFI is managed by a compact MEFI controller that needs no tuning or programming. The combination delivers a stout 396 ft-lbs with 345 hp.

The top-of-the-line ZZ6 crate engine is the ZZ6 platform, which produces more than 400 hp and torque. This package is the latest in the proven ZZ platform and is available as PN 19417576 for the Base model followed by a Turn-Key, an EFI Deluxe package, and an EFI Turn-Key model. ■

***Chevrolet Performance offers a number of crate engines ranging from long-blocks to complete turn-key packages that include a carburetor (or even EFI), front accessory drive, plug wires, and more. This example is the SP350/385 Turn-Key package available as PN 19417623. (Photo Courtesy Chevrolet Performance)***

## Discontinued and Obsolete Parts

Say you decide that you need a particular part and you check with Chevrolet Performance or even General Motors and find that the part is no longer made. Before your frustration level forces you to contemplate burning your project down, remember that the small-block V-8 was introduced in 1955—some of the parts may be up to 60 years old. As demand lessened for certain pieces, Chevrolet dropped production of those and went on to other designs. If you must have a certain part or casting number, part of the fun will be searching for it.

Before you start, make sure that you know everything you can about the identification of that part, so you know it when you see it. Also, find out what it is worth. Get an idea, before you buy, of the usual price range of the part, new and used. Swap meets, junkyards, and the internet can lead you to the parts you need. However, don't rely on the description given by the seller. Sometimes the seller doesn't know what he has or has misidentified the part either intentionally or innocently. Of course, most times the seller knows exactly what he has.

Keep trying. It never ceases to amaze me when I consider what some folks have stashed away in their garages and storage sheds. Be prepared to buy a part you need one week and then to find the same part the following week for one-tenth the price. It happens. I was searching for a particular intake manifold with a particular casting number and casting date to restore a numbers-matching Corvette. I found one in another state and was willing to pay the price, $150, to get it. I was happy to finish the project. Two weeks later, I went to a swap meet. In a pile of intakes, I found the same manifold, with the same casting numbers I needed for $10. One man's treasure was another man's junk.

Many parts are still available over the counter from a Chevrolet dealer, so try them first. If you don't succeed there, try a more specialized dealer or an authorized and licensed aftermarket supplier. Often, these parts are produced using the exact same blueprints and tooling that were originally used to make the parts. Not everything is being reproduced, but with more than 16,000 listed part items, one of them may have what you need. ■

## ZZ6 350 HO Crate Motor

The crate motor business is booming, and one of Chevrolet's most popular crate engines has been the ZZ-series of Gen I small-blocks. The latest version is the ZZ6 which delivers more than 400 hp and torque to match. Think about that, this crate engine delivers more power than any 350 small-block ever installed in a production vehicle! The ZZ6 is available in several iterations:

PN 19417576 is the base model and is supplied with an externally balanced flexplate, aluminum heads and intake, HEI distributor water pump, and damper topped with a set of distinctive center-bolt valve covers. (A short block is also available as PN 12670966.)

PN 19417622 is known as the ZZ6 Turn-Key package and is supplied with the base-model components along with a 770-cfm Holley carb, starter, fuel pump, air-conditioner compressor, power steering pump, alternator, plug wires, and a serpentine belt drive system.

Chevrolet Performance also offers two electronically fuel injected versions of the ZZ6. PN 19368149 is the EFI Deluxe engine that is topped with a port fuel injected intake with a throttle body mounted in place of the carb. An engine control unit (ECU), harness, and WB02 are supplied to finish the wiring and to get the engine fired up without the need for third-party tuning. A Turn-Key option is also offered for the ZZ6 EFI package, which comes with the accessory drive kit and more. ■

*The ZZ6 crate engine from Chevy Performance is the most powerful "production" small-block of all time with 405 hp and 406 ft-lbs. It is offered in a base model, a Turn-Key version, EFI Deluxe, and a Turn-Key EFI package. (Photo Courtesy Chevrolet Performance)*

## Vortec 5000 and 5700 Engines

In 1996, Chevrolet introduced the Vortec 5000 RPO L30 305-ci and Vortec 5700 RPO L31 350-ci engines and made them available in full-size trucks, Suburbans, and Blazers. These are enhanced Gen I one-piece rear main seal small-blocks, but they feature a number of changes that improve performance. All of these engines have steel hydraulic roller cams and roller lifters, and the blocks have minor lifter-bore changes to use roller lifters along with bolt bosses in the lifter valley to bolt the spiders, which help retain the roller lifters in their respective bores.

The Vortec cast-iron cylinder heads have revised, larger (170-cc volume) intake port runner dimensions and the combustion chambers have been changed to help increase compression. The 64-cc heart-shaped chambers have straight plugs, but the plug bosses move the plugs higher and closer to the chamber roof. The L31 head uses 1.94/1.5-inch valves with pressed-in rocker studs. The intake port openings are 0.080-inch taller than those on previous standard-production Gen I heads. The intake manifold bolt holes in the Vortec heads are positioned at 90 degrees to the head/manifold surface, but the bolt spacing is different and only four bolts are used on each side to mount the two-piece Vortec intake manifold. You must use a revised Vortec intake manifold gasket when using Vortec heads and related production or aftermarket intake manifolds.

Sequential electronic fuel injection with a mass airflow meter is used along with a two-piece intake manifold, which has an aluminum lower base piece and a composite plastic material upper half. Static compression has been increased and the coolant system has been revised to provide better bank-to-bank coolant flow balance. The coolant passages at each end of the heads are larger.

The vibration dampers on Vortec 5000 and 5700 motors incorporate a crankshaft trigger ring for their electronic ignitions and are not interchangeable with other Gen I engines. The Vortec small-block engine blocks also have an additional coolant bypass hole that is not used in other earlier Gen I powerplants.

The 1996 Vortec 5000 305 has increased output to 220 hp at 4,600 rpm and has 285 ft-lbs of torque at 2,800 rpm. The Vortec 5700 has 335 ft-lbs of torque at 2,800 rpm and delivers 250 hp at 4,600 rpm. These engines can still readily be found in donor vehicles and can make a good powerplant for hot rods and pickups, but you need to make sure to use the specific Vortec components from Chevrolet or the aftermarket. ■

number-3 and number-4. Remember, each cam bearing goes in a particular position front-to-back, since three different sizes are used. If you cannot find these older Chevy part numbers, turn to the aftermarket bearing companies.

You may have heard that a number of race engine builders are using roller cam bearings in their maximum-effort, "take no prisoners" engines. These are entirely unnecessary in stock and even most race engines.

### Main Caps

Gen I and II small-blocks have been offered with two- or four-bolt main caps. Most four-bolt main cap blocks have a two-bolt front cap and a two-bolt rear main cap. Now, before you run out and look for a four-bolt block or upgrade from two-bolt caps to four-bolt caps, keep in mind that a two-bolt block can withstand up to 500 hp, especially if you use quality main cap studs and nuts instead of the stock main cap bolts. The two-bolt bottom end has to be right, but it is often used in short-duration motors.

For stock street use and some performance and race use, a two-bolt block is more than adequate. If your power levels are going to be higher than this or if you are going to use large doses of nitrous, high-boost turbocharging, or supercharging, then go to a four-bolt block.

The Gen I and II main caps themselves are made of gray iron, nodular iron, or steel. Most factory-installed production blocks use two- or four-bolt gray-iron main caps, although some had nodular-iron caps (the nodular main caps have an "N" cast onto their surface). Most are straight caps, meaning the bolts enter the block surface at 90 degrees. However, some Bowtie four-bolt main steel caps are splayed, which means the two inner bolts enter the block at 90 degrees, while the two outside bolts enter the block at 70 degrees. They are splayed 20 degrees from perpendicular. The splayed caps provide more bottom end strength and perch in a place in the block that is subject to less distortion.

## SB2: Short Name, Big Design Jump

In 1996, Chevrolet offered an all-new Gen I–based small-block racing engine called the SB2. It's new-design block, aluminum cylinder heads, and two-piece, single, 4-barrel intake manifold made up the bulk of the changes. To make matters a little more confusing, Chevy introduced an SB2.2 engine design with further updates before being updated with the RO7 at least in NASCAR competition in 2007. Unless you're really searching for something unique to run in your hot rod or high-revving weekend warrior, there's not a big call for these engines any more. However, having something unique is what makes hot rodding fun, so let's take a quick look at what made the SB2.

The cast-iron block (PN 24502600) is based on the proven Bowtie 1184 block design. The splayed four-bolt blocks feature revised lifter angles and lifter bore locations that work with the new SB2 heads. The lifter bores could be enlarged to 0.875 inch and the cam bearing bores were sized for big-block Chevy-style cam bearings.

The SB2 aluminum heads featured non-siamesed mirror port intakes and revised raised intake runner angles, which each point directly toward the intake manifold plenum and carb. Also, the locations of the intake and exhaust valves have been changed from the standard production sequence. The valve sequence on these SB2 heads is I, E, I, E, E, I, E, I. This valve sequence calls for a different camshaft, and aftermarket cam makers are set up to produce the cams and left- and right-bank pistons you need.

SB2 heads can be used on a stock production block or Bowtie block, but you need the updated camshafts and 0.180-inch offset roller lifters in order to maintain rocker arm geometry. The raised intake port runners along with the SB2 intake manifold runners have been repositioned so that there is a direct line from the intake manifold plenum to each cylinder. The intake port openings are almost 1/2-inch higher than those found on the 18-degree, high-port Bowtie race heads.

Extra-long-stem 2.15/1.65-inch-diameter valves (5.550 inches overall) are required. These are slightly longer than those used on the 18-degree, high-port Bowtie heads. The SB2 uses a 1.950-inch spring installed height. The intake valve angle is decreased to 12 degrees, and the exhaust is angled at 8 degrees, toward the bore centerline. On the CNC-prepared SB2 head (PN 24502560), the combustion chamber is shallow and measures 38 cc on the CNC-prepped head, which gets you 15.0:1 static compression with a flat-top piston and 358 ci. The chamber can be opened up farther to 53 cc to run a 9.0:1 compression ratio.

The SB2's exhaust ports are raised and have a siamesed-port exit design with more coolant passages nearby to aid in cooling. The exhaust port openings feature revised exhaust header bolt patterns that are unique to the SB2 heads and require non-traditional tube header flange bolt holes to match.

Use head gasket PN 10185054 with these SB2 heads. The head calls for the standard head bolt pattern, but because of the revised port locations, some of the bolts pass through openings in the rocker arm valley and into the port runner floors. Screw-in AN plugs with O-rings are used to block off the head bolt access holes in the rocker valley.

The special, eight-bolt, cast-aluminum valve covers provide oil galleries and spray bars that can be added to shower the valve springs with pressurized oil. These help cool the valve springs to increase race durability.

The two-piece intake manifold uses a separate lower valley cover that provides for the coolant crossover, thermostat housing, and distributor mounting and keeps hot oil in the lifter valley off of the intake runners. The upper dry manifold runner spider and the single Holley 4-barrel carb with an open plenum are unique to the SB2 head intake ports and offer the advantages of easy removal of the upper manifold plenum and intake runners without having to remove the distributor or drain any coolant. ■

Keep these tips in mind: Whenever you replace the original main caps, you must have the new caps fitted to the block saddles in order to properly register the caps. The new caps must then be precision align-bored and align-honed in order to ensure that the crankshaft is properly centered in the block and that it is square with the front and back of the case and perpendicular to the cylinder barrels. Not all automotive machine shops are properly set up, or experienced enough, to do this kind of work. Make sure you patronize a shop that has the equipment and expertise to reliably align-bore and align-hone your engine.

When a block is align-bored, the distance from the crank centerline to the camshaft centerline may be altered. This alters the length of the timing chain needed on that block. Competition Cams, Cloyes,

## Places to Look for Small-Block Cores

Everybody knows that Chevrolet has been making small-block V-8s since 1955, but they also stopped putting them in production vehicles in the late 1990s as the Gen III took over. Finding rebuildable Chevy engine cores is not difficult; millions have been made. They have been used in passenger cars, station wagons, muscle cars, police and taxi vehicles, hot rods, boats, RVs, school buses, race cars, heavy-duty trucks, generators, and irrigation pumps. Some guys have even stuck them in airplanes.

Keep in mind that other GM divisions have used Chevrolet small-blocks to power some of their vehicles. Chevy 305 and 350 engines have been factory installed in Pontiac, Buick, Oldsmobile, and Cadillac cars. The 1977 to 1980 models are good places to look for carbureted Chevy small-block motors in BOP cars, and 1990 Cadillacs used a fuel-injected Chevrolet Gen I 350 with a roller cam and a one-piece seal. In 1991, Cadillac also used a 305 with fuel injection, hydraulic roller cam, and a one-piece rear main seal. Some Pontiac Firebirds in the 1990s have used Chevy LT1 Gen II motors.

Now don't confuse these Chevrolet-made engines with the 350-ci motors that Pontiac, Oldsmobile, and Buick designed and used in their cars. What am I saying? Any Bowtie lover can spot a Chevy small-block in a junkyard or an arroyo from 2 miles away, no matter what's wrapped around it. ■

and other companies offer timing chain sets that have shorter chains to accommodate align-bored blocks. If you install a new standard-length timing chain and gear set on an align-bored block, there is so much slack in the new chain it looks like a used one out of a taxicab engine with 300,000 miles on the clock.

It is a good idea to mark each main bearing cap (and rod cap) with a stamped-in number before you take an engine core apart. Each cap must go back into its respective position and the correct direction when it is reassembled. The factory puts an arrow on each cap to show the "front" direction. However, the caps are not numerically stamped. You need to stamp them before disassembly.

### Main Bearings

Main bearings are generally available in the following sizes: standard (Std.), 0.001, 0.010, 0.020, 0.030, and 0.040 inch. When a crankshaft is checked for wear, it may be necessary to grind the crank journals undersize in order to restore the journals to their correct roundness and to remove scratches. An oversize bearing must then be used to keep the required running clearances.

The most important thing is to make sure that the bearing surfaces are spotlessly clean—both the bearing itself and the bearing saddles in the block and the main caps. Check the clearances and follow the clearance recommendations. Chevrolet recommends main bearing clearances of 0.002 to 0.003 inch with a crank thrust clearance (also called crank end play) of 0.005 to 0.007 inch. If the crank has been reground, make sure that the radius from the crank cheeks to the journal are not going to interfere with the side edges of the bearing. Chamfered-edge bearings are available to clear cranks with large journal radii.

Chevrolet Performance offers a main bearing kit for a standard 350-ci engine as PN 12499102. Always use a main bearing set that has a groove cut in the half of the bearing that fits in the upper position in the bearing saddles of the block. The lower bearing half should not have a groove, and it fits in the main bearing cap. Do not use fully grooved bearing shells.

### Block Dowel Pins

Sometimes when you acquire a block, a number of the dowel pins are missing. Here are the GM replacement parts for Gen I blocks:

**Block Dowel Pin Part Numbers**

| Part | Part Number |
|---|---|
| Rear Block/Transmission Dowel Pins | 01453658 |
| Block Deck/Head Locating Pins | 585927 |
| One-piece Rear Oil Seal Housing/Block Locator Dowel Pin | 9441003 |

Some folks wish to offset the cylinder head locations from their original blueprint location for racing purposes. Offset head locator pins are available from aftermarket suppliers. However, this is not something a novice engine builder should try. At times, the block is misaligned to the transmission bellhousing locator pins on the rear of the block. Offset block/transmission dowel pins are also sold on the aftermarket.

## Generation II LT4

In 1996, Chevrolet also introduced the LT4 350 small-block V-8 as an engine option in the 1996 Corvettes. This Gen II small-block 350 engine has a number of changes when compared to the 1992 to 1995 Gen II LT1 350, which has 300 net hp and 330 ft-lbs of torque in production vehicles. The 1996 production LT4 engine is rated at 330 net hp, and used revised aluminum heads with 2.00/1.55-inch lightweight valves. The exhausts are hollow stem valves that are partially filled with a mixture of sodium and potassium to improve valve cooling and reduce weight. Static compression is 10.8:1 (the Gen II LT1 has 10.4:1) with the small chamber LT4 aluminum heads and revised pistons that have the smaller valve reliefs.

The LT4 heads (PN 12555689 or 12363287) have intake ports that are raised 0.100-inch higher than those found on the 1992 to 1996 LT1. The port contours have been reshaped and improved for more flow and increase the intake port volume to 185 cc. The exhaust port contours have been changed on the LT4 head for smoother flow. Stud-mounted, self-aligning Crane roller rockers with a 1.6:1 ratio are used along with single-coil 110/260-pound spring-pressure valve springs. The LT4 head (PN 12555689) uses a non-adjustable net lash shouldered rocker arm stud. A steel roller cam and hydraulic roller lifters increase the capabilities of the valvetrain to 6,300 rpm.

This motor used reverse-flow cooling and its heads can be interchanged onto the LT1 block, provided that you use the production LT4 electronic TPI manifold. Use the new-design LT4 intake manifold gaskets, which fit the revised intake manifold bolt-hole spacing and bolt angles. The LT4 uses a one-piece rear main seal crank, which is externally balanced, and 5.7-inch powdered metal rods. These engines may now be even more rare than the SB2 race engine. ■

### Used Engine Blocks

If you are about to buy a used block, here are some things to think about before buying: How has the block or complete engine been stored? Has it been kept inside in a clean, dry place or has it been sitting outside? Has it been covered up? Why is it being sold? Did a rod bearing spin? Was it burning large amounts of oil before it was pulled out? Is it covered with rust, dirt, or 200,000 miles of grease? If water was left in the block when it was stored or if rain or snow has gotten into it, has the block suffered a freeze crack? Some cracks are practically impossible to spot when the block is covered with rust, oil, grease, or who knows what. If the crank and rods are still in the block, can you turn the motor over? Is it locked up or does it turn over smoothly?

Check the casting numbers and dates. What do they tell you? If the heads are off the block or if the seller lets you remove the heads, check the bore of the motor. Has the block already been bored 0.040 inch over or larger? Are the cylinder walls clean, rusty, or cracked?

Look at the threaded bolt holes on the block. Have any of the threads been stripped? Are bolts broken off in the holes? Are all of the main bearing caps still on the engine? Are dowel pins missing?

Some problems may not be found on a used block until you take it to a machine shop and have it cleaned. You may find cracked cylinder barrels, cracked water jackets, or cracks caused by broken connecting rods hitting pan rails, oil passages, or cylinder barrels. The main caps may be mismatched or from another block.

Some of these problems can be fixed. Cylinders can be sleeved, threaded holes can be heli-coiled, and cylinders can be bored out and cleaned—up to a point. Some problems cannot be fixed. Cast-iron blocks with cracks in the outboard water jackets, with major damage from a broken connecting rod, or with more than one cracked cylinder barrel need to go directly to the dump or metal recycler or back to the guy who sold it to you.

The point is, there are times when the cost of fixing a used block is too high. Keep looking for a block that doesn't need major repair. Try to find a used engine that is still running in a vehicle so you can hear it and maybe drive it to get a better idea of its condition. Millions of Chevy Gen I and II small-blocks are out there, so you shouldn't have any trouble finding a good, rebuildable core motor with the features that you want.

CHAPTER 2

# Gaskets and Fasteners

When it comes to sealing your small-block Chevy, there several areas you'll need to address due to design changes. First, you must determine whether you are building an engine using the familiar two-piece rear main oil seal or with the new-style one-piece rear main seal that was first introduced in Gen I blocks in 1986. Adapters are available, both from Chevrolet Performance and aftermarket suppliers, which allow you to use a one-piece, rear-main-seal-style block with an earlier two-piece seal crank.

When searching for gaskets, it is important to note that many different materials and applications are available from Chevy and aftermarket suppliers. Also, Chevrolet has discontinued many different gaskets and seals over the years but gasket companies such as Fel-Pro Gaskets, SCE Gaskets, Cometic Gaskets, and others that specialize in sealing engine components may have exactly what you're looking for.

## Intake Manifold Gaskets

There are now five different production intake manifold gasket types, and which one you use depends on whether you are building a Gen I, Gen II LT1, Gen II LT4, or Vortec small-block. The intake manifold bolt angles, the bolt spacing, and the position in the cylinder heads and intake manifolds, and some production port positions have been altered from what you may be familiar with. Coolant crossover passages have been moved or in some motors eliminated. These intake manifold/head bolt hole changes began with the 1987 models. Intake manifold gaskets of interest include the following:

*There are a variety of intakes and heads available, so make sure you have the correct intake setup for your application. Most GM intake manifolds are supplied with rubber end gaskets that fit on the block between the two head surfaces. Many aftermarket manifolds recommend using a gasket sealer instead.*

PN 10147994 fits all Gen I 262 to 400 small-blocks with standard port locations and sizes. This gasket does not work with 1996-or-later Vortec heads or intake manifolds. Do not use this intake manifold gasket on Gen II motors. This gasket has a heat riser passage. Using an intake manifold gasket with a blocked heat riser passage can help keep the temperatures in the intake manifold cooler; however, blocking the heat riser passage makes cold morning operation more difficult.

The PN 19301685 Intake Gasket is designed for the Chevrolet Performance Fast Burn Aluminum Vortec heads (PN 12558060, PN 19300955, and PN 19300956) only. The gaskets are 0.120-inch thick and have both the early six-bolt pattern and the Vortec four-bolt pattern.

For production Vortec heads, use gasket PN 89017465 with four bolt attachments to the heads. This installation requires attaching bolt PN 12550027 because the bolt has a ball

*Many aftermarket gaskets are available with larger intake port openings, but unless you've port matched your intake and heads for all-out performance, stick with the original sizes.*

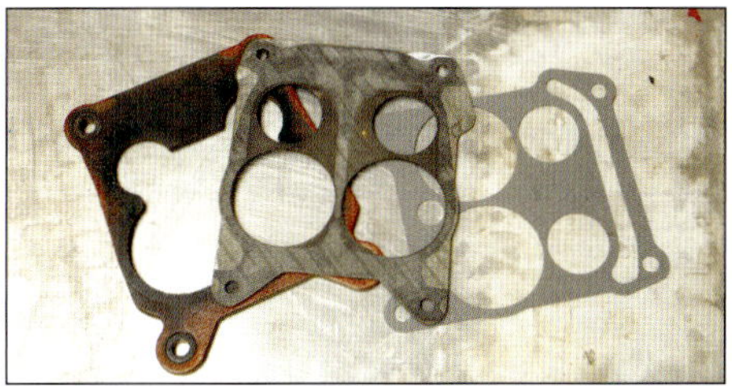

*Chevrolet used a variety of carbs and intakes over the years, which means there are a lot of different gaskets. On many of the intake manifolds made in the 1960s, a heat riser channel was cut across the carb mounting deck, which required a traditional gasket and a metal gasket. Newer-model gaskets do not seal these. In short, be aware of the year of the intake you are using to get the correct carburetor gasket.*

design on the end that sits in the head so it will not crush the intake manifold gasket.

If you plan to swap an LT1 (Gen II) engine to accept a carburetor and distributor, use intake gasket PN 12524653.

PN 12528884 is made for Gen II 350 LT4 raised intake port heads. There is no coolant passage in the gasket because these are reverse-flow heads. The manifold bolt holes have also been relocated (used on engine PN 12371172).

Chevrolet Performance offers other unique intake gaskets for use with different performance and racing cylinder heads. PN 10185042 is required with splayed valve heads (PN 24502517). For 18-degree high port heads (PN 10134363 and PN 24502580), use gasket kit PN 10185007.

Aftermarket gasket makers also can supply intake manifold gaskets with larger port openings for racers who are using heads with large port opening dimensions. Be sensible here. Don't buy the largest intake port gasket you can get, thinking that if you open the port opening to the gasket size, you'll improve the performance of the engine.

If you are building a street engine, the only thing you need to remember is to make sure that the intake manifold port opening and head port opening match and that there is no ledge formed by the gasket or the head to impede flow. If you are building a race motor and you have substantially improved the flow in the port runners and increased the size of the head port opening, think about increasing the gasket size opening to match the port sizes.

## Carb Gaskets

Over four decades of small-block production, a number of different carburetors have been used, and all these carburetors used different-style gaskets between the carb base and the top surface of the intake manifold.

Heat riser passages were built into some intake manifolds to feed warm air to the base of the carb to warm it up when first started on cold mornings. The carb gaskets must match the heat riser passages in these manifolds. You can check the intake manifold casting date to help determine which carburetor and carb gasket are correct for your application. The intake may require the use of a Rochester 2-barrel, Carter WCFB or AFB, Rochester Four Jet, Rochester Quadrajet, or Holley 4-barrel. One of the more common misapplications I have seen is the use of a later-style Quadrajet carb gasket on a 1969 or earlier Quadrajet intake, which has cast-in heat riser passages and a channel that runs across the front side of the carb mounting surface. This channel requires a particular carb gasket to seal it. If a later-style Quadrajet gasket is used on the 1969 and earlier intakes, the result is an air leak, because the later gasket doesn't seal the intake surface and the heat riser channel completely.

Chevrolet used to offer two types of carb heat shields that fit between the intake manifold and the base of the carb and incorporate a carb gasket into the heat shield. PN 3969835 fit Holley square-flange 4-barrels and PN 3969837 fit Rochester Quadrajet spreadbore carbs on 1970-on intakes. These heat shields can reduce heat absorption by carb fuel bowls and can cure some fuel percolation problems. Aftermarket models are available.

## Head Gaskets

Most production engines that have cast-iron heads were built using factory steel shim head gaskets. Engines with aluminum heads always received a composition-style head gasket. Composition head gaskets can be used with iron heads, but never use a steel shim gasket with aluminum heads.

Head gaskets are made in various compressed thicknesses and

## Bolts, Studs, and Torquing Tips

Unless you're building a turbocharged or supercharged engine that sees extended periods of severe service in a race car or a boat, there is little reason to use cylinder head studs. Studs are needed to ensure even gasket crush and promote proper sealing in engines with very high cylinder pressures. The brake mean effective pressure (BMEP) in the average street engine rarely approaches the point where gasket integrity is threatened. Blown head gaskets are normally the result of improperly torqued bolts, detonation, or improperly faced surfaces on the head or block.

For street and bracket racing applications, it is usually safe to use stock Chevy head bolts. Factory fasteners have the proper elasticity to provide effective clamping at the recommended torque specs. Aftermarket bolts—such as those available from ARP or Milodon, and others—perform very well.

If you angle-cut the heads to gain compression, be certain to have the machinist spot face all the head bolt seats to make them parallel to the deck surface. Remember also that the bosses along the outside of the head for the short bolts can get very thin after angle milling. It is possible to break or crack the head in this area if care is not exercised when torquing the bolts.

Another good move is to install the head and gasket on the bare block and observe their relationship through the empty cylinders. In this manner, you can determine if any part of the gasket or combustion chamber is overhanging the bore. This problem can be remedied by using the correct head gasket for your bore size and by lightly blending the edges of the combustion chambers to match the bore size. ■

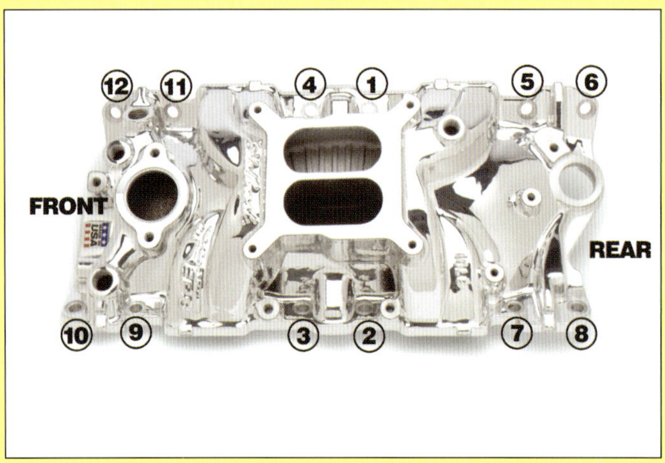

***The head gaskets for a 400 small-block have six additional steam holes between the cylinder barrels to help keep these siamesed blocks cool.***

bore sizes. Altering the thickness of the gasket affects the measured static compression ratio of the engine. It also affects the clearance between the open valves and pistons and between the piston deck and the head deck. You need a minimum of 0.035- to 0.040-inch clearance between the piston deck and the head quench area deck with steel rods. When using aluminum rods, your engine may need more piston-deck-to-head-deck clearance to accommodate aluminum rod stretch.

Steel shim or copper gaskets must be coated with a head gasket sealer before installation.

Some gaskets do not require hot re-torquing. However, it is not a bad idea to do a hot re-torquing on any head gasket. Follow the recommended head bolt torquing sequence and torque to the proper amounts.

PN 3830711 is a production steel shim gasket for 4-inch-bore Gen I engines. It is 0.026-inch thick when compressed and should only be used with cast-iron cylinder heads.

PN 10105117 is a composition head gasket with stainless steel surfaces. This gasket is used on 4-inch-bore Gen I motors and has a 0.028-inch compressed thickness. It can be used with cast-iron or aluminum heads and is recommended for marine engine use.

PN 12557236 was used on the ZZ4 crate engine and other 350 HO engines. This composition gasket has a compressed thickness of 0.051 inch and can be used with other cast-iron or aluminum heads and 4-inch bores.

PN 10185054 is a heavy-duty, competition composition gasket that is Teflon coated with solid wire fire rings. Compressed thickness is 0.040 inch and it should be used with 4.0- to 4.165-inch-bore Gen I blocks. This gasket does not have any steam holes for use on street-driven siamesed bore 400 blocks. If used on the street, drill the steam holes in the gasket and use heads with steam holes.

PN 14096405 composition gasket has a stainless steel face on one side and graphite coating on the other. Compressed thickness is 0.028 inch and it is for 4-inch-bore Gen I blocks.

PN 10168457 is a composite head gasket for the 1992–2001 aluminum headed LT1 engine. It has a compressed thickness of 0.050-inch.

If you are building a siamesed 400 production block and you intend to use the motor on the street, you need to use a 400-style head gasket with extra steam holes and be sure there are matching steam holes in the heads you use. If the heads you intend to use do not have the required steam holes in their deck, you can use a 400 head gasket as a template to locate and drill the six extra steam holes in each head. If you are going to race a 400 small-block full-time, there is no need to drill the matching steam holes in the heads. Coolant flow at engine speeds above 3,500 rpm is sufficient to keep things cooled down.

Chevrolet Performance offers a Cylinder Head Installation Kit for the 5.7L L31 engine (1986 and newer Gen I engines). PN 12499223 is supplied with two head gaskets (PN 10105117), two center-bolt valve cover gaskets (PN 10046089), and intake (PN 89017465) and exhaust gaskets (PN 12550033).

When overhauling an engine, it's best to go with a complete gasket set. Chevy Performance offers two kits that are supplied with gaskets for the following surfaces: heads, oil pan, intake, rear main seal housing, water outlet, front cover, fuel pump adapter, water pump, valve covers, distributor, and rear main seal. Kit PN 19201171 is for the 350 HO, HT383, and Circle Track crate engines (PN 88958602 and PN 88869602). Gasket Kit PN 19201172 is designed for the Fast Burn 385, ZZ5, SP383/350, and ZZ6.

## Valve Cover Gaskets

For decades, the Gen I small-block was notorious for valve cover oil leaks. When the new center-bolt valve covers were introduced in 1987, valve cover leaks were prevented by using a new mating surface and gasket on the covers and a machined gasket surface on the rails on the cylinder heads. If you have the old-style valve covers, you can use a bar retainer (plain steel PN 14082321 or chrome PN 14044820) to help the bolts hold down the cover by distributing the clamping force over a greater area. There is also a torx stud (PN 14082320) and nut (PN 14051876) for the older type of flange bolted cover, which makes mounting the valve cover gaskets easier.

The old-style cork valve cover gasket, used from 1955 to 1986, is PN 3933964. The gasket for center-bolt valve covers is PN 10046089. Each bolt on the center bolt valve covers has a small O-ring gasket under the bolt head which is available new as a kit with PN 12497980.

## Clearances

| | |
|---|---|
| Main Bearings | 0.002 to 0.003 inch |
| Crank End Thrust | 0.005 to 0.007 inch |
| Rod Bearings | 0.002 to 0.0025 inch |
| Rod Side Clearance | 0.010 to 0.020 inch |
| Piston to Bore | Follow recommendations of piston maker |
| Valve Lash | Follow recommendations of cam maker |
| Minimum Piston Ring End Gap | Follow recommendations of ring maker |
| Minimum Piston Deck to Head Deck | 0.035 to 0.040 inch with steel rods, more may be needed with aluminum rods |
| Open Valve to Piston Deck | Minimum of 0.045 inch on a stock engine, 0.100 inch on a high-performance or race engine |
| Spark Plug Gap | 0.035 inch with GM point ignition |
| | 0.045 inch with GM HEI ignition |
| | 0.035 to 0.060 inch with GM/MSD ignition |
| Cam End Play with Cam Button | 0.004 to 0.006 inch |

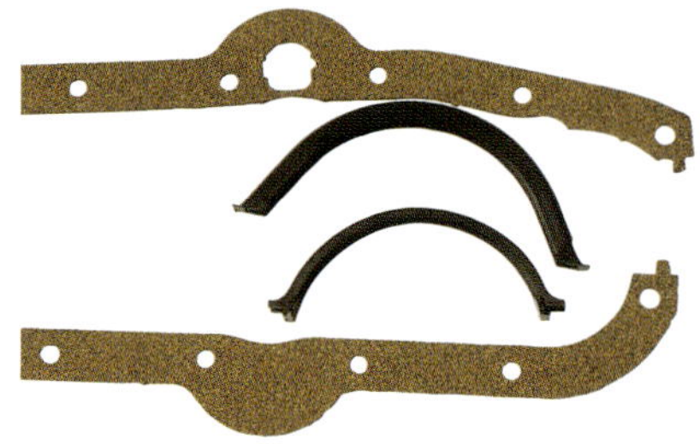

***This is a traditional oil pan gasket set for a Gen I engine with a two-piece rear main seal. You need to get the pan gaskets that match the dipstick bulge location on your block and pan. Then determine whether your pan needs either the thin or thick front pan gasket. The 1955 to 1975 blocks and pans used the thin, 1/4-inch rubber seals, while the 1976 to 1985 engines used thicker 3/8-inch seals.***

Bowtie splayed valve heads (PN 10185040) use valve cover gasket PN 10185043.

### Oil Pan Gaskets

Determine which side of the engine is set up for the oil dipstick location. You'll want an oil pan that matches the block's dipstick position. Oil pan gaskets are made to match whichever side the dipstick fits, and the block, pan, and the oil pan gaskets all must match. Some replacement and Bowtie blocks were made with provisions to put the dipstick on either side.

Gen I engines from 1955 through 1985 with two-piece rear main seals used four separate gaskets to seal the oil pan to the bottom of the block. Check the seal thickness used to seal the front of the oil pan to the bottom sealing surface of the timing chain cover. Two different thicknesses have been used over the years, and you may also have an oil pan that came from a different year engine than the block you are using. It's no problem; most gasket sets come with both gasket sizes.

Here's how to tell which front pan gasket to use: On engines from 1955 to 1974, a 1/4-inch-thick gasket was used, and from 1975 to 1985, a 3/8-inch-thick gasket was used. Take the oil pan you are going to use and place a straightedge across the pan rails and over the front gasket half-moon opening. Now measure the distance from the seal surface to the bottom of the straightedge. If the distance is 2$^1/_4$ inches, use the 1/4-inch-thick seal. If the distance is 2$^3/_8$ inches, use the 3/8-inch-thick seal.

Oil pans and oil pan gaskets for 1986-on one-piece rear main seal engines are different from those found on pre-1986 two-piece rear seal blocks. The one-piece seal blocks use a one-piece neoprene gasket (PN 10108676) to fit the redesigned oil pan found on Gen I one-piece seal engines. Use metal oil pan rail reinforcements (PN 12553058 LH and 12553059 RH) with one-piece-style oil pans. Gen II L99, LT1, and LT4 pans can use oil pan gasket PN 10108676.

### Gasket Sealants

Since the head bolts go through the water jackets on production blocks, it is necessary to use thread sealant on these bolts to prevent water from seeping up the bolt columns. Sealants are used elsewhere in the motor, but use these sealants sparingly.

Excessive sealants are pushed out as bolts are torqued down and pieces can begin to circulate in the motor. They can wind up clogging the oil pickup screen and cutting off the oil supply. Blobs of sealant can move into small passages and prevent oil circulation in other parts of the motor. Gasket cements hold a gasket where you need it, and there is less chance of any excess gasket cement squeezing out and moving through the motor.

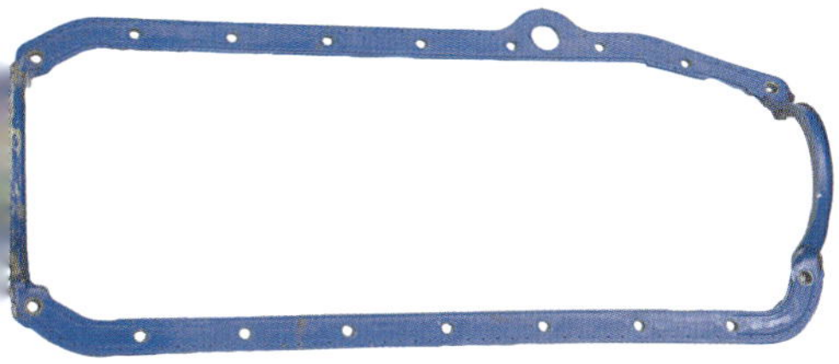

*Gen I and Gen II engines with a one-piece rear main seal and matching crank use a single, one-piece oil pan gasket. These are also now available for earlier blocks as well.*

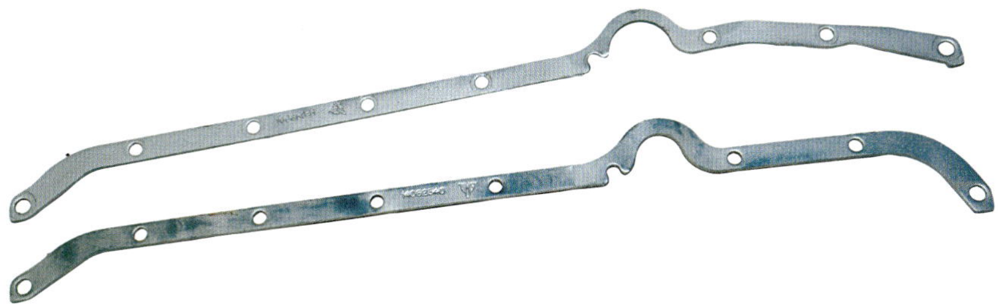

*To help seal the first-generation small-block oil pans, Chevrolet Performance offers these oil pan rails that help spread the torque of the bolts over the mounting area.*

## Recommended Bolt Torque

| Cast-Iron Engines | | | |
|---|---|---|---|
| Main Cap | 7/16-inch bolts | 65 ft-lbs (outer) | Oil or Moly lube |
| | | 70 ft-lbs (inner) | Oil or Moly lube |
| | 3/8-inch bolts | 40 ft-lbs (outer) | Oil or Moly lube |
| | 7/16-inch studs | 65 ft-lbs (inner) | Oil or Moly lube |
| | | 60 ft-lbs (outer) | Oil or Moly lube |
| | 3/8-inch studs | 60 ft-lbs (outer) | Oil or Moly lube |
| Connecting Rod | 11/32 inch | 40–45 ft-lbs | Oil or Moly lube |
| | 3/8 inch | 45–50 ft-lbs | Oil or Moly lube (0.006-inch stretch) |
| (PN 14011092) | 7/16 inch | 70 ft-lbs | Oil or Moly lube (0.005- to .006-inch stretch) |
| Cylinder Head | | 65 ft-lbs | Sealant (Blind bolt holes in Bowtie blocks require oil on head bolt threads.) |
| Rocker Arm Screw-In Stud | | 50 ft-lbs | Sealant |
| Camshaft Sprocket | | 20 ft-lbs | Oil |
| Intake Manifold | | 30 ft-lbs | Oil |
| Flywheel or Flexplate | | 60 ft-lbs | Oil |
| Front Damper Bolt | | 60 ft-lbs | Oil |
| Exhaust Manifold | | 25 ft-lbs | Anti-seize |
| **Aluminum Engines** | | | |
| Main Cap | 3/8-inch bolts | 40 ft-lbs (outer) | Oil or Moly lube |
| | 7/16-inch studs | 65 ft-lbs (inner) | Oil or Moly lube |
| | | 60 ft-lbs (outer) | Oil or Moly lube |
| | 3/8-inch studs | 60 ft-lbs (outer) | Oil or Moly lube |
| Connecting Rod | 11/32 inch | 40–45 ft-lbs | Oil or Moly lube |
| | 3/8 inch | 45–50 ft-lbs | Oil or Moly lube (0.006-inch stretch) |
| (PN 14011092) | 7/16 inch | 70 ft-lbs | Oil or Moly lube (0.005- to 0.006-inch stretch) |
| Cylinder Head | | 65 ft-lbs (long) | Oil or Sealant |
| | | 60 ft-lbs (short) | Oil or Sealant (Blind bolt holes in Bowtie blocks require oil on head bolt threads.) |
| Rocker Arm Screw-In Stud | | 50 ft-lbs | Sealant |
| Camshaft Sprocket | | 20 ft-lbs | Oil |
| Intake Manifold | | 30 ft-lbs | Oil |
| with Aluminum Heads | | 25 ft-lbs | Anti-seize |
| Flywheel or Flexplate | | 60 ft-lbs | Oil |
| Front Damper Bolt | | 60 ft-lbs | Oil |
| Exhaust Manifold | | 25 ft-lbs | Anti-seize |

When using aluminum heads, make sure you use a hardened steel flat washer under the head bolts or stud nuts. Use a steel shim or spring cup under valve springs used with aluminum heads. When using main cap studs, place a hardened steel washer under the stud nut. ■

If the engine is going into a vehicle that has an oxygen sensor in the exhaust system, use sealants that are oxygen sensor safe. Some of the sealants on the market produce gases while curing that can damage the oxygen sensor.

## Fasteners

Each bolt and stud manufacturer, whether it is from Chevrolet or an aftermarket company specializing in fasteners, has a recommended torque value or stretch value for each type of fastener. Follow the manufacturer's recommendation for the proper amount of torque or stretch required for the bolt or stud. Also, each fastener type, depending on its application, requires some type of lubricant on the threads in order to achieve the proper torque or stretch amounts. This lubricant could be sealants, oils, anti-seize, or some form of moly-based lubricant. Follow the recommendations.

Each fastener that is torqued must be drawn up to its recommended torque value in stages and in the proper bolt-torquing sequence. This is especially important when tightening main cap fasteners, head fasteners, and rod bolts. Follow the recommendations, take your time, and double-check your work.

Of equal importance is that every fastener must be clean. Clean the threads and holes in the block and remove any rust, corrosion, and old sealants. If a threaded hole is damaged, it needs to be repaired; the threads on a fastener must be spotless as well. Make sure that the fastener threads are not damaged or stripped.

Like many gaskets, if you cannot find a specific fastener from Chevrolet any more, chances are that one of the aftermarket fastener companies such as ARP or Milodon will have what you need.

## Main Cap Bolts and Studs

Small-journal Gen I blocks used a different length main cap bolt than later medium- and large-journal Gen I blocks, which were about 1/4 inch longer. Use the correct bolts or aftermarket studs. Also, the main cap bolt spacing is different between the small, medium, and large journal blocks, and so the main caps are not interchangeable between the small, medium, and large journal (400) blocks.

The production main cap bolts used by Chevrolet work just fine in all street applications and you don't need to use a stud kit in a stock or street performance engine. Stud kits offer the advantage of reducing the amount of wear and tear on block threads, if you are frequently tearing the motor down. Some race situations can benefit by using a stud kit, especially if you are using a two-bolt block. A main cap stud kit adds strength to the bottom end of the two-bolt block. In large nitrous, supercharger, or turbocharger, high-RPM and high-power applications, a four-bolt block with a stud kit can help. Nodular-iron caps are stronger than the production gray iron caps, and steel caps are stronger still. Also, a splayed main cap offers more strength than a straight main cap.

A four-bolt production block uses 10 inner main cap bolts (PN 3932480) and 6 shorter outer bolts (PN 3877669). Chevy Performance offers a Main Bearing Bolt Kit for its Sportsman Blocks as PN 12480108. These bolts are Grade-8 with 12-point heads and an oxide coating.

If you have a small main journal (2.30 inches) two-bolt block, you can use windage tray mounting studs in five of the main cap bolt positions. This stud (PN 3872718) is 5 1/4 inches long. A similar windage tray stud for use with 2.45 main journal blocks is PN 14087508. These studs are 5 5/8 inches long and can be used with two-bolt blocks or as the inner studs on a four-bolt block.

Four-bolt blocks with straight main caps not using a windage tray can use the 7/16-inch main cap stud kit (PN 10185033). PN 14011001 stud is used in the inner position and PN 14011002 in the outer stud position. These outer studs should not be used on splayed main bearing caps. PN 10046007 is a mounting bolt for the oil pump, which has a stud portion that holds the rear edge of a windage tray. Use a hardened steel flat 7/16-inch stud washer (PN 14087508) with 12-point 7/16-inch x 20 nut (PN 3942410) or 6-point 7/16-inch x 20 nut (PN 3942410).

Two main cap stud kits are offered for four-bolt blocks. PN 14011039 has all of the studs required for one block with straight main caps but does not include the washers and nuts.

Main stud kit PN 10185033 includes the washers and nuts and has 10 (7/16-inch) inner studs, 14 (7/16-inch) outboard studs, and 4 (3/8-inch) outboard studs, all of which are made from 4340 steel.

## Cylinder Head Bolts and Stud Kits

Cylinder head/block deck dowel pins are used to help position the head on the block. These dowel pins are 5/16 x 9/16-inch (PN 585927). Offset dowel pins (available from aftermarket suppliers) are sometimes used by experienced engine builders and machinists to relocate the combustion chambers on the head in relation to the cylinder barrels.

Gen I production small-blocks use three different length head bolts to secure the cylinder heads to the blocks. Long head bolts (PN 10168525) are 7/16-14 x 3.75 inches. You need 14 of these. The medium-length bolts (PN 10168526) are 7/16-14 x 3.00 inches. Four are required per motor. The bottom row of short head bolts use PN 10168527 and are 7/16-14 x 1.75 inches. Sixteen are used. A kit with all of the bolts is available as PN 12495499.

Aluminum D-port Corvette heads PN 10185086 and 10185087 (casting number 10088113) require different head bolts with flat washers under the bolt head to protect the aluminum surface of the heads. Use long bolt PN 10168525 (7/16-14 x $3^{13}/_{16}$ inches), medium-length bolt PN 10168526 (7/16-14 x $3^{1}/_{16}$ inches), and short bolt PN 10168527 (7/17-14 x $1^{3}/_{4}$ inches). These bolts come with the correct flat washer.

A cylinder head stud kit is offered under PN 14014408 and can be used on conventional production cast-iron and aluminum raised runner Bowtie heads. This kit does not include flat washers or nuts. Short head studs are available individually as PN 14011035 (7/16-14 x 2.69 inches). Long-length head studs are PN 14011036 (7/16-14 x 4.73 inches). The medium-length studs are PN 14011037 (7/16-14 x 3.99 inches).

These head studs can be used with 1038 steel stud nut PN 3942410, which has six points and is 7/16-20, or the 12-point 4037 steel stud nut PN 14044866 (7/16-20). Both of these stud nuts are magnafluxed at the factory. Hardened steel flat washers are under PN 1005115, which has a 0.45-inch ID and 0.750-inch OD and should be used on Phase 6 Bowtie aluminum heads for clearance, or on other heads, you can use flat washer PN 14011040, which is 0.45-inch ID and 0.778-inch OD.

GM head stud kits are not made for the Bowtie 18-degree, 15-degree, splayed valve, or SB2 race heads. These must be obtained from aftermarket suppliers.

Something to consider when using head stud kits is that you may not be able to remove the cylinder heads from the engine once the engine is in your vehicle. Depending on the size of your engine compartment, firewall position, air conditioner, and heater box size and location, brake boosters, etc., you may not have enough room to slide the heads on or off the studs. You may have to remove the engine from the vehicle in order to get the heads off.

If you are using small-block heads on a race motor and these heads have been angle milled (which is quite common), remember to have the surfaces on the heads, where the head bolt holes are, spot faced to the correct angles to match the angle milling of the head deck surface. If you do not do this or if your machinist fails to do this after angle milling the cylinder heads, the heads of the bolts (or the nuts used with a head stud kit), do not bear down on the head surface squarely and correctly.

*Gen I and II engines used three different lengths of head bolts.*

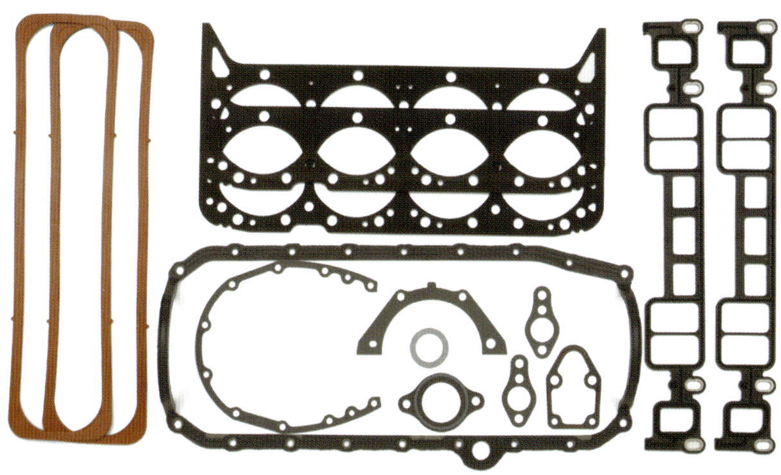

*If you need to refresh your 350 HO engine, Chevy Performance offers a complete gasket kit (PN 19201171) that includes head gaskets, oil pan, intake, fuel pump, timing chain cover, rear main seal, and valve cover gaskets. (Photo Courtesy Chevrolet Performance)*

CHAPTER 3

# Rotating Assemblies

Often when you look at a crank counterweight to check the casting number, only the last four digits of it are there. Check it against the crank casting number list by looking at the last four digits of those numbers. Casting dates are also found on crankshafts.

The 265, 283, and some 302 cranks use a 3-inch stroke with small journals. The 1968 and 1969 302 cranks have a 3-inch stroke with medium journals.

The short-lived 1975 to 1976 Gen I 262-ci engines had a cast crank stroke of 3.10 inches with medium journals.

The 307 and 327 engines used crank strokes of 3.25 inches. All 307 cranks are medium journal cranks, while 327 cranks were made in both small and medium journals. You can use a 350 medium journal four-bolt block, then use a rebalanced 307 cast medium journal crank to build a four-bolt 327-ci engine.

The 267, 305, and 350 cranks used a 3.48-inch stroke length with medium journals.

The 400 engines that were made from 1970 to 1980 used larger-diameter-crank main journals (2.65 inches) and the same rod journal size as medium journal cranks (2.10 inches) but with a crank stroke of 3.75 inches. These cranks require external balancing by using specific vibration dampers, flywheels, or flexplates for the 400 engine. This is also true if you build a popular non-factory combination: a 400 crank with the main journals cut down to 2.45 inches in a 350 block. You must use the externally balanced 400 damper and 400 flywheel or flexplate. It is possible to internally balance a 400 crank by having an experienced machine shop add heavy metal slugs to the counterweights. Do not use an externally balanced 400 damper, flywheel, or flexplate on an internally balanced engine. I bring this up because on several occasions, folks have shown up at my shop with a running 350 small-block that had a huge vibration or a newly rebuilt 350 that had broken some rods or suffered some other major disaster. When we checked the engine, I noticed that the 350 engine had a 400 vibration damper or a 400 flywheel or flexplate. The owners didn't know the difference, and they had unknowingly pulled a tired 400 engine out of the vehicle, replaced it with a rebuilt 350, and used the 400 damper and flexplate on the new internally balanced 350 engine. It doesn't work for long.

***Crankshafts have casting numbers and casting dates so you can learn more about what you have or are looking at.***

***A forged 350 steel crank (casting number 3941182) has casting numbers on the front counterweight. However, only three digits (182) are discernable here.***

In 1986, Chevrolet introduced the one-piece rear main oil seal and made related changes in cranks, oil pans, gaskets, and blocks. The medium journal cranks, used in one-piece seal blocks, are all externally balanced and require the use of matching 1986-or-later flywheels and flexplates. The flange on the rear of the new-style cranks was changed to fit the one-piece seals, and the bolt pattern for flywheels and flexplates was reduced to a 3-inch diameter from the 3.58-inch bolt pattern used on two-piece seal cranks from 1955 through 1985.

Cranks were balanced with whatever size engine and related rotating components it received at the factory. A 307 crank is not balanced the same as a medium journal 327 crank, even though they physically interchange with each other and have the same stroke. If you mix and interchange rotating parts from different engines, have the rotating assembly rebalanced.

Some cast, 2.45-inch main journal, 3.48-inch stroke, two-piece cranks have the same casting number (3932442), but are balanced differently. Cast cranks used on 267, 305, and 350 motors should not be interchanged from one engine size to another because of possible balancing problems, even though they have the same stroke and physically interchange in medium journal blocks.

## Two-Piece Seal Cranks

Since Chevrolet switched to a one-piece seal more than 30 years ago, it does not offer a new crankshaft for the original two-piece seal blocks. Following are some of the more popular crankshafts that were available to help in your search or identification of used or NOS cranks that you may come across.

PN 3932444 is a nodular cast-iron 350 Gen I crank with a 3.48-inch stroke. This crank is used with a two-piece rear main oil seal and has 2.45/2.10-inch journals.

PN 24502460 is a raw 5140 alloy forging used to build large journal cranks of various journal sizes and strokes. This crank is no longer available from Chevrolet.

PN 3941180/casting number 1182 is a 1053 forged steel crank with a 3.48-inch stroke and 2.45/2.10-inch journals.

PN 10051168 is a 4340 alloy, raw, non-twist forging with 3.20- to 4.0-inch strokes possible. It comes with 2.900-inch unmachined journals that can be cut to fit 400 small-block 2.65-inch main journals.

PN 3951527 is a cast 400 crank, 3.75-inch stroke, 2.65/2.10-inch journals in ductile iron. It requires external balancing by using an appropriate 400 front damper and 400 flywheel or flexplate.

Some crank surface treatments, such as nitriding, only penetrate the surface of the metal a few thousandths of an inch. If the crank journals are later cut or reground, the treated surface may be cut or ground off and the crank does have to be retreated. Some aftermarket crank makers use a hardening treatment that penetrates 0.010 to 0.015 inch and is still there after a reduction in journal diameter of 0.010 inch.

## One-Piece Rear Seal Cranks

All 1986-and-later one-piece rear main oil seal cranks are externally balanced, have medium-size journals, and have a smaller bolt circle (3.0 inches) pattern on the rear crank flange. This requires the use of matching late-model flywheels and flexplates, which have mounting bolt-hole patterns that match the cranks for one-piece rear main seal engines. Flywheels and flexplates for two-piece rear main seal cranks do not interchange with one-piece seal cranks.

*This is the one-piece rear main seal crank, which first came into use in 1986 on all production engines. Compare the rear flange area to the earlier Gen I two-piece rear main seal crank.*

*Shown are the rear flange and journals of a Gen I crank that uses a two-piece rear main seal.*

PN 14088526 is a nodular cast-iron crankshaft for use with a one-piece rear main seal. This is a 3.48-inch stroke crank with 2.45- and 2.10-inch journals.

PN 14096036 is a 1053 alloy forged crank with 2.45/2.10-inch journals and 3.48-inch stroke. The original ZZ1 and ZZ2 350 HO crate engines received this crank, while the ZZ3 and ZZ4 engines used PN 14088533. Both are discontinued.

PN 14088533 is a 1053 alloy forged crank with 2.45/2.10-inch journals and 3.48-inch stroke. It requires a one-piece rear main oil seal. This crank was used in the ZZ3 and ZZ4 crate engines and on the ZZ3 short-block partial assembly.

PN 12670965 is also a 1053 forged steel crank that is used in ZZ5 and ZZ6 engines as well as in post–November 1998 ZZ4 engines. It must be used with rod PN 10108688 and piston PN 10159436.

PN 12489436 is a forged 4340 steel crank used to produce 383 ci with a 3.800-inch stroke. Mains are standard 350 size and 2.100-inch rod journals.

## Used Cranks

When you are looking at a used small-block crank, determine if it is a cast or forged crank. You can expect to pay more for a forged one due to added strength. The cast crank has a thin parting line on its throw arms, while a forged crank has a much thicker or wider parting line.

Check the casting number and casting dates to determine what stroke it is. Does it use a one-piece or two-piece rear main oil seal? Measure the rod and main journals. Has the crank been previously cut down? Machine shops that recondition cranks usually stamp the amount they have cut the crank on the front crank throw arm. If your measurements show that the crank journals have been previously cut more than 0.010 inch, walk away. You can find another one.

Are the threaded holes in the rear flange stripped? Has the drilled hole for the pilot bearing at the rear of the crank been elongated or damaged? Has the thrust surface on the crank been worn or damaged? How about the threaded hole in the crank front snout? Some early crank snouts are not drilled or tapped for a vibration damper retention bolt. You can get the snout tapped and threaded for the bolt at a machine shop. Also, some early cranks that were used in automatic transmission cars did not have a hole drilled in the rear of the crank for a manual transmission pilot bushing.

Remember, when you get the crank to the machine shop, ask the crew to clean it, check for cracks and straightness, clean out the threaded holes and oil passages, and possibly have it ground and micropolished. If any of the journals have been damaged, you may be able to have the journal welded or chromed then cut back to acceptable size. However, you need to compare the cost of fixing a damaged crank to the cost of buying an undamaged one. At some point, it's cheaper and easier to find an undamaged used crank or to buy a new one than to repair a damaged one.

***Check the crank journal diameters to see if the crank has been previously cut and to determine the size of the bearings you need.***

***A cast crank can be distinguished from a forged crank by its thinner parting line.***

***Notice the thicker parting line of this 350 forged crank.***

## Cast Versus Forged Cranks

Chevy stock cranks are either nodular cast iron or forged steel. To figure out which yours is, check the parting line, which is left from the molds when the crank is poured. A cast crank has a thin parting line, while a forged crank line is thicker or wider. Tap a crank lightly with something hard, and a cast crank emits a thudding noise. A forged crank rings like a bell; it is a quite distinctive sound. Of course, you can also check the casting number.

Some people who build high-performance motors believe that they must have a forged crank and that cast cranks just don't cut the mustard. They would rather shell out the extra money for a forged crank.

The truth of this belief depends on your situation. Up to a point, cast cranks are fine. In a short-duration, normally aspirated bracket drag race engine, 450 genuine horsepower is around the upper limit for a small-block cast crank. Almost any true street-cruising application can get along just fine with a cast crank. At horsepower levels higher than 450, or if you are planning a nitrous or high-boost blower or turbo application, move to a forged steel crank.

Good used cast cranks are more numerous and less expensive than forged cranks. You can take the money you saved and spend it on something else. Just be sure the crank is magnafluxed and properly prepped and use a high-quality vibration damper (especially with a cast crank).

These days, a large number of forged cranks are available from aftermarket suppliers for a large range of applications, stroke lengths, steel alloys (most use a very strong 4340 alloy), and total weights. These aftermarket cranks can also be prepared in various ways. All of the counterweights can be knife-edged to reduce weight and windage. The crank pins

## Crank Stroke and Journal Sizes

Crank strokes with small journals (2.30-inch mains/2.00-inch rods) include the 3.00-inch strokes on the Gen I 265, 283, and the 1967 302 Z28 engines. The 3.25-inch stroke lengths were used on 327s from 1962 through 1967 with small journals. The 5.7-inch rods with small rod journals and 11/32-inch rod bolts were used with these cranks.

Strokes with medium-size journals (2.45-inch mains/2.10-inch rods) include the 1968 to 1969 302 Z28 with a 3.00-inch stroke, a 3.10-inch stroke used on the 262, 3.25-inch used on the 307 and 1968 327s, and 3.48-inch strokes on the 267, 305, and 350. The Gen II 265-ci V-8 uses these journal sizes with a 3.0-inch stroke and one-piece rear main oil seal. The 5.7-inch rods with 2.10-inch rod journal sizes are used with these medium journal cranks with the exception of the Gen II 265 L99 motor, which uses a 5.940-inch rod. Production rods for medium-size journals have 3/8-inch rod bolts.

The 400 used a 3.75-inch stroke with larger main journal diameters of 2.65 inches and rod journals of 2.10 inches. The 400 uses a shorter 5.565-inch length rod with 3/8-inch rod bolts. These 400 rod bolts have a unique head on the bolt, which helped provide more clearance between the bolt head and cam lobes and the block itself.

Gen II 265 and 350 engines have used the same stroke lengths as their Gen I cousins but have a medium journal size and use one-piece rear seals.

Factory cast or forged steel cranks have been made. Forged steel cranks have only been made in 3.00 inches for the 265, 283, and 302 engines, the 3.25-inch stroke for the 327, and the 3.48-inch stroke for 350 engines. Some 283, 327, and 350 cranks are cast.

Gen I 262, 267, 305, 307, and 400 production cranks were all cast. There were no factory production steel cranks made for these engines. Aftermarket suppliers make cast and forged cranks in a variety of stroke lengths, steel alloys, and journal diameters.

All Gen I small-block engines prior to 1986 used a two-piece rear main oil seal and associated cranks and oil pans. The 400 small-block was externally balanced and used a specific vibration damper and flywheel or flexplate.

In 1986, Chevrolet changed its production crank designs so that a one-piece rear main seal could be used. All one-piece rear main oil seal Gen I and II production blocks from 1986-on are externally balanced. All 1986-and-newer production small-blocks use specific externally balanced vibration dampers and flywheels and flexplates on these engines. Cranks, dampers, flywheels, and flexplates are not interchangeable between one-piece rear seal blocks and the earlier blocks that used a two-piece rear main seal. There are adapters that enable you to put a crank designed for a two-piece seal into a block for a one-piece seal, but you must still use the appropriate damper, flywheel, or flexplate to match the crank.

Vibration dampers used on the small-block have also varied over the years. Chevrolet also makes an over-the-counter damper that can be used with aftermarket cranks that have an even larger crank snout that is the same diameter as the big-block Chevy but has production-size main and rod journals. This enables you to use a big-block balancer with these cranks. ■

on the rod journals can be drilled to further reduce weight. Extra-wide radius journal fillets add strength. Counterweights can be reduced in radius to reduce rotating mass. Special coatings are available that reduce oil cling, and chemical, vibration, and heat treatments are available that further harden and relieve the metals.

Several aftermarket companies such as Callies, Crower, Trick Flow, Lunati, Eagle, and others offer high-quality forged cranks with up to 4.00-inch strokes. Remember, a stock Chevy steel crank takes a tremendous amount of abuse. It all depends on what your intentions are for your engine.

### Crank Prep

Make the following checks on any used or new cranks you are considering purchasing. Take a good look at the entire crank for damage. Check the thrust surface and the journals for damage and wear. Do any of the journals look blue from lack of oil and overheating? Measure the journals. Have the journals been cut down from their standard sizes? Are the journals worn, scratched, or out of round? Check the crank key slots for damage or wear. Look at the threaded holes in the crank snout and the crank flange, and check the bore at the rear of the crank. Any damage to the pilot bearing hole? Some cranks used in vehicles with automatic transmissions were not bored for a pilot bushing.

The crank can be set up on V-shaped blocks so that it can be rotated and you can check for straightness and run out with a dial indicator; it should be no more than 0.000 to 0.0005 inch. You can also slip the crank into an engine block with just the main bearings and main caps torqued down to see if it spins easily at the touch of just your fingers. If it is straight and the journals are round, clean it thoroughly and get into the oil supply holes with a brush. Gun bore-cleaning brushes work fine in this application.

After it is clean, have the crank magnafluxed for any cracks. Don't skip this step. You may not be able to see cracks with the naked eye. Magnafluxing can save you a lot of time and money. It is easy to replace a cracked crank with another before you put it into a motor. Yes, you can wait until you build an engine, put it in a vehicle, and run it to locate a crack in the crank, but this is not an easy task and it's cheaper to magnaflux it before you use it. Small surface cracks in journals may be removed when the journal is cut undersize.

If you are racing, check the crank stroke length to make sure each rod journal is equally long and index the crank to make sure each throw is 90 degrees to the other in turn. Don't forget to have the rotating assembly balanced. Another common practice with externally balanced cranks is to internally balance them by using heavy Mallory metal plugs. When the rotating assembly is balanced, the correct position for the weight is determined and holes are drilled into crank counterweights. The heavy metal plugs are then inserted into these holes to achieve an internal balance. Then you can use a standard internal-balance, front-vibration damper and standard internal-balance flywheel or flexplate. Cross drilling the oil passages in the main journals aids the survival of any small-block crank by ensuring a steady, pressurized oil supply to the bearings during the entire rotation of the crank.

Some repairs can be made to the crank if necessary. Journals can be welded up and recut back to standard, and they may also be chromed, built back up, and then recut to standard. Some bent cranks can be straightened. Damaged threaded holes can be heli-coiled. Cracked cranks or cranks with damaged thrust surfaces, however, should be sent to the nearest junk pile or metal recycler.

It's all relative to how much you want to spend. Sometimes it is cheaper to obtain another crank that doesn't need as much repair. On the other hand, if you have a $2,500 Super Gas aftermarket crank with all the bells and whistles, then it may be worth it to try to repair it; and it's definitely cheaper than buying a new one. That's a decision that you, your crank grinder, and your significant other must make.

With all of that out of the way, the crank journals, if necessary, can be cut undersized and the journals polished. Make sure that the crank grinder leaves a large radius in the journal fillet, which is a much stronger formation than a tight, small radius in the journal fillet. Also, the oil holes in the journals should be chamfered lightly to help distribute oil to the bearings.

If you are building a non-production combination of parts, like a 383 motor using a 350 block and a 400 crank, make sure there is clearance between the rotating crank counterweights and the block. In addition, check other clearances, such as cam lobe clearance and rod bolt and rod-to-block clearances.

## Rod Bearings

There are many options when it comes to rod bearings from Chevy Performance to a number of aftermarket companies. The most important thing is to get the clearances correct. One minimum clearance rule of thumb is 0.001 inch for every 1 inch of journal diameter. For example, a 2.10-inch-diameter journal requires a minimum bearing clearance of 0.0021 inch (which is 2.10 times 0.001 inch). I prefer the tighter side of the clearances rather than running the bearings on the wide side. Chevrolet recommends 0.002- to 0.0025-inch clearance on the rod bearings. Side clearance between rods should be 0.010 to 0.020 inch.

The bearings and their respective mating surfaces on the main and rod caps must be spotless clean. One tiny piece of metal grit, dirt, or lint from a shop rag on the back of the bearings or the caps can keep the bearing from sitting properly on these surfaces. Any measurement you then make is incorrect and false.

The quality of the machining work on the crank, block, and rods also affects these clearances and your ability to maintain them when you actually assemble the engine. If the machine work was sloppy or incorrect, the problems seem to multiply.

Oversize bearings are available in sizes 0.010, 0.020, 0.030, and 0.040 inch. Bearing sets can also be ordered that are 0.001-inch oversize or undersize, if you have a particular situation in which you need to use them. Chevy Performance offers a Connecting Rod Bearing Kit for 350 and 383 engines as PN 17800761. This set of eight bearings is the second design without chamfer.

# Crankshaft Casting Numbers

## Crankshafts Using Two-Piece Seals

| Casting Number | CI | Material | Stroke (inches) | Comments |
|---|---|---|---|---|
| 1130 | 327 | Forged | 3.25 | Medium journal |
| 1178 | 302 | Forged | 3.00 | Medium journal |
| 1181 | 305, 350 | Cast | 3.48 | Medium journal |
| 1182 | 350 | Forged | 3.48 | Medium journal |
| 2680 | 327 | Forged | 3.25 | Small journal |
| 2690 | 350 | Forged | 3.48 | Medium journal |
| 3279 | 302 | Forged | 3.00 | Medium journal |
| 4577 | 327 | Forged | 3.25 | Small journal |
| 4672 | 327 | Forged | 3.25 | Medium journal |
| 310514 | 350 | Cast | 3.48 | Medium journal |
| 330550 | 350 | Cast | 3.48 | Medium journal |
| 354431 | 262 | Cast | 3.10 | Medium journal |
| 3727449 | 283 | Forged | 3.00 | Small journal |
| 3729449 | 265 | Forged | 3.00 | Small journal |
| 3734627 | 327 | Forged | 3.25 | Small journal |
| 3735236 | 265, 283 | Forged | 3.00 | Small journal |
| 3735263 | 283 | Forged | 3.00 | Small journal |
| 3782680 | 327 | Forged | 3.25 | Small journal |
| 3814671 | 327 | Forged | 3.25 | Small journal |
| 3815822 | 265, 283, 302 | Forged | 3.00 | Small journal |
| 3835236 | 283 | Forged | 3.00 | Small journal |
| 3836266 | 283 | Forged | 3.00 | Small journal |
| 3848847 | 283 | Forged or cast | 3.00 | Small journal |
| 3849847 | 283 | Forged | 3.00 | Small journal |
| 3876764 | 283 | Forged or cast | 3.00 | Small journal |
| 3876768 | 283 | Forged | 3.00 | Small journal |
| 3884577 | 327 | Forged | 3.25 | Small journal |
| 3892690 | 350 | Forged | 3.48 | Medium journal |
| 3911001 | 307, 327 | Cast | 3.25 | Medium journal |
| 3911011 | 307, 327 | Cast | 3.25 | Medium journal |
| 3914672 | 327 | Forged | 3.25 | Medium journal |
| 3923279 | 302 | Forged | 3.00 | Medium journal |
| 3932442 | 267, 305, 350 | Cast | 3.48 | Medium journal |
| 3941174 | 307, 327 | Cast | 3.25 | Medium journal |
| 3941178 | 302 | Forged | 3.00 | Medium journal |
| 3941182 | 350 | Forged | 3.48 | Medium journal |
| 3941188 | 350 | Forged | 3.48 | Medium journal |
| 3949847 | 283 | Forged or cast | 3.00 | Small journal |
| 3951130 | 327 | Forged | 3.25 | Medium journal |
| 3951529 | 400 | Cast | 3.75 | Large journal |

## Crankshafts Using One-Piece Seals

| Casting Number | CI | Material | Stroke (inches) | Comments |
|---|---|---|---|---|
| 10168568 | 265 | Cast | 3.00 | Medium journal |
| 12489436 | 383 | Forged | 3.80 | Medium journal |
| 12670965 | 350 | Forged | 3.48 | Medium journal |
| 14088526 | 305, 350 | Cast | 3.48 | Medium journal |
| 14088532 | 350 | Forged | 3.48 | Medium journal |
| 14088535 | 305, 350 | Cast | 3.48 | Medium journal |
| 14088552 | 350 | Forged | 3.48 | Medium journal |

# Coatings

A number of high-tech coatings are available on the market for various engine parts. Pistons, combustion chambers, valves, valve springs, other rotating parts, and exhaust headers can be coated with materials that reduce heat absorption or friction, or shed oil quickly. The increases in power with these coatings may seem marginal; however, the sum of all the parts could be important when every bit of horsepower counts.

The major benefits are an increase in the durability and life of the coated parts. Engine bearings using a high-tech coating can help protect the bearing when oil pressures fall because of oil pump aeration. High temperatures in piston decks are reduced and, as a result, so are fatigue failures. Piston skirt coatings can reduce friction, so wear on the part is minimized. Valves' faces and stems can be coated to reduce heat absorption and erosion. Coated valve stems have reduced wear and fewer tendencies to seize and gall in the guides. Valve springs seem to last longer before the open pressures decline, since heat in the springs is reduced. Heat-induced fatigue failures also decline. This is an area that has seen a lot of advances over the years as new materials and application techniques were discovered and improved.

Dry film, liquid, and sprayed-on molten coatings are available. Not all of them penetrate the metal itself. Some of the coatings are intended for nonferrous aluminum parts, such as pistons or aluminum heads, while others are used on ferrous material, such as cast-iron heads. Most form an extremely thin layer—some are 0.0003- to 0.0005-inch thick, others are 0.001- to 0.002-inch thick—on the top surface of the coated material. The thickness of these layers may require you to take this into account when you are checking clearances on the engine. Check with the coating manufacturer for its recommendations. ■

If you have had your crank journals ground with large fillet radii, some stock bearings may not have enough clearance on the side edges to clear a large journal fillet radius. The bearing side edges may need to be chamfered slightly to obtain clearance. Aftermarket bearings are produced with a large chamfer already on the bearings for this type of situation. Aluminum rods use a dowel pin to help position and retain the bearing. You can obtain bearings that have pre-drilled dowel holes, or you can buy a tool fixture that allows you to drill the dowel hole in the bearing shells yourself.

Chevrolet Performance offers a set of high-quality 5.700-inch powdered metal rods that are ideal for engines up to about 500 hp. This kit (PN 12495071) replaces the well-known "pink rods" and it has the same rods used in the Gen II LT1 and LT4 Vette engines. Another set (PN 19332460) is used for 383-ci small-blocks. These rods have been machined for clearance and use a standard 0.927-inch pin and a journal size of 2.100 inches.

If you are racing, you must make regular, periodic inspections of the engine bearings. Observation of the wear pattern on the bearings, if any, can give you an indication of any problems. The idea is to catch and correct any problems before a major disaster strikes. Specialty rod bearings are available with various amounts of eccentricity. That is, when measured in the rod, the bearing is slightly wider in the inside diameter at the parting lines of the cap than they are when measured 90 degrees from the parting line axis. These can be helpful if you find that the wear pattern on previous bearings is too narrow or too wide.

*This is one style of earlier vibration damper found on a 1956 265 motor. It is narrow and mounted to it is a single V-belt pulley for the water pump and the generator.*

## Pilot Bushings

You should always install a new pilot bearing in the rear of the crank if you are using a manual transmission. Make sure your crank has been drilled to accept a pilot bushing; not all cranks are drilled for it. Do yourself, your clutch plate, and your transmission a favor and use a needle bearing roller pilot bearing. Chevy Performance offers one as PN 14061685.

## Vibration Dampers

Gen I small-blocks that have two-piece rear main oil seals were internally balanced. The one exception, however, was the 400 small-block, which was externally balanced. The 400 used a unique front damper and externally balanced flywheel or flexplate.

All of the one-piece rear main seal Gen I engines made from 1986 to the present are externally balanced and use different flywheels or flexplates with smaller 3.00-inch bolt circle patterns on the crank rear flange.

The 1996-and-later enhanced Gen I Vortec 5000 305s and Vortec 5700 350s use a front vibration damper, which also has an ignition trigger ring. These dampers are not interchangeable with other Gen I dampers.

Gen II 265 4.3-liter and Gen II 350 5.7-liter engines are externally balanced and have one-piece rear main seals and matching crankshafts. The front balancers are not interchangeable with Gen I or III engines. These dual-mass, two-piece dampers use a serpentine belt crank pulley as part of the vibration damper.

As the pistons go up and down in an engine, vibrations are transmitted

*This is a 400 balancer for externally balanced, Gen I engines. Note that a section of the outside diameter is undercut when this damper is made. This provides the necessary external balance for the 400 engines and helps you identify it. You also need an externally balanced flywheel or flexplate with the 400. If you are building a non-factory combination using a 400 crank in a 350 block (commonly called a 383), you again need to use the 400-style damper and the 400 externally balanced flywheels and flexplates.*

*Note the groove worn into the front seal surface of the damper. A sleeve can be purchased at most parts stores that slides over the snout. Given the deteriorating state of the rubber, this damper is a good candidate for replacement.*

*The dual-mass front vibration damper found on externally balanced Gen II engines is a two-piece design that incorporates the crank serpentine belt pulley. These dampers do not interchange with Gen I small-blocks.*

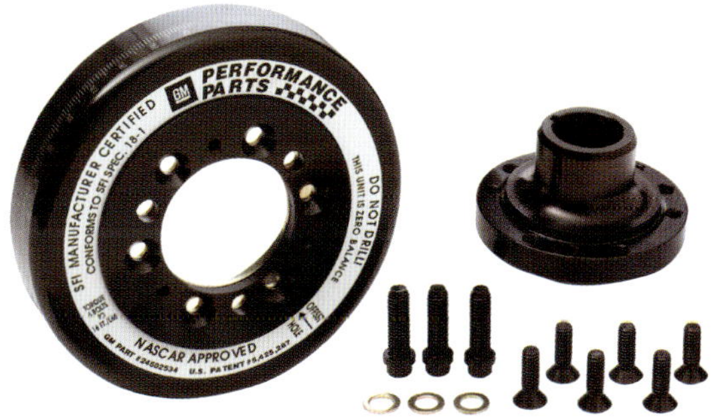


*For even higher RPM racing, such as NASCAR, Chevy Performance provides an approved unit that is specially tuned. The two-piece design uses either a standard hub (PN 24502534) or a 1.598-inch hub (PN 24502535). (Photo Courtesy Chevrolet Performance)*

*Chevrolet Performance Parts offer a variety of stock replacement and higher-performance balancers. PN 19301706 is an 8-inch diameter, nodular iron balancer for externally balanced engines.*

to the crankshaft. The crank twists slightly as these forces act on the arms of each crank arm. The crank throws rebound as the forces acting on the crank change directions. The vibration damper mounted on the end of the crank snout helps absorb these crank vibrations and prevent their transmission to other parts of the engine. For decades, Gen I production engines have used dampers that consisted of two metal rings with each ring separated by an elastomer rubber seal. The top dead center (TDC) timing mark was cut into the surface of the damper's outer metal ring.

Chevrolet tuned the production dampers to work in the RPM ranges normally experienced by a production street motor. In other words, these dampers work best in the street-driving low-RPM situations experienced by the majority of stock small-block engines. High-performance production engines received larger-diameter balancers that worked best at a higher engine RPM.

There are a number of things you must consider when you are choosing a balancer and before the engine is assembled. A variety of damper diameters have been used over the years. The diameter has been matched with a stationary timing scale tab that is located on the timing chain cover. Some of these tabs were spot welded onto the cover and some were bolted to the covers. The timing tabs were placed in a position that would just clear the circumference of the rotating dampers.

Also, the timing mark on the damper's outer ring and the matching timing tab on the timing cover were moved to other locations after 1969. You can check the location by looking at the timing mark position in relation to the crank keyway slot in the inside diameter of the damper. You must match the timing tab position correctly to accurately match the diameter of the damper and whichever style of timing mark position is on the damper. Otherwise, there is difficulty properly setting the initial ignition timing.

If you find that the engine doesn't run like you think it should when you've set ignition timing at the correct amount, or you find the engine likes to run with about 20 degrees of advanced or retarded initial timing at idle, I suspect that you may have a mismatched damper timing mark and timing tab. Another possibility is that the outer ring on the damper may be moving in relation to the inner damper ring. One way to check for the correct combination of parts is to use a dial indicator to determine TDC during a trial assembly of the motor and verify that the timing mark on the damper is lining up with the 0-degree TDC mark on the timing tab.

In addition, be aware of another possible problem with production elastomer cast-iron dampers: Over time, the elastomer rubber dries out and cracks. The outer metal ring then has room to move around in relation to the inner metal ring on the damper. The outside ring can also move rearward or forward in relation to the inner ring, which changes the timing marks in relation to the crank keyway. Once again, properly setting initial timing can become a problem. For instance,

## Small-Block Vibration Dampers

| Part Number | Diameter (inches) | Timing Mark Position | Timing Tab | Comments |
|---|---|---|---|---|
| 12551537 | 6.75 | 10-degrees before crank keyway | 3991435 | Smaller size for limited clearance |
| 19301706 | 8 | – | 3991436 | Nodular iron, for externally balanced engines |
| 12498008 | 8 | – | – | For externally balanced engines, counterweight can be removed for neutral balance, use with 383 engine |
| 24502534 | 7 | 2-degrees before crank keyway | – | NASCAR approved (tuned for up to 9,000 rpm), standard crank hub diameter |
| 24502535 | 7 | 2-degrees before crank keyway | – | NASCAR approved and specially tuned, use with large-diameter 1.598-inch crank hub |

Remember, if you are building an engine using a 400 crank and a 350 block to build the popular 383 combination, you must use a 400-style front vibration damper and flywheel or flexplate for externally balanced 400 motors.

The crankshaft/front damper retaining bolt PN 3815933 is 7/16-20 x 2 1/4-inches. The correct flat washer to use with this bolt is PN 19355269.

Gen II engines use a dual-mass vibration damper that is unique. This damper and hub does not mate to the crank snout in the manner most Gen I small-block enthusiasts are used to, and consequently, it cannot be interchanged with Gen I engines. The dual-mass damper has two independent inertia rings mounted on a common hub, which enables it to work over a wider range of engine RPM than previous designs. Rather than have a separate pulley for a serpentine belt, this damper incorporates the belt ribs and grooves as part of the damper. All Gen II engines are externally balanced. ■

you may check the timing with a timing light and set the mark at one position, and then when you check it again, the mark might be in a different position. A more dangerous problem is the possibility that the outer ring might move rearward and cut into the timing chain cover. Most dangerous is when the outer ring moves forward. It can come off and fly through the hood, fenders, hoses, and anything else in its way.

Look at the damper that you are using and examine the elastomer rubber between the two metal rings closely. Does it look cracked? Are portions of the elastomer missing? Does the rubber look like it is pushed outward or inward from its normal flush position? Is the timing mark in its correct position in relation to the crank keyway slot or has the timing mark moved? Does the face of the damper look like it has been repeatedly hit and dented with a hammer or sledge in an incorrect effort to put it on? If so, get rid of it and buy a new one.

Many dampers show signs of damage because someone used the incorrect removal and installation tools. In their efforts to remove a damper, they mistakenly used a large three-armed gear puller. This improper use of the wrong tool can pull the outer ring right off a production balancer. Likewise, a hammer or sledge is not the correct installation tool.

On a Gen I–style damper, check the three threaded holes for the bolts that hold the crank pulley on. Over the years, Chevrolet has used coarse- or fine-threaded bolts to hold the crank pulley to the damper. Not everyone checks to see which thread type was used on a particular damper. Consequently, a fine-threaded damper may have had coarse-threaded bolts run into it, ruining the threads in the damper. The reverse also happens. If the threads are damaged, you can have

*Here are two dampers for internally balanced small-blocks. Note that the timing indicators do not align with the keyway. Make sure you use the matching timing cover and timing pointer with each damper. Otherwise, the TDC mark is not in its proper position with the timing pointer. Also note the wear grooves on the left version above and that the right version already has a repair sleeve pressed over the snout.*

heli-coil thread inserts placed in the damper to repair it.

Also, examine used dampers to determine if a groove has developed on the surface that the front oil seal rides on. If there is a groove, an inexpensive repair sleeve can be pressed on over the original surface. If you don't repair it, you probably have an oil leak from the front seal.

Many of the early small journal cranks have crank snouts that were not drilled and tapped for a vibration damper retaining bolt. The early dampers were held on the crank by an interference fit only. If your crank is not drilled and tapped for the damper retaining bolt, you can have your local machine shop do the work before your engine is assembled.

## Flywheels and Flexplates

All Gen I engines with two-piece rear main seals were internally balanced engines, with one exception: the externally balanced Gen I 400 small-block. All two-piece seal cranks have a rear flange bolt pattern of 3.58 inches to fit their flywheels and flexplates.

*The 454 big-block flexplates have a thicker balance weight than the 400 small-block flexplate. Don't mix them up. The flexplate side with the weight goes toward the block.*

*Casting numbers can be found on flywheels and flexplates and can help identify which one you have.*

*Balance plates can be used to provide the external balance to most flywheels or flexplates.*

*This flexplate reminds the installer which way to install it. If reversed, there are issues when bolting the torque converter into place.*

*Flywheels are made in different diameters and use different-size clutch and pressure plate diameters. This example is an externally balanced, one-piece rear main seal design from a RamJet 350 crate engine.*

*The flywheels for 400 small-blocks have extra balance weights cast into them to provide the necessary material to balance them. The 1986-on Gen I and Gen II small-block flywheels (such as this one) are also externally balanced; however, their flywheels and flexplates can be distinguished by their smaller 3.0-inch crank flange bolt pattern, which was used on all one-piece rear main seal cranks. Also note the machining holes on the clutch side of the flywheel.*

## Flywheels and Flexplates

### Flywheels

| Part Number | Diameter (inches) | Teeth | Comments |
|---|---|---|---|
| 3991469 | 14 | 168 | Use with two-piece seal, internal balance |
| 14085720 | 12-3/4 | 153 | Lightweight (15 pounds), nodular-iron, two-piece seal, internal balance |
| 14088646 | 12-3/4 | 153 | 1986-on, lightweight (15 pounds), nodular-iron, one-piece rear seal, external balance (discontinued) |
| 14088648 | 14 | 168 | 1986-on, one-piece rear seal, external balance |

Flywheels are drilled for different diameter clutch assemblies: 10.4, 11.0, and 11.85 inches are available. Some flywheels are drilled for two different clutch-diameter patterns.

### Flexplates

| Part Number | Diameter (inches) | Teeth | Comments |
|---|---|---|---|
| 471529 | 12-3/4 | 153 | Two-piece seal blocks, internal balance |
| 471598 | 14 | 168 | Two-piece seal blocks, internal balance |
| 12554824 | 14 | 168 | Externally balanced, one-piece seal |
| 14088761 | 14 | 168 | 1989-on 350 HO, one-piece rear seal, external balance |
| 14088765 | 12-3/4 | 153 | 1986-on, one-piece rear seal, external balance |

Flexplates are drilled for different torque converter mounting bolt patterns. Some flexplates are drilled for two different patterns. Torque converter bolt patterns on flexplates have been 9.75, 10.75, and 11.5 inches. Flywheels and flexplates for one-piece rear seal blocks have a smaller 3.0-inch bolt pattern. Make sure that you use the proper flywheel and flexplates, bolts, and star-shaped washers. A flywheel bolt (PN 12337973, 7/16-20 x 1-inch) is 1-1/8-inch overall and a flexplate bolt (PN 3727207, 7/16-20 x 27/32-inch) is 7/8-inch overall. Don't mix them up; use the correct fastener. ■

All Gen I and II small-blocks made after 1986 that have one-piece rear main seals are externally balanced and require the use of flywheels and flexplates that provide the correct external balance. The cranks used in one-piece seal blocks have a smaller rear flange bolt pattern, measuring 3.00 inches, to fit their matching flywheels and flexplates. The 1990 V-6 flywheels and flexplates are interchangeable with small-block V-8s. The 4.3-liter 1990 V-6s are built with the same bore and stroke and share many parts with the Chevy 350 V-8. However, the 4.3-liter V-6 is missing two of the cylinders found in the 350 V-8.

Nodular-iron, lighter weight Gen I flywheels are available from General Motors, if you are trying to reduce rotating mass.

Aftermarket balance plates are manufactured that enable you to use a Gen I internal-balance-type 14-inch flywheel or flexplate with a 400-style external-balance crank. These balance plates fit between the crank flange and flywheel or flexplate and give the extra external balance weight you need for a 400 crank.

One note of caution, you may think that the externally balanced 400 flywheels and flexplates are the same as those used on the externally balanced 454 big-block Chevys. They are not the same. While they look similar and physically bolt up and interchange, the 454 and 502 big-blocks use a flywheel or flexplate that has a heavier counterweight added to provide the necessary balance for the big-block externally balanced motors.

*If you are racing, tech inspectors look for this sticker from the SFI Foundation certifying that the part has met the safety requirements.*

*A safety "blow-proof" clutch bellhousing, when using a manual transmission, is required by most racing associations. If your clutch or pressure plate decides it has had enough "fun" and disintegrates, this bellhousing and an engine plate contain the pieces and keep your legs and feet attached to the rest of your body.*

## Starter Tips

*The dual starter bolt pattern found on most blocks allows the use of a $12\frac{3}{4}$- or 14-inch flywheel or flexplate with the matching starter.*

*Two starter shims of different thicknesses help get the teeth on starter gears correctly meshing with flywheel or flexplate teeth. These shims are not always necessary, but may be required if excessive starter noise or drag is encountered.*

*Chevy Performance offers a lighter-weight, high-torque starter that fits either size flywheel or flexplate. This mini starter (PN 12361146) uses less amperage than a conventional starter.*

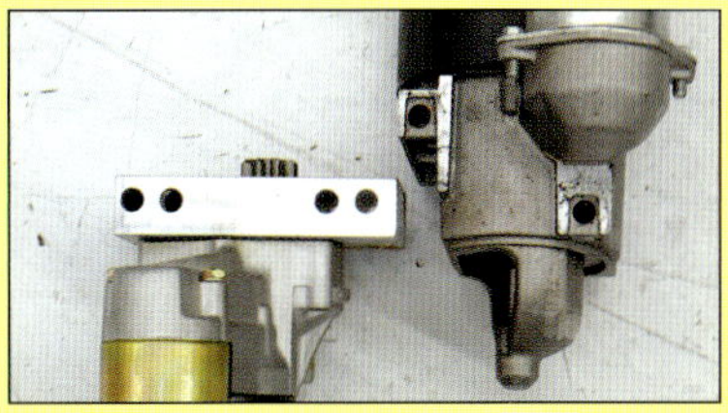

*There are two types of conventional starters for the small-block. The one on the left has starter bolt holes that are straight across for $12\frac{3}{4}$ inch flywheels or flexplates. The starter on the right, with staggered bolt holes, is for 14-inch flywheels or flexplates. The starter noses themselves are slightly different and are interchangeable between starters.*

### Starters

Chevrolet has basically used two different starters to match the number of teeth found on the starter ring gears of flywheels and flexplates. The starters used with a $12\frac{3}{4}$-inch-diameter, 153-tooth flywheel or flexplate have one type of starter nose, while the starter used with the 14-inch diameter, 168 flywheels and flexplates use another type of starter nose.

Starters for 14-inch-diameter, 168-tooth flywheels or flexplates have mounting bolt holes that are diagonal. Starters for $12\frac{3}{4}$-inch flywheels or flexplates have their mounting holes straight across. Some of the small starter body mini-starters have both mounting bolt holes. Your engine block must have the correct starter mounting bolt holes. Most blocks have bolt holes that mount either starter, but some blocks have only been drilled for one type of starter mount. Check your block for these mounting holes.

The body of the starters has been changed over the years, with some being larger or smaller than others. The smaller starter bodies may be helpful if you have a tight situation in the engine compartment, such as when chassis parts, kickout oil pans, or tube exhaust headers sit close to the starter.

Many Chevy small-block, big-block, and V-6 1990 starters are interchangeable as long as they are used with their matching flywheel or flexplate diameters. Conventional-size starters weigh about 19 to 20 pounds, while the mini-starters weigh about 10 pounds.

If you are having trouble with starter heat soak, which is a common problem after switching from stock cast-iron exhaust manifolds to tube headers, use a starter heat shield to lower the radiant heat absorbed by the starter solenoid. One aftermarket system uses a separate solenoid, mounted on the inside fender well, and a small jumper wire to bypass the Chevy starter solenoid. This also solves the heat soak problem and gives you a more convenient location at which to hook up a remote push-button starter when you are working under the hood alone.

If you have built a high-static compression engine (greater than 11.5:1 CR), you can give your starter a mechanical advantage by using a 14-inch flywheel or flexplate and a high-torque, heavy-duty starter. Several companies in the aftermarket such as Powermaster, MSD, and Meziere offer starters with higher torque ratings to aid in cranking race engines over.

### Connecting Rods

Many of the small-block rotating assembly components are interchangeable. However, you must

## Starter Numbers

**PN 10465143** is a remanufactured starter for heavy-duty use with $12^{3}/_{4}$-inch OD ring gears.

**PN 1876552** is a heavy-duty starter for 14-inch OD ring gears.

**PN 12361146** is a Bowtie high-torque, gear reduction, mini-starter. It weighs one-half (10.5 pounds) that of a conventional starter. It fits either 14- or $12^{3}/_{4}$-inch OD ring gears. It provides more clearance for tube headers and oil pans because of its smaller size.

**PN 12363128** is a chrome, high-torque, mini-starter and fits both $12^{3}/_{4}$- and 14-inch flywheels or flexplates.

**PN 10455702** is another high-torque, gear reduction, mini-starter, originally used on 1988 small-block Corvettes. It weighs 10.14 pounds, but it only fits $12^{3}/_{4}$-inch OD ring gears.

Bolts for starters are unique because they have knurled sections and shoulders, which are required to properly register the starter to the block surface. Always use the correct starter bolts. Two sizes are used: short 3/8-16 x 12-7/32 or long 3/8-16 x 41/64 inches. Mini-starters come with their own bolts and starter shims as part of the assembly. Use a starter mounting brace (PN 345353) to help support the front of a conventional-size starter motor. ■

rebalance the rotating assembly when you mix and match parts from different engines. Also, the use of an externally balanced 400-ci-style crank requires a 400 vibration damper and flywheel or flexplate. Or you can have the assembly internally balanced using heavy metal or other techniques. With crank strokes of 3.75-inches or longer, you may need to add clearance for the block, rod big ends, and rod bolts to clear the cam lobes, piston skirts, or cylinder barrels. Do a trial assembly and make sure everything fits.

If you use a different-stroke crank or a longer or shorter rod, make sure that the compression or pin height of the piston matches the rod length and available total deck height of the block you use. You can check this by adding half the crank stroke with the connecting rod's center-to-center length and the piston pin height (also called the piston compression height). This sum along with any piston-deck-to-block-deck clearance should not exceed the total available deck height of the block. Here is an example:

| | |
|---|---|
| 1/2 350 crank stroke | 1.74 inches |
| Rod center-to-center length | 5.70 inches |
| Stock 350 piston pin height | 1.56 inches |
| Total | 9.00 inches |

Most uncut production blocks have an available total block deck height of 9.025 inches. In this example, there would be 0.025 inch of piston-deck-to-block-deck clearance when the piston is at TDC, which is okay.

The 265 and 283 Gen I cranks with 3-inch stroke lengths used rod journal diameters of 2.00 inches. Production 265/283 connecting rods used 11/32-inch rod bolts, and many of these early rods have an oil weep hole and groove at the parting line of the rod cap. These rods used a pressed-on piston pin and the beams were narrow. They are the weakest small-block rods, relatively speaking.

*Notice the oil weep groove on the left side of this rod cap. These were found on most small journal production rods used with 265, 283, and some small journal 327s.*

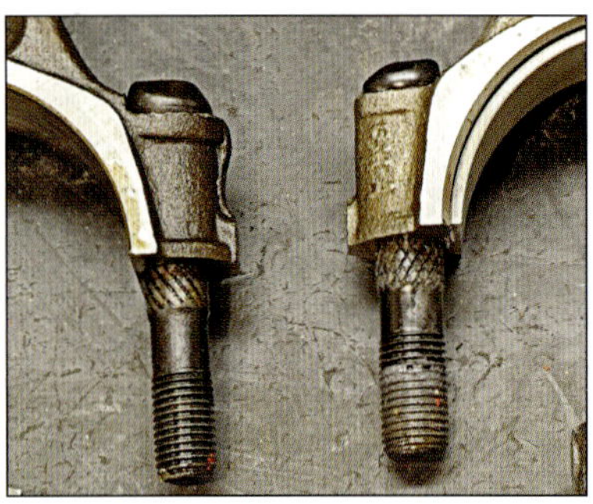

*The rod and bolt on the left is from a 283 Gen I engine and the example on the right is from a 350. The 283 is a 2.00-inch small journal and uses 11/32-inch bolts. The 350 version has a 2.10-inch journal and is held together with stronger 3/8-inch retainers.*

*A 400 rod is on the left with a 350 on the right. Both rods share a 2.10-inch medium-rod journal size, though the 400 rod has a shorter 5.565-inch center-to-center length. A standard 350 rod is 5.7 inches.*

## Detonation and Preignition

Two of the major things to avoid in any engine are detonation and preignition. If these problems occur, sometimes even if only for a few seconds, it decreases maximum power and causes engine damage. When a gaseous mixture of air and fuel is compressed, the pressures increase and the temperature of the gaseous mixture rises. In any performance engine, you want to increase these pressures, since this has a direct effect on how much torque an engine makes.

Best power is usually found at cylinder pressures and temperatures just below the detonation level. However, if pressures increase too much or too quickly or if the temperatures get too high, the gaseous mixture self-ignites. The idea is to reach high cylinder pressures without detonation occurring. Increasing the dynamic compression of any engine increases the mechanical efficiency of the engine. You want the mixture to be ignited by the spark plug at the optimum moment to produce the best power. In an effort to reach these maximum power goals, race motors are often run right at the edge of detonation and sometimes the line is crossed.

If you are lucky, when detonation occurs the engine just begins to miss and lies down on power. If you are unlucky, parts break or melt down and you receive an expensive lesson in humility and the destructive power of the internal combustion engine.

Many things can cause detonation, such as using too high a compression ratio without adequate fuel octane levels. An example would be someone who built a 12.5:1 static compression ratio motor, and then tried to run the engine on 86-octane pump unleaded gasoline. Or someone who didn't match the camshaft to the dynamic compression ratio and built more cylinder pressure than the octane level of the fuel could handle. An inadequate cooling system allows the coolant temperature to rise above normal, causing the cylinder heads' temperature to rise because they can't be cooled quickly enough. The additional heat is not rejected from the heads to the cooling system and the increased temperatures prematurely ignite the air/fuel mix.

Hot spots in the piston deck surfaces or dome or combustion chamber can get hot enough to ignite the mix. Carbon deposits or sharp edges on piston domes, valves, or spark plug threads that protrude into the combustion chamber can become hot enough to glow red and set off the incoming fuel charge. Spark plugs that are the wrong heat range are unable to convey heat to the engine coolant quickly enough and heat continues to build in the center electrode or the side ground wire. This can also light off the fuel.

An air/fuel ratio that is too lean causes rapid cylinder temperature increases and again, the mixture can go off by itself. Ignition timing that is too far advanced for the particular engine combination can cause a preignition problem.

Improper piston dome shapes or too much piston-deck-to-head-deck height can create small spaces that prevent the smooth travel of the flame front across the piston surface. Weird cylinder pressure spikes can be caused by burning off a little of the fuel in one part of the combustion chamber followed by a separate burning in another part of the chamber.

Oil that gets past piston rings or valve stem seals to contaminate the fuel mixture in the combustion chamber can also cause a detonation problem.

Detonation probably does not occur in every cylinder at one time. You may have one cylinder that does not receive the same amount of fuel as the other cylinders and thus runs leaner. Unequal fuel distribution can be a problem. Coolant circulation on high-power engines can also be a problem if one or more cylinders run hotter than others. This might be caused by a water pump that gives unequal or inadequate coolant distribution to each side of the engine. Gen II small-blocks with reverse coolant flow circulate the coolant to the heads first, then to the block to reduce cylinder head temperatures and the onset of detonation.

Too much nitrous or improper nitrous/fuel/air ratios can cause cylinder pressures and temperatures to rise so much that detonation occurs. Too much blower boost results in the same thing.

Remember also that the temperature of the air being ingested into the engine can have an effect on the engine temperature. Avoid using hot air from inside the engine compartment, if possible. Feeding an engine cooler outside air, either with scoops sealed to the top of the carb or by ducting cooler outside air to the induction, helps. Intercoolers on turbos or blowers lower incoming air temperatures. Adding cooler induction air has the added benefit of making more engine power. Nitrous oxide or methanol fuels can also have a cooling effect on the incoming intake charge.

Aluminum heads offer some advantages over a cast-iron head. One is that aluminum heads reject heat more quickly than cast-irons. Head temperatures are usually lower and

## Detonation and Preignition *(Continued)*

this reduces the chances of detonation. Static compression can be increased a bit before detonation starts to be a concern again, when compared to the same engine with cast-iron cylinder heads.

Some of the new high-tech coatings applied to pistons, valves, and combustion chambers can help reduce hot spot temperatures and keep detonation from occurring, in addition to reducing heat-induced fatigue in parts. ■

## Cubic-Inch Displacement

To determine the cubic-inch displacement of your engine, use the following formula.

CID = bore x bore x stroke x 0.7854 x number of cylinders
CID = 4.030 x 4.030 x 3.48 x 0.7854 x 8
CID = 4.030 x 4.030 x 3.48 x 6.2832
CID = 355.11597, which is what you get when you bore a 350 SBC 0.030-inch over but keep the stock 3.48-inch stroke. ■

Center-to-center length is 5.7 inches.

The 1962 through 1967 327 small journal (2.00-inch) rods have 11/32-inch rod bolts, have oil weep holes at the parting line, and use a pressed-on piston pin. In 1968 and 1969, the 327 motors used a better rod on larger 2.10-inch journal cranks and 3/8-inch rod bolts. The beam section is a little wider and stronger, and there is no oil weep hole at the parting line. Center-to-center length is 5.7 inches.

The 1967 302 Z28 engines used a 5.7-inch-long small journal (2.00-inch) rod (PN 3927145) with high-strength 11/32-inch bolts. The 1968 and 1969 302s used a 3/8-inch rod bolt and fit onto larger 2.10-inch crank journals.

During 1968, the rod was changed from a pressed-on design to a full-floating piston pin design. All 302 Z28 rods were shot-peened, magnafluxed, and heat-treated at the factory. In 1968 to 1969, the 302 Z28 rod (originally PN 3946841) used 3/8-inch rod bolts that were better than other production 3/8-inch bolt rods.

The 262, 267, 305, 307, and 350 production engines have used a 3/8-inch rod bolt and used 2.10-inch journal cranks with a pressed-on piston pin. The 1970 to 1972 LT1 350 engines used pink rods that were heat-treated, magnafluxed, and shot-peened at the factory. They used the better Z28 3/8-inch rod bolts. Rod length was still 5.7 inches.

The 1970 to 1980 400 small-blocks came with a shorter 5.565-inch center-to-center connecting rod. The rod bolts are also shorter on the 400 stock rods with a differently shaped bolt head that provided additional clearance between the rod bolt head, the block, and cam lobes. The big end on the 400 rod is also sized for the 2.10-inch rod journals on the 400 cranks. These changes allowed the stroke of the crank to be increased to 3.75 inches, yet still fit within the existing small-block outside dimensions. These rods are otherwise dimensionally the same as the stock production 350 medium journal rod and use a pressed-on piston pin.

The Gen II 265 L99 V-8 uses a powdered metal rod that is 5.940 inches in length with 3/8-inch rod bolts, while the LT1 and LT4 engines use a 5.7-inch powdered metal rod. These rods use a 2.10-inch rod journal.

PN 12495071 is a set of 5.700-inch powdered metal rods designed for engines up to 500 hp. These replace the old "pink rods" and were used in the Gen II LT1 and Corvette LT4. The rods are available individually as PN 10108688.

For 383 engines, use PN 19332460, a kit for the third design engine. These are powdered metal and use a standard 0.927-inch pin and 2.100-inch journal.

PN 10108688 was the standard-production forged steel connecting rod. Center-to-center length is 5.7 inches, and this rod comes with production 3/8-inch rod bolts. The rod fits 2.10-inch rod journals, and it uses a pressed-on piston pin.

PN 00361933 was the stock 1970 to 1980 400 small-block rod with a 3/8-inch rod bolt that is specific to the 400 rod. Rod length is 5.565 inches, and it fits 2.10-inch rod journals. Press-on piston pins are used with these rods. This part is discontinued.

PN 14096846 was the high-performance pink rod. This 5.7-inch length rod fits 2.10-inch journal cranks, and it has 3/8-inch bolts. It is heat-treated, magnafluxed, and shot-peened at the factory and made from 1038 forged steel. This rod was used with pressed-on piston pins. It was used on the production LT1, Z28, and L82 engines and on the ZZ3 and ZZ4 350 crate motor small-blocks. It is color coded with a dab of pink or purple paint.

PN 10108697 is a 5.940-inch-long powdered metal rod used in the Gen II 265-ci L99 4.3-liter V-8. This rod is similar to the pink rod in terms of its strength and performance, but it is longer in length. It uses a pressed-on piston pin and fits 2.10-inch medium journal cranks though is discontinued.

Rods with 5.7 inches, 6.0 inches, and shorter or longer center-to-center length made from aluminum, stainless steel, forged steel, and titanium are also available from aftermarket suppliers. Aluminum rods should only be used in short-duration race engines. They must be inspected often, and you should replace them before they work-harden and fail. Do not use aluminum rods in a street-operated engine.

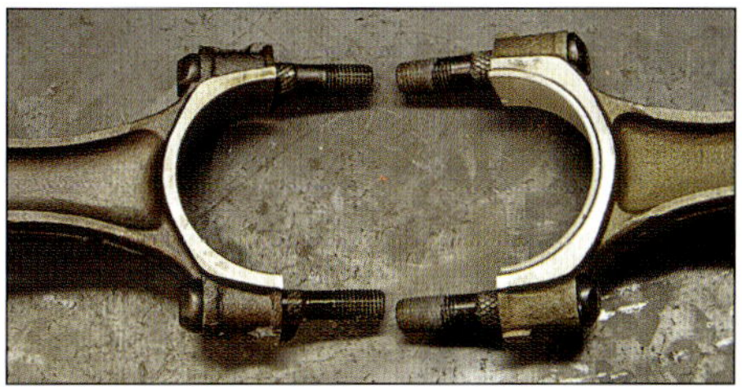

*The rod on the left is from a 1966 283. This is a small journal rod with an 11/32-inch rod bolt. The rod on the right is a production medium journal rod for a 350 with a 3/8-inch rod bolt. Notice the added material to the 350 rod in the high tension areas for increased strength. Also, the 350 beams were made thicker and wider. The early 265 and 283 rods were similar to the rods on the left. These are the weakest small-block rods, relatively speaking. The small journal rods also have an oil weep groove at the parting line of the cap. Medium journal rods do not have the oil weep groove.*

*Tru-Arc retainers are used in many floating piston pins. Spirolox and Teflon buttons can also be used in these applications (shown in the piston). These retainers keep the piston pin from moving side-to-side (and damaging the cylinder bores) in a piston with floating pins. Never reuse them if they have been removed. Pressed-on piston pins do not require a pin retainer.*

## Rod Bolts

One of the things to do with any used rod is to replace the rod bolts when rebuilding a motor. The old bolts are pressed out and the new bolts pressed in. (Rod bolts are not installed by hitting them in with a hammer.) When the bolts are replaced, the big end of the rod must be resized at the machine shop so that the bearing bore in the rod provides the necessary crush to the bearing ends and to have the proper clearances.

The production sized rod bolts and nuts are perfectly adequate for most street-driven applications. Chevy Performance offers a set for its 383 engines as PN 12491166. However, if you are building a high-performance or race engine, move up to the better 3/8- or 7/16-inch rod bolts that are produced by the aftermarket. ARP and Milodon make rod bolts of high quality and increased strength.

## Piston Pins

Remember that the piston pin is one of the most highly stressed parts of the rotating assembly. Most pins that come with the new pistons you buy are reliable and strong enough for most applications. However, if you are building a race engine that is going to produce a large amount of cylinder pressure, say from very high compression levels or large amounts of nitrous or blower boost, or that it is used at extreme RPM levels, then you can look into upgrading the pin to a different design or total weight. Some weight savings can be made. Talk to your piston maker about what you need for your particular combination.

## Floating Versus Pressed-On Piston Pins

There isn't much difference between a rod that takes a pressed-on piston pin and one that takes a floating pin. It is more a question of the convenience of assembly and disassembly. When using a pressed-on pin, the rod is placed in a rod oven and the small end is heated. The pressed-on pin has an interference fit in the rod (0.0012 inch), so when the pin end is heated and its inside diameter opens slightly, the piston and cooler pin can be fit on the rod. When the rod cools, the pin is held tightly by the rod and the piston swivels on the pin. To remove a piston that uses a pressed-on pin, a heavy hydraulic press is used to push the pin out of the rod. However, as sometimes

*Shown is a dished piston used in low-compression engines. Dished pistons are found in many stock 400 small-blocks.*

*These crusty cast pistons feature four valve reliefs to help ensure valve clearance in a range of different cam and power applications from the factory. These are a common-looking piston and have reliefs on both sides for easy positioning during assembly line work.*

*Hypereutectic pistons are used in a variety of performance applications. This style of piston is strong and remains stable through heat cycles. Note the additional coating on the skirt.*

*This is what can happen if you use too much nitrous in your application: meltdown. And it only takes a few seconds.*

happens, the piston can be damaged in the act of pressing the pin out of the rod and piston.

With a floating pin, assembly and disassembly is much easier. The pin rides on a small clearance in the rod end, and it can be slipped in and out of the rod by hand. The piston pin is held in the piston by placing circular retainers in grooves in the piston pin bosses that are located at each end of the pins. These retainers keep the pin from moving side-to-side in the piston. To take the floating pin assembly apart, you remove the pin retainers and slide the pin out of the piston and rod.

If you are going to be taking an engine apart frequently, either between rounds or between race seasons, this is one of those small things that makes life easier. If you don't expect to be taking your engine apart until it has 100,000 miles on it, a pressed-on piston pin and rod assembly will do just fine.

Pin retainers, used with floating pins, basically come in two styles: two C-clips (also called Tru-Arcs) on each end of the piston pin, or a single Spirolox or round wire retainer on each end. Some engine builders feel that the Spirolox retainers are better, but they are difficult to remove once they are installed in their respective grooves. Whichever you use, don't reuse them once they have been removed during rebuilds. Always use new pin retainers.

Many Chevrolet pistons and most aftermarket performance piston makers design their pistons so that they can be used either with a pressed-on pin or a floating pin. If you use a floating-pin setup, make sure that when you insert the pin retainers, there is a 0- to 0.0005-inch clearance between the end of the pin and the retainers. A larger clearance allows the pins to pound out the retainers. Make sure that the piston you use has some provision for pin oiling in the piston pin boss. The pin should have a side clearance of 0.0004 to 0.0008 inch in the piston pin boss. Some pistons in race engines have floating pins that are retained by pin buttons. Made of Teflon, these buttons fit into each end of the pin bores. These buttons actually ride close to the cylinder wall and prevent the pin from moving side-to-side in the rod and piston.

To convert your stock rod from a pressed-on pin to a floating pin, hone the pin end of the rod to give 0.00015- to 0.0008-inch clearance between the floating pin and the rod bore. To ensure that oil lubes the floating pin in the rod, drill a 1/8-inch hole into the top of the small end of the rod for pin oiling. Counterbore the 1/8-inch hole with a 1/4-inch bit to chamfer the opening. Deburr the pin bore, then hone to the correct side clearance for the piston pin.

An alternative way to ensure that oil gets to the floating pin and rod surface is to place two very shallow oiling grooves into the inner bore surface of the small rod end bore. Each oiling groove should be 90 degrees to the top of the rod pin bore.

Some folks have the small end bushed when using a floating pin. Others feel that this reduces the overall strength of the stock rod end because it reduces the thickness of the metal on the rod surrounding the piston pin. They run a floating pin in the rod without using a bushing. Many aftermarket rods are made with more material on the small end and are fitted with a pin bushing. Since these rods were designed initially with a pin bushing in mind, there's no problem with them. A floating piston with a pin bushing does have an advantage. Any wear occurs to the pin and the bushing, and a worn bushing can be replaced without the need to junk the rod.

## Piston Dome and Dish Volumes

You can usually get information on the amount of piston dome and dish volume from the piston makers. However, sometimes you can't or if the pistons have been machined for some reason (such as a reduction in dome height or the deepening of valve reliefs) after they were purchased, you need to measure their present volumes in order to determine the static compression ratio of your parts combination. It's easy.

Put a piston with a top ring on it into a cylinder, placing a little petroleum jelly or white grease on the top ring so it seals. Push the piston deck, not the dome or dish, down in the cylinder exactly 1/2 inch or exactly 1 inch from the top of the block deck to the top of the piston deck.

Make sure you wipe off any excess petroleum jelly or grease from the cylinder walls. Use a plastic plate to seal the top of the cylinder barrel. Now use your large-volume syringe or burette and measure how many cubic centimeters of solvent or other liquid it takes to fill the cylinder barrel to the top of the block deck. When you finish and you know how much solvent was used, you can do the following calculations.

Determine how many cubic centimeters are in the cylinder without the dome or dish. You do this by taking the depth that you placed the piston deck in the bore, in this case either 1/2 or 1 inch down from the block deck, then multiplying the bore diameter by the decimal factor 0.7854.

Total volume = bore x bore x amount the piston is placed x 0.7854

Total volume = 4.030 x 4.030 x 0.5 x 0.7854

Total Volume = 6.377801 ci

Now convert that cubic-inch sum to cubic centimeters by multiplying it by 16.387.

6.377801 ci x 16.387 = 104.51302 cc

Now, you can compare this calculated cubic centimeter figure to the amount of volume in cubic centimeters that you actually found from your cylinder measurement. The difference between the two figures is the volume amount of dome or dish or valve relief your piston has.

It takes less time to calculate if you use the "1/2-inch down" measurement. But if you have an especially large, tall piston dome, it may be better to use the "1-inch down" amount. ■

## Pistons for the Chevy Small-Block

| Part Number | Engine Size | Comp Ratio | Head Chamber Volume | Size | Notes |
|---|---|---|---|---|---|
| 93422884 | 350 | 8.5:1 | 76 cc | Standard | 350/290 hp |
| 10159436 | 350 | 10:01 | 58 cc | Standard | 5.7L HO, ZZ4 and LT1, high silicone aluminum |
| 12514101 | 350 | 9.1:1 | 64 cc | Standard | 300- and 330-hp service engine with "SP" ID |
| 88962542 | 383 | 9.1:1/9.7:1* | 64 cc/62 cc | Standard | First or second design |
| 88962748 | 383 | 9.1:1/9.7:1* | 64 cc/62 cc | 0.005 | Second design |
| 88962749 | 383 | 9.1:1/9.7:1* | 64 cc/62 cc | 0.030 | First or second design |
| 12499103 | 383 | 9.1:1/9.7:1* | 64 cc/62 cc | 0.005 | Kit of eight PN 88962748 |
| 12499104 | 383 | 9.1:1/9.7:1* | 64 cc/62 cc | 0.030 | Kit of eight PN 88962749 |

*Compression ratio based on a 0.028-inch thick head gasket

Always calculate the actual measured static compression ratio for your particular parts combination, which includes bore, stroke, piston dome or dish volumes, chamber volumes, piston-deck-to-block-deck clearance, and head gasket compressed thickness. The pistons listed are all pressed pin. If you are using a domed piston, check to see if the pistons work in any cylinder bore or if they must be used in particular cylinder barrel positions. ■

## Production Piston Compression Heights

Piston compression height is measured from the center of the piston pin bore hole to the deck of the piston, not to the top of any dome or bottom of any dish. Depending on the crank stroke, rod center-to-center length, total block deck height (measured from the centerline of the crank main journal to the top of the block deck), piston-deck-to-block-deck clearance, and head gasket compressed thickness, other piston compression heights can be used. Aftermarket piston makers offer a dizzying array of pistons with different pin heights for the small-block Chevy.

Determine the total package height by taking half of the total crank stroke and adding the center-to-center length of the rod, then adding the compression or pin height of the piston. For instance, if you look at a 350 engine, the crank stroke is 3.48 inches. So, divide that by 2 and you get one-half of the stroke, or 1.74 inches. Add the standard 350 rod length of 5.7 inches, and you get 7.44 inches. Now, add the compression height of the 350 production piston, which is 1.56 inches, and you get a total of 9.00 inches. The nominal total small-block block deck height is 9.025 inches. This combination leaves 0.025 inch of nominal deck height above the piston deck when it is at TDC.

Make allowances for the piston-deck-to-block-deck height at TDC, the compressed head gasket thickness, and the minimum block-deck-to-head-deck clearance. The nominal total block deck height for a standard deck small-block is 9.025 inches, but your block may not be that height because of production casting and machining tolerances, or because the block had been previously decked at a machine shop to ensure flatness or to produce a 0 deck height. ■

| Displacement (ci) | Bore (inches) | Stroke (inches) | Rod Length (inches) | Piston Compression (or Pin) Height (inches) |
|---|---|---|---|---|
| 262 | 3.671 | 3.1 | 5.7 | 1.75 |
| 265 | 3.75 | 3.0 | 5.7 | 1.8 Gen I |
| 265 | 3.75 | 3.0 | 5.94 | 1.56 Gen II L99 |
| 267 | 3.5 | 3.48 | 5.7 | 1.56 |
| 283 | 3.875 | 3.0 | 5.7 | 1.8 |
| 302 | 4.0 | 3.0 | 5.7 | 1.8 |
| 305 | 3.736 | 3.48 | 5.7 | 1.56 |
| 307 | 3.875 | 3.25 | 5.7 | 1.675 |
| 327 | 4.0 | 3.25 | 5.7 | 1.675 |
| 350 | 4.0 | 3.48 | 5.7 | 1.56 |
| 400 | 4.125 | 3.75 | 5.565 | 1.56 |

### Rod Prep

When buying rods, examine them individually to determine if any damage has occurred, even brand-new rods. Are the bearing bores of the large end scored or nicked? If they are used rods, have they turned blue or black from overheating due to a spun bearing? Does the small end show any damage? A used rod should be cleaned and magnafluxed to check for any cracks. Also check the rod for straightness or twist.

If you are building a performance or race engine, decide whether the mold's parting lines on the side beams of a stock rod need to be ground and polished. This smooths out the rough portions of the beam to help prevent stress cracks from forming. You do not want to eliminate weight from the side beams, nor do you want to take so much metal off that you compromise the strength of the rod rather than improve it. The rod beams can be shot-peened to further improve the surface and to help resist cracks.

The balance pads on stock rods can be reduced in size to lessen the overall weight of the rod, but you must leave a little on the balance pads of the rod so that when the rotating assembly is balanced, you have something to work with to weight match all eight rods.

Throw away used rod bolts, especially if they are the stock production 11/32- or 3/8-inch variety, and install new aftermarket premium rod bolts. Don't skimp on cost. The new bolts must be installed properly with a suitably large press.

The rod bearing bore diameter must be checked; measure it at 90 degrees to the parting line of the rod cap. Big ends that are out of spec can be resized. Many rods used in high-RPM engines are deliberately resized and honed in a way that makes the big-end diameter slightly larger

## Maximum Average Piston Speeds

The following is a listing of average maximum piston speeds for various parts combinations. Keep to a conservative maximum average speed limit of 4,000 feet per minute (fpm) or less if you are using stock small-block rotating parts. On some short-duration, very serious drag race engines, using premium aftermarket rotating parts that are lighter and much stronger than stock parts, the maximum average piston speeds can reach 6,000 fpm.

Using the 4,000 fpm figure helps you make other decisions concerning parts selections that operate within the RPM range of your engine. Keep in mind that the maximum average piston speed has nothing to do with where in the RPM range your particular engine produces its best power. This is a calculation that helps you determine the reliability, durability, and longevity of a specific parts combination.

The formula for determining maximum average piston speed is (Crank Stroke x RPM)/6.
The formula for determining the engine RPM at a maximum average piston speed of 4,000 fpm is 24,000/stroke.
The formula for determining the engine RPM at a maximum average piston speed of 4,500 fpm is 27,000/stroke.
The formula for determining the engine RPM at a maximum average piston speed of 5,000 fpm is 30,000/stroke.
To find the engine RPM at a maximum average piston speed of 5,500 fpm the formula is 33,000/stroke.
The formula for RPM at 6,000 fpm maximum average piston speed is 36,000/stroke.

| RPM Where Piston Speed Will Average | | | | | |
|---|---|---|---|---|---|
| Stroke (inches) | 4,000 fpm | 4,500 fpm | 5,000 fpm | 5,500 fpm | 6,000 fpm |
| 2.80 | 8,571 | 9,643 | 10,714 | 11,786 | 12,857 |
| 2.90 | 8,276 | 9,310 | 10,345 | 11,379 | 12,414 |
| 3.00 | 8,000 | 9,000 | 10,000 | 11,000 | 12,000 |
| 3.25 | 7,385 | 8,308 | 9,231 | 10,154 | 11,077 |
| 3.48 | 6,897 | 7,759 | 8,621 | 9,483 | 10,345 |
| 3.60 | 6,667 | 7,500 | 8,333 | 9,167 | 10,000 |
| 3.76 | 6,283 | 7,181 | 7,979 | 8,777 | 9,674 |
| 4.00 | 6,000 | 6,750 | 7,500 | 8,250 | 9,000 |
| 4.125 | 5,818 | 6,545 | 7,273 | 8,000 | 8,727 |
| 4.25 | 5,647 | 6,353 | 7,059 | 7,765 | 8,471 |

Be cautious! If you are building a small-block street engine, use the 4,000 fpm average piston speed limit or less. This helps the rotating assembly live longer and reduce the amount of stress on the parts. Going above 4,000 fpm requires lighter, much stronger premium aftermarket rotating assemblies that can take the amount of stress and force encountered at very high RPM levels in a race engine. Keep these piston speed limits in mind when you are making your parts selections. Also note that maximum average piston speed is not the same as peak piston speed. ■

when measured at the parting line, as compared to the diameter when measured at 90 degrees to the parting line. As the RPM and the speed and G forces on the rod and piston increase, the bore on the big end of the rod may ovalize (it is no longer round). If this ovalizing becomes too large, the crush on the rod bearing weakens and the bearing spins in the rod bore, then onto the crank journal surface. Bearing and crank journal failure is what happens next. In an effort to compensate for this high-RPM ovalizing, the rod bore is finished in the manner described above, so that as the forces acting on the rod increase, the big-end bore goes from a deliberate oval shape to a round shape.

### Pistons

Chevrolet has used three types of aluminum pistons: cast, hypereutectic, and forged. Cast pistons are found in most stock-production, low-performance engines. They give long service in this type of application because of the tight piston to cylinder wall clearances allowed. Hypereutectic pistons are aluminum pistons produced with additional silicon in the alloy. They have more heat resistance and strength than a cast piston. Because they don't expand as much as a forged piston, hypereutectic pistons can be fit with tight piston-to-cylinder-wall clearances and have the stability of a

## Measured Static Compression Ratio

This gets involved but is easy to do. A piece of paper and a pocket calculator are all you need. If you have a computer with a spreadsheet program, you can place the calculations on the computer; then all you need do is enter the variables to solve for the compression ratio. You need to know the piston-deck-to-block-deck height, head gasket compressed thickness, combustion chamber volume, engine bore and stroke, and piston dome volume (which may be positive, if it has a dome, or negative, if it is a dished piston or has valve reliefs in a flat top). When you purchase pistons, the specs include information on dome or dish volume, and head gasket specs include the compressed gasket thickness or compressed gasket volume. These measurements are given in cc, not inches, so our equation converts from cc to inches by dividing the number of cc by 16.39.

You must measure the actual piston-deck-to-block-deck height. This is done with a dial indicator and a deck bridge. Just bring the piston up to TDC and measure how far down the deck of the piston (not the dome) is from the deck of the block. This measurement usually runs from 0.008 to 0.025 inch. If the block has been previously decked at a machine shop to ensure flat surfaces, the deck height distance may be reduced from normal. You can port the chamber volume in the head to measure that amount.

Okay, let's see what we found in our example 350 + 0.030-inch engine.

Bore = 4.030 inches
Stoke = 3.48 inches
Measured Combustion Chamber Volume = 64 cc
Head Gasket Compressed Gasket Thickness = 0.039 inch (GM composition-type gasket)
Measured Piston-Deck-to-Block-Deck Height = 0.025 inch
Piston Dome Volume = + 2.4 cc (TRW # 2304F + 0.030-inch forged)

We need to convert the combustion chamber volume from cc to ci. So,
Chamber Volume = 64 cc / 16.39 = 3.90482 ci

We need to convert the head gasket compressed thickness to volume in cubic inches. So,
Head Gasket Volume = 0.039-inch gasket thickness x 0.7854 x 4.030-inch bore x 4.030-inch bore = 0.4974685 ci

Now, we need to convert the piston deck height into a measurement of volume in inches.
Piston-to-Deck Volume = 0.025-inch deck clearance x 0.7854 x 4.030-inch bore x 4.030-inch bore = 0.31889 ci

Convert piston dome cc to ci: 2.4 cc / 16.39 = 0.1464307 ci

Now, let's finish it up.
Actual Measured Static Compression Ratio = 1 + (0.7854 x 4.030-inch bore x 4.030-inch bore x 3.48-inch stroke) / [(3.90482 chamber volume + 0.4974685 head gasket volume + 0.31889 deck height volume) – (0.1464307 piston dome volume)]. So,

CR = 1 + (44.389494) / [(4.7211785) – (0.1464307)]
CR = 1 + (44.389494 ci / 4.5747478 ci)
CR = 1 + (9.70331565)
CR = 10.703156 or 10.70:1

If you use a piston that has a dish or is a flat-top with valve reliefs, then instead of subtracting the dome volume, add the volume of the dish or valve relief volumes. ■

cast piston. Forged pistons are the strongest pistons and can take the most heat and pressure of the three types, but they expand more than other types of pistons. They require a larger piston-to-cylinder-wall clearance when installed, and may clatter a bit when the engine is cold and the piston has not expanded completely.

Piston decks are made with flat tops, domes, or recessed dish shapes. Most have reliefs for valve clearance in their deck surfaces. These shapes and the resulting volumes have a direct effect on the amount of static compression a cylinder has. Other engine dimensions are involved, and you need to know what amount of static compression your parts combination produces. Engines that have cast-iron heads and run on the street with pump gasoline should not exceed a 9.5:1 static compression ratio in order to avoid detonation. Bore, stroke, cylinder head chamber volume, head gasket compressed thickness, deck clearance, piston dome, and valve relief volume must all be measured or known, in order to figure out the static compression ratio. Aluminum-headed engines can use approximately one more compression point and still run pump fuels, but everything else (ignition, ignition timing, cooling system, cam timing, intake air temperature, etc.) must be right to avoid detonation.

Some domed small-block pistons have two different dome styles to match either left- or right-hand cylinder banks. Flat-top or dished pistons can usually be used on either side of the engine. In any case, make sure you figure out what your static compression is when you make your parts selection.

If you want to use a very high compression ratio, large doses of nitrous, or a blower with high boost, expect high cylinder temperatures and pressures. A forged piston with a thicker deck or that has a lower top ring groove in relation to the piston deck may help the piston survive. Check with your piston maker for designs made for these applications. High-tech piston coatings can help the piston reject the increased temperatures, increase parts survival, and keep the high temperatures and pressures in the combustion chamber where they can work on the top of the piston to produce power.

Some pistons (particularly domed pistons) are manufactured to fit in particular cylinder barrels on one side of the engine or the other. Always check to see if you have a universal-fit piston, and if not, that it is installed into the correct barrel to match the valve sequences and chamber shapes. The pistons listed here do not work with 18-degree, 15-degree, splayed-valve, or SB2 cylinder heads because of differences in combustion chamber shape, piston dome shapes, depth, and cam lobe and valve sequencing. These heads require special pistons, which are available on the aftermarket. Many other pistons and piston types are available from aftermarket suppliers.

If you are assembling a high-performance street or mild bracket race engine, you can use a hypereutectic piston with a pressed-on pin. This type of piston is stronger than a cast piston, and it can take more abuse. It costs only a few dollars more than a cast piston and it can be fitted with tight piston-to-cylinder-wall clearances for quiet operation.

When building a very-high-performance street engine or a serious race engine, use a forged piston, especially if you plan to use a turbocharger, supercharger, or nitrous oxide with any static compression ratio, or if you plan to use a carbureted engine with a static compression ratio higher than 10.5:1. These types of engines can develop high heat and cylinder pressures that might melt or break a cast piston. Forged pistons expand more than other types of pistons, so you must use a larger clearance between the piston and the cylinder wall. Follow the manufacturer's recommendations for piston to cylinder wall clearances.

When your block is being bored, bring the pistons you are using. Each piston is measured and fit to a particular cylinder barrel. The block is bored out until the cylinder diameter is just shy of the desired size. The pistons' diameters are individually measured, and the final block honing brings the cylinder diameter out to the correct diameter. This includes whatever piston-to-cylinder-wall clearance is required. If you are building a performance street or a race engine, make sure that the final cylinder honing is done with a block torque plate in place. This ensures that the cylinder barrels are round when everything is bolted together and torqued down, and piston ring seal is improved.

Cast and hypereutectic pistons generally need a 0.0007- to 0.002-inch cylinder wall clearance. Forged pistons, which have a greater expansion rate, may have a required clearance of 0.004 to 0.007 inch. It is important that you follow the manufacturer's recommendations for the proper clearance for a particular piston. The manufacturer also states where on the piston skirt you must measure to determine the piston diameter, usually 90 degrees from the piston pin centerline axis.

Check the valve to piston deck clearance, especially if you are using a camshaft with higher-than-stock lifts or have increased the rocker arm ratio. A stock cam requires a minimum of 0.060-inch clearance and any cam intended for racing requires a minimum of 0.100 inch. Check for this clearance from 20 degrees before TDC to 20 degrees after TDC; some valve-to-piston interference can occur at these points, not just at TDC. Rotate the assembly through a few entire revolutions to be sure. Keep this in mind if you are installing a cam in an advanced or retarded position. Too many folks neglect to check these clearances, and suffer the consequences.

Increasing the compression ratio on any motor increases the engine's mechanical efficiency. Now, you may be tempted to use a piston with the biggest dome you can find and fit it into the heads you plan to use. But what is the static compression? A street engine with cast-iron heads, running on low-octane, unleaded pump gasoline should have a static compression ratio lower than 9.5:1. In a race engine, a large piston dome has some disadvantages because the large dome inhibits good flame travel; the flame front must go over the top of the dome. Current thinking in high-performance and race engine design is to increase static compression by using smaller cylinder head combustion chambers and flat tops or the smallest piston dome volume required to obtain high compression ratios and good flame front travel speed.

Bowtie SB2 heads, which are the 1996 Gen I race heads, have small 38-cc combustion chambers. Many aftermarket heads have small combustion chambers and thick head decks. These head decks can be shaved down to produce even smaller combustion chamber volumes. Very high compression ratios can be made with flat-top pistons or small piston domes if you use a small combustion chamber volume. Flame travel is enhanced and more power is produced when compared to large combustion chamber and big piston dome combinations.

Race engine builders usually must spend a lot of time massaging the domes on pistons to remove sharp edges and generally smoothen out dome contours, which results in a piston dome shape they feel is conducive to good flame travel, and to reduce hot spots. Now, however, many aftermarket piston makers can deliver pistons with fully machined domes that greatly reduce the amount of hand finishing you

## Basic Piston and Ring Clearances

### Piston Skirt Clearances

| Source | Type | Street and Performance | Competition |
|---|---|---|---|
| Chevrolet | Cast aluminum | 0.0015 to 0.0025 | Not recommended |
| Chevrolet | Forged | 0.004 to 0.006 | 0.0055 to 0.0065 |
| Chevrolet | Hypereutectic | 0.0015 to 0.0020 | Not recommended |
| TRW/Speed Pro | Hypereutectic | 0.0015 to 0.0020 | Not recommended |
| TRQ/Speed Pro | Forged | 0.003 to 0.0055 | 0.0055 to 0.0065 |

### Ring End-Gap Clearance Recommendations

| For 5/64 and 1/16 Ductile Iron Top Rings and 0.043 and 0.031 Pressure Back/Head Land Top Rings | | For Regular (Plain) Iron Second Rings | |
|---|---|---|---|
| **Using Special Fuels:** | | | |
| Supercharged/injected nitro engines | 0.022/0.024 | Supercharged/injected nitro engines | 0.014/0.016 |
| Supercharged/injected alcohol engines | 0.018/0.020 | Supercharged/injected alcohol engines | 0.012/0.014 |
| **Using Gasoline:** | | | |
| Supercharged/injected gasoline engines | 0.022/0.024 | Supercharged/injected gasoline engines | 0.012/0.014 |
| Oval track rectangular rings | 0.018/0.020 | Oval track | 0.012/0.014 |
| Oval Track head land rings | 0.024/0.026 | | 0.012/0.014 |
| Oval track pressure back rings | 0.020/0.022 | | 0.012/0.014 |
| Pro Stock, Comp Eliminator, Modified Production, ect. | 0.018/0.020 | Pro Stock, Comp Eliminator, Modified Production, ect. | 0.012/0.014 |
| Super Stock | 0.018/0.020 | Super Stock | 0.010/0.012 |
| Stock | 0.016/0.018 | Stock | 0.010/0.012 |
| Street engines | 0.016/0.018 | Street engines | 0.010/0.012 |

Note: These Speed Pro end-gap recommendations will be appropriate in most cases. They stress that this chart should be used as a guide to normal ring fitting, and that the ideal end gap may be different for specific combinations. If you're ever in doubt, check with other engine builders or add 0.002 inch to the recommended end gap. Racers with plenty of experience often close up the gaps from 0.002 to 0.004 inch, but you have to be willing to sacrifice a motor if you guess wrong.

Setting piston-to-cylinder-wall (skirt) and end-gap clearances are critical steps in building a reliable small-block. Use these charts as a starting point, and discuss your specific applications with your machine shop. ■

may want to do. Pistons can also be lightened and balanced by the manufacturer, eliminating another step for you if you are building a performance engine.

Aftermarket piston makers supply just about any piston size, design, and weight you could ask for. Pistons with the ring package moved up on the piston are available, as well as high-tech piston coatings that help the piston live longer in a race engine. Various pin heights are made, including those for popular stroker combinations. If they don't have what you want, they can custom-make it. Call and get advice before you buy.

### Piston Rings

Piston ring grooves are cut for different ring widths for low-performance and high-performance piston rings. Chevy High Performance and many aftermarket forged pistons use rings that have a top and second ring width of 1/16 inch with an oil ring width of 3/16 inch. Cast pistons use piston rings with a wider width of 5/64 inch for the top and second ring and 3/16 inch for the oil ring.

Piston top rings are made from various materials: plain cast-iron, ductile iron, chrome-faced, plasma-ceramic-faced, and moly-faced. Also, second rings can be made with various zero-gap features, if you are looking for better cylinder sealing. Third or oil rings are also offered in low-tension forms for race engines. Some ring sets are 0.005-inch oversize and these require that you file the ring ends to make a custom ring end gap the size you want.

There is some power to be gained here by getting the ring gap exactly right. However, if you reduce the gap by too much, the ends of the ring can butt up against each other after they heat up and expand. If this occurs, power falls off and there may be some damage to the cylinder walls as a result.

For gasoline-fueled engines, one rule of thumb for minimum top ring end gaps is 0.004-inch gap for every 1 inch of cylinder bore. For example, a 4-inch cylinder bore requires a minimum top ring end gap of 0.016 inch with gasoline. Be careful here. Any ring gap measurement you make is made when the piston and rings are cold.

If you get the gap too small, the ends may hit each other when the ring is heated up and expands. The top ring is hotter than the second or third rings because it is so close to the piston top and combustion chamber heat.

Start out with a larger, more conservative ring end gap and work your way down to smaller gaps when the motor is freshened. (This requires that you keep accurate records of the actual clearances given when the motor is first assembled.) If there is no sign that the rings' gap ends have been rubbing or butting against each other, you can reduce the gap 0.001 inch from the previous clearance, but you have to be able to risk the engine if you go too far.

If cylinder temperatures are going to be high, such as in a high-compression or nitrous engine, blower engine, or with hypereutectic pistons, the minimum top ring end gaps must be larger. Use of alcohol or nitro fuels also requires changes in the minimum ring end gap. Always follow the manufacturer's recommendations for minimum ring end gaps.

On a street-operated, gasoline-fueled engine, you don't need fancy or expensive rings. A pre-gapped, moly-faced top ring; a pre-gapped, cast-iron second ring; and a standard-tension oil ring assembly do just fine and give excellent service. Minimum ring end gaps for a street-driven engine can be larger and more conservative. The top ring gap should be 0.018 to 0.022 inch, the second ring gaps should measure 0.012 to 0.014 inch, and the oil ring support rail gaps should be 0.012 to 0.014 inch. If you are using an effective crankcase vacuum extraction system on a race engine, move to a low-tension oil ring setup, which frees up a little more power by reducing oil ring friction on the cylinder walls.

## 377 and 383 Engine Combinations

Since engine parts interchanges are easy to do with Chevy Gen I small-blocks, two non-factory engine combinations have become commonplace. Both combinations take parts from two different production engine sizes and combine them to gain advantages not found in other production engines.

The 377-ci engine is built using a 400-style block and a 350 medium journal crank. Depending on the size of the 400-block cylinder bores, you get the large bore size of the 400 with the higher RPM capabilities of the shorter 3.48-inch stroke of the 350 crank.

The main bearing journals of the 400 block are set up

## 377 and 383 Engine Combinations *(Continued)*

for the 2.65-inch main journal diameters of a 400 crank. The main journals on a 350 crank are 2.45 inches. The rod bearing journal diameters are the same on 350 and 400 cranks (2.10 inches). So something must be done to make up the difference between the 400-block main journal sizes and the smaller diameter main journals on the 350 cranks. There are a number of things you can do.

All of the major bearing makers can supply an extra-thick main bearing set for this interchange. Federal-Mogul makes a set under PN 4981. These thick bearings fit inside the 400-block main bearing saddles and then provide the proper clearance for a 350 crank. The extra-thick bearing sets work fine and are convenient, but they are expensive. A cheaper alternative is to use a bearing spacer insert that snaps into the 400-block saddles and then you use production 350-style main bearings on top of the spacers. Competition Cams can provide the bearing spacers under PN 5620. A third alternative, but even more expensive, is to use an aftermarket forged crank that has the 3.48-inch 350 stroke and main journals that are sized for the 400 block and 400-main bearing crank diameters.

The 5.7-inch-length connecting rods of the 350 are then used with a 400-style piston. A 6-inch rod could be used, but you would need an aftermarket piston with the appropriate changes in piston pin compression height. Using the 5.7-inch 350 rods and 400 pistons keep your costs down.

The 377 delivers the larger bore sizes not available with the 350 production setup, while keeping the shorter 350 stroke and 5.7-inch rod length for higher RPM operation. Use a 350-style internally balanced front vibration damper and internally balanced flywheel or flexplate.

Another common non-factory combination to build is the 383, but it has different power generation and RPM operating range characteristics. For the 383, you use a 400 crank in a 350 block. The main journals of the 400 cast crank (there were no forged factory production cranks used in the 400 engines) are cut down by a crank grinder from the 2.65-inch diameter to a 2.45-inch diameter to fit inside the main bearing saddles of the 350 block.

You then use whichever 350 main and rod bearings you need. You can use the 5.7-inch rods from the 350 and an aftermarket piston with the appropriate changes in pin compression height. You can use the 5.565-inch 400 rod or 5.7-inch 350 rod or an even longer rod, but you must carefully check the clearances between the head of the rod bolts and the camshaft lobes, the bottom of the cylinder barrels, and the skirts of the pistons you choose. You may have to grind material from the rod bolt heads and the side of the big end of the rods to get the required 0.050-inch clearances. In most instances, you find that some, not all, of the rods and rod bolts require a little grinding to get the clearances needed. You can use a small base circle camshaft to help provide additional clearance.

The easiest 383 parts combination uses the 400 (5.565-inch) rods and a 350 production piston. If you use this combination, generally, there are no cam clearance problems at all. However, you still need to check the crank/block clearances. Make sure by doing a trial assembly of your parts. Some folks don't care for this 400 short-rod combination because the long stroke of the 400 crank when matched with the short 400 rod and 350 piston, gives a rod ratio of 1.47:1. However, the ease of this combination and the usual lack of any major interference or clearance problems make this combo a common choice.

Aftermarket piston makers now have a wide variety of pistons for the 383 combination and for use with either hypereutectic or forged pistons and for the 5.565-inch 400 rod, the 5.7-inch 350 rod, or a 6-inch rod. Prices for the hypereutectic pistons are reasonable, with the forged pistons costing more. Of course, depending on which combination of parts you use and your intentions, you may be able to use production-style cast pistons.

The 383 delivers more low- and mid-RPM-range torque due to the longer 400 crank stroke. However, the high-RPM potential is limited because of the stroke and rod ratios involved. With the 400 crank, you must use a 400-style externally balanced front vibration damper and 400-style externally balanced flywheel or flexplate. You can have the entire rotating assembly internally balanced by using heavy metal plugs in the crank counterweights, but this is an expensive alternative proposition.

One other combination is to use a 400 crank with the main journals cut down in a Gen I 305 block. The main journals of the 400 crank are reduced to fit the 2.45-inch main journals of the 305. The 400 rods and production 305 pistons are used to finish off the short block. The use of a 400 crank puts more torque and bottom end into the engine. Depending on the block bore size, you can build a 329.7-ci (3.736-inch standard bore) or up to a 336.8-ci engine. ■

## Setting Piston Ring End Gaps

Properly setting the end gap on oversize (gappable) ring sets can be a tedious, error-prone process. However, done precisely, it almost certainly improves horsepower, reliability, and fuel economy, and extends engine life. Done incorrectly, it takes the fine edge off an otherwise excellent engine or, in the worst case, results in severe ring damage and greatly shortened engine life.

Properly gapping rings places two demands on the engine builder: 1) The precise amount of material (exact, to one thousandth of an inch) must be removed from the end of each ring; and 2) the resulting gap must be parallel and have no burrs or sharp edges that can scratch the bore. Until recently, there were two common ways to gap rings, both of them less than satisfactory: filing the ring while holding it in a vise or using a simple cutting-wheel tool. Both of these methods require substantial experience and manual dexterity. And even with experience, it's easy to ruin a ring or two (luckily most machine shops sell individual rings).

There are now a number of ring gapping tools that will help get the job done correctly, but it is still an exercise in patience. ■

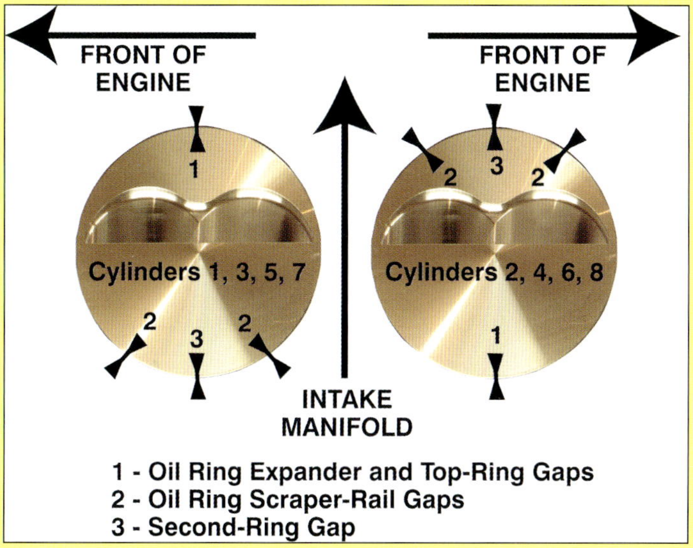


*Install all piston rings with end gaps staggered as shown here. With properly gapped rings and properly honed cylinder walls, this procedure provides the best cylinder sealing and most efficient oil control. Install rings on pistons with the proper expander tool whenever possible.*

*Oversize ring sets are available, but you have to set the gaps on each ring individually. When gapping your own rings, always take your time; cut a little and measure, then do it again. It only takes a few turns of the wheel to remove material and if you take off too much, the ring is unusable, and you have to purchase a replacement ring.*

CHAPTER 4

# Lubrication Systems

The Chevy small-block lubrication system is very reliable and presents no design defects to worry about. Just keep everything clean. Change the oil and filter on a regular basis, and your engine will provide good service for more than 100,000 miles. If the recommended main and rod bearing and rod side clearances are maintained, a stock volume oil pump is all that is required. A high-volume or high-pressure pump or an oil pump from a big-block Chevy are not needed in most street applications. These other pumps take additional horsepower to run and add more strain on the cam/distributor drive gears and driveshaft.

Checking the operating clearances on the stock oil pump and optimizing them, if necessary, ensures adequate oil pressure. The clearance between the pump gears and the pump gear cover should be 0.002 to 0.0025 inch. If there is more clearance, take a sheet of 400-grit sandpaper and some oil, then move the main pump body in a figure-eight motion over the wet sandpaper to remove material until the clearance is correct. If there is less than the minimum clearance, you can sand the pump gears. Remember to Loctite the pump cover bolts when you put the pump back together.

Two different oil pump intermediate driveshafts have been used in Gen I blocks. All Gen I blocks except the 400 use a driveshaft that is $5^{3}/_{4}$ inch long overall and is the same shaft diameter its entire length up to where the plastic or metal coupling sleeve attaches. The 400-style shaft is the same length, but the diameter is necked down in a portion of the shaft to clear the wider journal 400 main caps.

The oil pump driveshaft for a Chevy big-block is longer ($6^{1}/_{2}$ inches overall) and is not interchangeable. Gen II engines that have a front-mounted Opti-Spark distributor use an oil pump driveshaft stub, which connects the gear on the rear of the cam to the oil pump. If you have a Gen II long-block and elect to use a Bowtie 4-barrel carburetor, aluminum intake, and a rear-mounted distributor, you must change the oil pump stub driveshaft to the conventional intermediate driveshaft found on Gen I engines.

Have the oil pump screen and pickup tube welded to the pump body. Remove the pump's pressure bypass spring in the pump before you do any welding to prevent heat damage to the spring. There are some aftermarket pickup screens and tubes that bolt to the pump and give positive retention of the pickup instead of welding. Check that there is 1/4- to 3/8-inch clearance between the lowest point of the pickup screen and the bottom of the oil pan before securing the pickup in place.

***The stock standard-volume small-block oil pump gives excellent service in most applications. Make sure that the pickup screen you use fits the depth of the oil pan and that the pickup tube is welded or bolted to the pump body.***

Make sure you prime the oil pump before you install it. Squirt some oil into the pump or stick the pickup down into some oil and turn the pump shaft by hand to coat the pump gears. This ensures that the pump moves oil as soon as the new engine is turned over the first time you start it. It's also a good practice to use a priming tool on an assembled engine before it is started for the

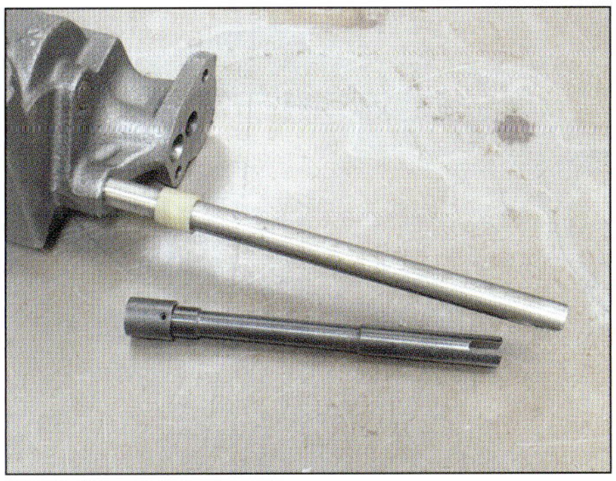

*The oil pump driveshaft is connected to the oil pump with a small plastic connector. In high-performance applications, it is recommended to go with a more robust shaft with a steel coupler. Also, note that the center section of the heavy-duty version (on the bottom) for the 400-ci small-block is necked down in the center portion to clear the wider main caps found on the 400.*

*You can increase the operating oil pressure in a standard-volume oil pump by changing the pressure relief spring to the PN 3848911. With this high-pressure spring, there is no need for washer shims or carb jets. Operating pressures are 65 to 70 pounds.*

first time. Oil can then be pumped throughout the engine. Continue to use the priming tool until you see oil come out of all the rocker arm oiling holes.

Generally, the rule of thumb for oil pressure is 10 pounds of pressure for every 1,000 rpm. For example, you should have 40 pounds of hot oil pressure at 4,000 rpm, 50 pounds at 5,000 rpm, and 60 pounds at 6,000 rpm. Chevrolet makes a high-pressure relief spring (PN 3848911). It is color-coded white and provides a maximum of approximately 70 pounds of oil pressure. This spring is used in high-performance oil pump PN 3848907 and is for use in the Gen II LT1/LT4 pump (PN 93427692). You can add this spring to a stock standard-volume oil pump for increased line pressure.

PN 3848907 is a standard-volume oil pump with a Z28 pressure relief spring.

PN 14044872 is a high-volume oil pump with 1.50-inch gears creating approximately 25 percent more capacity than a standard pump.

PN 3855152 is an oil pump pickup screen and tube that is used with PN 465220 Z28 oil pan and standard-volume Z28 pump.

PN 10046007 is an oil pump mounting bolt.

PN 3998287 is an oil pump/distributor driveshaft. Use it with plastic retainer/connector PN 3764554.

PN 24241872 is a magnetic drain plug. This is an effective tool to catch and hold small metallic debris that can cause engine damage. It's also helpful to inspect when changing the oil.

If you do use a high-volume or high-pressure oil pump, use a pump driveshaft that has a metal coupler instead of using the stock plastic coupler.

## Oil Pans

First, make sure whichever oil pan you use fits inside your engine compartment without hitting the front suspension crossmembers. Also determine on which side of the engine the dipstick goes. It must match the dipstick location in the block and the oil pan. If you mistakenly put an oil pan with a passenger-side dipstick location onto a block with a driver-side dipstick location, you can develop an oil leak. Check these things before you build the engine and certainly before you install the engine into the vehicle.

Over the years, two-piece rear main oil seal pans used two different thicknesses of seals between the front oil pan surface and the timing chain cover. Here's how to tell which front pan gasket to use: On engines from 1955 to 1974, a thin 1/4-inch gasket was used; from 1975 to 1985, a 3/8-inch-thick gasket was used. Take the oil pan you're going to use and place a straightedge across the pan rails over the front gasket's half-moon opening. Measure the distance from the seal surface to the bottom of the straightedge. If the distance is $2^{1}/_{4}$ inches, use the thin 1/4-inch seal. If the distance is $2^{3}/_{8}$ inches, use the 3/8-inch seal. You can use a two-piece seal oil pan with a thick gasket on a block that originally used a thin gasket and pan, if you must. Just make sure you use the appropriate front pan seal and that the pan has the dipstick location that matches the block and location that you need.

Also, make sure you use a pan for a two-piece rear main oil seal with a block that has the two-piece rear seal. Likewise, a one-piece rear main seal block and crank requires an oil pan suited for this application. Chevrolet and some aftermarket suppliers do make adapters to mount a two-piece seal crank into a one-piece seal block and use the appropriate pan. Make

## Dipsticks and Dipstick Tubes

There are a number of things to check when you are selecting oiling system parts to build a small-block Chevy. The oil pan must match the block you are using. The block and pan may mount the oil dipstick tube on the driver's or passenger's side. The pan you decide to use may mount the dipstick directly into the side of the pan itself without passing through the pan rail of the block. Your block may be the type that uses a one-piece or a two-piece rear main seal. If so, you need a matching oil pan. You can use an adapter to fit a two-piece rear main seal and crank into a block designed to use a one-piece seal and related crank.

The oil pan gaskets must match the style of block and pan you use.

Dipsticks and the dipstick tubes that were used over the years have changed considerably. The length of the tube and the matching dipstick have changed. The FULL line on the dipstick has been moved to different locations, depending on the length of the tube and where it entered the crankcase. It is very easy to mix up parts if you are pulling used pieces from different engines and intend to use them. Some dipstick tubes are merely pressed into the dipstick tube hole on the block. A second tube is pressed into the block pan rail and extended down into the crankcase. Others have little brackets that are then bolted to the engine to secure the dipstick and tube. Some older models have two little bumps on the exhaust manifold that hold the dipstick tube.

If you are removing the dipstick and tube from an engine core, try to keep them together. Keep in mind also that some small-block exhaust manifolds only work when you are using a block that has the dipstick on the passenger's side. These exhaust manifolds may bolt right up, but they may cover and obstruct the hole to the dipstick on the driver's side. If you don't check while you are building the engine, you may not find out until the engine is in a vehicle and you try to place the dipstick and tube, finding you can't do it.

It is not uncommon to find a used engine with a mismatched setup. Often, the crankcase is then overfilled or underfilled. I had one customer come into the shop who complained that his engine was smoking excessively and using oil. The engine was also down on power and hard to start. When I checked the oil level on the dipstick, it read FULL, but the combination of dipstick and tube just didn't look right to me. I drained the oil, and from an oil pan that should have held four quarts, I drained 10 quarts. The engine had so much oil in it that I had to quickly reach for a second drain pan to hold all of the fluid. The dipstick he had used was too short and it had taken 10 quarts to get it to read FULL. We refilled his crankcase with 4 quarts and got him the correct dipstick and dipstick tube for his application. The engine no longer smoked, the power was back to where it should have been, it started easily, and oil consumption ceased to be a problem.

It is a good practice to check the dipstick and tube you are going to use by filling the crankcase with the proper amount of oil, installing the dipstick and tube, then checking that the dipstick's shown FULL level is correct. Do this before the engine is installed in the vehicle. ■

*A Moroso deep-sump oil pan allows for increased oil volume. Note the trap door baffle to keep oil around the oil pump pickup screen during acceleration and cornering.*

sure you figure this all out and make your parts selection before you build the engine.

The following are a number of oil pans used in different small-block applications. Some are obsolete from the Chevy Performance line, but I wanted to share them as a reference for used or NOS searches.

PN 12557558 is a 4-quart pan used on ZZ4 crate engines and 1986–1992 Camaros. It is designed for a

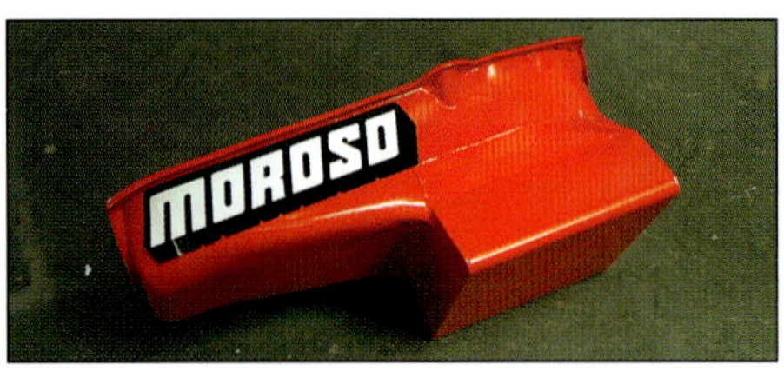


*Make sure that the type of pan you have chosen fits in the engine compartment of your vehicle and does not interfere with suspension or exhaust components. This deep-sump Moroso pan increases oil volume, but it isn't for every application. Also note the kickout on the driver-side pan rail as well as the dipstick location. Keep this in mind when selecting a pan.*

one-piece seal and has internal baffling with a right-hand dipstick.

PN 25534353 is a circle track "factory stock" pan with 8-quart capacity. Since it is for circle track racing, it has a 3.5-inch kickout with a louvered windage tray, three trap doors, and an oil scraper. It is used on the Circle Track crate engine PN 88869602.

PN 359942 is a 5-quart oil pan with trap door baffles and a bigger sump. It was used on Gen I engines in Corvettes with a two-piece rear oil seal block; driver-side dipstick position. This pan fits pre-1986 Corvettes but may not fit your application due to crossmember clearance problems with the larger sump.

Chevy Performance offers late-model circle track racers a high-volume pan with a kickout, windage tray, trap doors, and other racing features as PN 25534354.

PN 360866 is a Corvette 4-quart Gen I oil pan with a driver-side dipstick and is used with two-piece rear main oil seals.

PN 465220 is a 1969 Z28 Camaro oil pan with better baffling for use with two-piece rear seals. This pan has a 4-quart capacity and a driver-side dipstick for use with Gen I blocks.

PN 465221 is the standard-production Gen I 4-quart oil pan. Chevy windage trays do not fit this pan. It is used with two-piece rear seals and has a driver-side dipstick location.

PN 10055765 is a 1986-on Corvette 5-quart Gen I and II pan for use with one-piece rear main seals. It has a passenger-side dipstick location.

PN 10066039 is a 4-quart pan for two-piece rear seals and is used on the Gen I Goodwrench 350/190- and 350/285-hp crate motors. It clears and fits most front crossmembers.

PN 10110837 is a 1986-on Corvette and 350 HO Camaro 4-quart oil pan. Use it with the Gen I and II one-piece rear seal and passenger-side dipstick.

To help seal the oil pan gasket for leak-free performance, Chevrolet created a thin metal strip that is positioned between the pan flange and the retaining bolts. This helps distribute the clamping force of the bolts for a better seal.

PN 14082340 is an oil pan reinforcement for pre-1986 Gen I blocks; passenger's side.

PN 14082341 is an oil pan reinforcement for pre-1986 Gen I blocks; driver's side.

PN 14088501 is an oil pan reinforcement for 1986-on Gen I and II; driver's side.

PN 14088502 is an oil pan reinforcement for 1986-on Gen I and II; passenger's side.

The 1955 265 small-blocks did not have or use an oil filter.

On the 1955 to 1979 blocks, the dipstick was on the driver's side.

On the 1980 to 1985 blocks, the dipstick was on the passenger's side.

On 1986-on production, one-piece rear seal blocks, the dipstick is located on the passenger's side.

Cast-iron Bowtie blocks have provisions to mount the dipstick tube on either side, although the holes may not be drilled in the dipstick bulges in the block pan rails. Aluminum Bowtie blocks use a driver-side-mounted dipstick tube and related oil pans.

Some engine parts combinations or engine swaps are aided by using an oil pan on which the dipstick enters into the side of the pan itself without passing through the block. This arrangement may give you the dipstick clearance you need to go around certain exhaust manifolds or tube headers. PN 464607 is a 4-quart two-piece rear seal pan with a dipstick located on the driver's side going directly into the side of the pan. Use this pan with two-piece seal blocks that have the dipstick bulge on the driver's side. I have used this pan in small-block V-8 conversions in S-10 and S-15 Chevy two-wheel-drive pickups and Blazers when using late-model Camaro seven-hole cast-iron exhaust manifolds that run above the spark plugs and block access to the normal driver-side dipstick tube location.

A smart piece to add and use on your oil pan is a magnetic drain plug offered by Chevrolet as PN 24241872. It attracts metal particles and keep them from circulating in the engine and it can give you an early indication of problems. PN 14079398 is an oil pan gasket kit for pre-1986 engines with two-piece rear main seals. PN 14088505 is a pan gasket set for a one-piece rear main seal on 1986-and-later Gen I blocks and on later Gen II blocks. PN 10108676 is a one-piece oil pan gasket made for 1986-and-newer engines (one-piece rear main seal).

If you have a late-model one-piece rear main seal block, you can use a rear seal adapter (PN 10051118) that enables you to use a crankshaft designed for a two-piece rear main seal. However, with this GM seal adapter you must use an oil pan that was designed for a one-piece rear main seal. Aftermarket suppliers make rear seal adapters that allow you to install a two-piece seal crank into a one-piece rear-seal block, and then use an oil pan from a two-piece seal engine. Bowtie CNC Race Prepared blueprinted blocks come with a rear-seal adapter that allows the use of a crank and oil pan that were designed for two-piece rear main seals.

Rocket blocks require an aftermarket oil pan because the distance between the oil pan rails, side-to-side, is wider than that on production Chevy small-blocks.

If you are doing a small-block swap into a mid- or late-1970s Chevy Vega or Monza, Buick Skyhawk, Pontiac Astre, or Oldsmobile Starfire, which were all H-Bodies, use the V-8 pan and V-8 engine mounts installed in the 1975 to 1980 262 and 305 V-8 Monzas. This unique 4-quart oil pan clears the crossmembers in these H-Bodies. Aftermarket suppliers also supply pans that fit this small-block vehicle combination.

## Windage Trays

Windage trays help keep oil from clinging to a spinning crankshaft. At high RPM, the crank can collect a large amount of oil, which reduces the amount of horsepower the engine can make. These trays are not necessary on a stock street engine, but above 6,000 rpm they can help produce more power.

Chevrolet makes windage trays for the small-block, and they are also available from aftermarket suppliers. You need main cap bolts or studs that are made to mount the tray. Make sure that the windage tray you use fits inside your oil pan, and that you rotate the crank and rods after installation to make sure there is enough clearance for rotating parts. You can adjust the installed height of the tray accordingly.

Chevy windage trays are solid trays made to fit with certain pans. They do not fit 4-quart production pans. They are not full-length trays because of production clearance problems with frame crossmembers that necessitate the use of a rear sump on the pan. Marine applications that use an aftermarket oil pan with a full-length sump can use a full-length windage tray. Likewise, if you have enough crossmember clearance, such as that found in a tube-chassis race car, you may be able to use a full-length sump pan and windage tray.

PN 3927136 is for use with oil pan PN 360450 and requires five mounting studs (PN 14087508) for 1968-and-newer blocks or PN 3872718 for pre-1968 blocks.

PN 12554816 is a flat oil pan baffle used originally with Corvette pan PN 10055765 (1986–1996).

PN 14087508 is the windage tray main cap studs ($5\frac{5}{8}$ inches) for medium journal cranks in 1968-and-newer blocks.

PN 3872718 is the windage tray main cap studs ($5\frac{1}{4}$ inches) for small journal cranks in 1955 to 1967 blocks.

PN 9422297 is the windage tray nuts.

PN 3927136 is a Z28, 1970 350 LT1 semi-circular windage tray. Use it with driver-side dipstick and pan (PN 465220).

PN 14071077 is a flat windage tray for the Corvette 5-quart oil pan (PN 10055765) with one-piece rear main seal. Use it with a passenger-side dipstick.

PN 10166191 is a flat windage tray used on the 350/300-hp CC crate motor. Use it with oil pan (PN 12524504), one-piece rear oil seals, and passenger-side dipstick.

When installing a factory windage tray on a 400 block with 2.65-inch main journal diameters, the wider main journals of these blocks cause wider main cap bolt or stud spacing than other blocks. You may have to elongate the bolt holes in the windage tray to get the tray to fit properly on a 400 block.

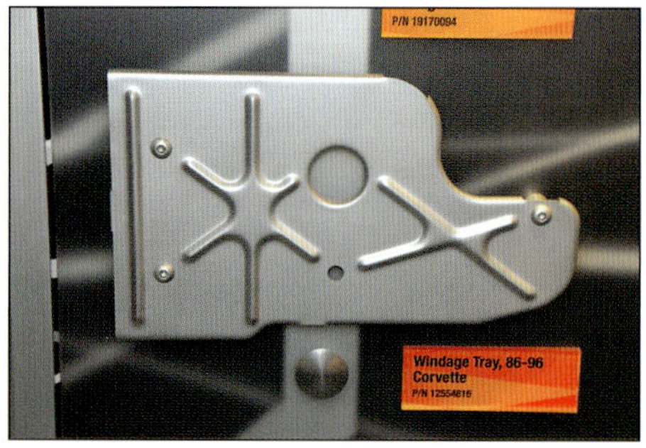


*Windage trays, such as PN 3927136, help control oil in the pan and may add some power at higher RPM, but not all oil pans have room to fit them. Generally, you need a 5-quart or larger capacity pan.*

There has been some discussion about whether you should use a solid tray or a screen-type windage tray. Some folks feel that the aftermarket screen-type trays do a better job of removing oil from the crank, while the solid trays allow oil to bounce back off the tray and back onto the crank. Oil pan crank scrapers and pan side kickouts can help solve the windage problems found on a race engine.

## Oil Filters and Block Adapters

On Gen I and Bowtie blocks there is a small, press-in plug located in the main oil passage in the block below the rear main cap. This plug blocks a hole that was drilled when the block was manufactured. The plug prevents oil from bypassing the oil filter. It is often removed from the block when a used block is cleaned. Sometimes it doesn't get put back in. Always check that the plug is in position, otherwise the oil does not go through the oil filter and the oil pressure may be artificially low.

The 1955 265 V-8 blocks did not have a boss for an oil filter. Chevrolet and GMC/Truck used two different

*To install a windage tray, different main cap bolts are required that have a stud to mount the tray.*

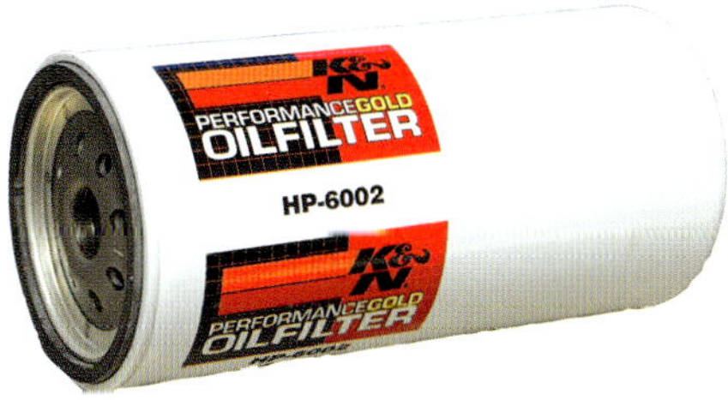


*If you have the room and ground clearance, larger capacity oil filters are available. These filters are generally used in large truck applications and can hold $1^1/_2$ or 2 quarts to increase total oil capacity and filter surface area.*

*Sometimes engine-room clearance dictates the use of a remote-mounted oil filter. Kits are available to move the oil filter practically anywhere you want to, and they include single or dual filter mounts. Just add the length of hose you need and hose clamps.*

block oil filter adapters over the years. Engines made from 1956 through 1967 used an adapter (PN 5573979) that then allowed a metal oil filter canister (PN 5574535) and a through-bolt to hold a separate replaceable paper oil filter cartridge. In 1968-and-later car engines, the inner surface on the block oil filter pad was changed slightly and a different block oil filter adapter (PN 3952301) was used to mount a spin-on type of filter. Half-quart oil filters were used on cars, while 1-quart filters were used on trucks. K&N makes some of the freest flowing oil filters on the aftermarket, and they come with high-burst-strength outside metal coverings that withstand more pressure. Keep this in mind if you have blocked off the oil bypass valve in the stock GM oil filter/block adapter.

*Early canister-type oil filters used a bolt-on housing to cover a replaceable filter element. They can be converted to a spin-on oil filter by adding an aftermarket adapter kit.*

After 1968, some trucks and some police packaged cars continued to use the early paper cartridge, metal canister-style filter assembly but with an adapter. You can change from one system to the other, but whichever one you use, you must then use the correct filter assembly that goes with it. Some people like the convenience of a spin-on filter, while others prefer the larger filtration capacity and lower cost of the cartridge style. Take your choice. Chevrolet made a conversion kit (PN 5574538) to change a spin-on filter setup to an early metal-canister-style oil filter, and there are others available through the aftermarket.

The 1992-and-later Gen II 350 LT1 Corvettes use a new offset oil filter/block adapter, which can be interchanged and fitted to any small- or big-block that used a spin-on oil filter. The offset adapter on the Gen II LT1 may give you the additional room you may need to fit headers or get other engine-room clearance on the driver's side, especially if you are doing an engine swap. It uses the longer and narrower oil filter for even more clearance by moving it close to the side of the oil pan. Here are the Gen II 350 LT1 part numbers for the filter, adapter block, and required parts.

| Part | Part Number |
|---|---|
| Oil filter | (AC) PF-52 |
| Filter/block adapter | 12554305 |
| O-ring gasket | 10244495 |
| Gasket | 12551589 |
| Adapter bolts (2) | 10233496 |
| Washers (2) | 10218873 |

Aftermarket sources can provide adapters and lines to remotely position the oil filter. These are helpful when you use an exhaust header system that comes too close to an engine-mounted filter or routes header tubes right where the oil filter would be if left on the engine. They also make adapters to convert a cartridge-style oil filter to a spin-on type filter or vice versa. Make sure that you install these conversion kits properly. One problem I have often seen concerns the conversion from an old-style metal canister and filter cartridge to the spin-on filters. A lot of folks take the old metal-canister-style block/oil filter adapter and throw it away and then put on the new conversion adapter. They don't realize that the new adapter uses the old block adapter in addition to the new conversion adapter. The problem is that if you don't use both pieces, the new spin-on filter fits and won't leak oil, but the oil does bypass the filter after filling it up.

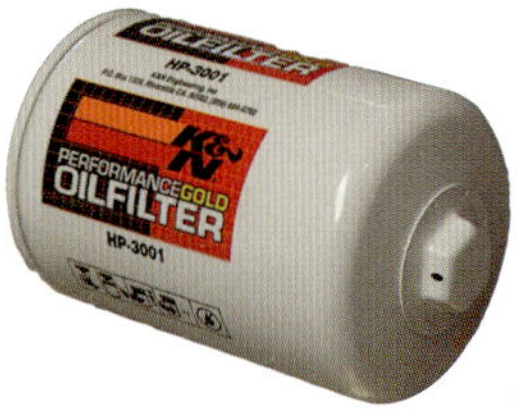


*K&N makes a high-quality line of air filters and oil filters. Their oil filters feature excellent filtration with high flow. They have high-burst pressure shells and a convenient hex head for wrenching them off. They also can be safety wired.*

*Notice that these valve covers have no provision for an oil filler cap or positive crankcase ventilation (PCV) system. The oil filler tube on the front of the manifold was used on engines prior to 1969. There was a road draft tube in the rear of the block that took care of crankcase ventilation. If you use an intake made from 1969 or later, you must use valve covers with some provision to add oil and to hook up a vacuum line to a PCV valve or breather caps.*

## Oil Coolers

There are a number of sandwich adapters that fit between the oil filter and the block oil filter boss. External oil lines can be mounted to the two threaded holes in the adapter and then run to whatever type of cooler you want to install.

Chevrolet offers a number of types of oil coolers that can be used on 1968-and-later small-blocks. PN 997033 is a kit that uses an adapter/spacer bolted to the oil filter pad on the block. This adapter sandwiches between the block and the oil filter. It includes hoses, an auxiliary radiator, adapter/spacer, and couplings. Your regular spin-on oil filter screws on to the adapter/spacer. These kits can also be adapted to cool transmission fluid.

Another sandwich oil cooler adapter (PN 14092394) was used on 1988 big-block trucks with four-wheel drive. This adapter can be fitted to a Gen I 1968-or-later small-block and mounts the oil filter beneath the adapter but parallel to the ground. This adapter is helpful if you have a clearance problem when the filter is mounted straight up and down, and it works with stock cast-iron exhaust manifolds. The two oil cooler line ports on the adapter face forward.

PN 14084369 was an optional kit assembly used in late-model 1986 to 1991 Corvettes with small-block 350 engines, that can be used on 1968-on Gen I small-block engines. This heat exchanger uses an adapter/spacer that allows 1/2-inch lines from the engine's water cooling system to cool and stabilize the temperature of the engine oil. The kit includes the heat exchanger adapter/spacer, gaskets, seals, and connectors, all of which can be bought separately if you wish. A standard spin-on oil filter screws onto the heat exchanger.

If you are rebuilding an engine that previously used an oil cooler, it is a good practice to completely flush out the old oil cooler lines and the oil cooler radiator or replace the cooler and lines completely. You don't want any metal particles that may have built up in the old cooler to contaminate your new engine.

## Oil Gauges

If you are racing, install an oil temperature gauge and try to maintain a hot oil temperature of 220°F or less. If your engine combination does this without an oil cooler, then leave it alone. An oil cooler that you don't need just adds weight and more fittings that can leak. If oil temperatures exceed 220 degrees, then get a cooler.

Always use an oil pressure gauge instead of relying on a stock idiot light. An oil pressure gauge warns you of a drop in pressure; an idiot light only comes on when it's too late. In addition to the pressure gauge, racers can also install a warning light that comes on when oil pressure falls to a predetermined level. These warning lights are helpful if you don't have enough time in a race to watch a regular oil pressure gauge. You can also set up a low oil pressure warning system to automatically cut electrical power to the ignition if the oil pressure drops below a certain point and possibly save an engine. Most aftermarket gauge companies can help you with these types of alert systems.

*Engine oils have improved over the years with various additive packages creating oils tailored for specific applications. Zinc and phosphorus additives are important to use with flat tappet cams, and for the initial startup of your small-block there are special break-in oils. When shopping for engine oil, you'll come across mineral-based oils, synthetic oils, and unique blends of both. Follow the recommendations of the engine builder or cam specs.*

# Cylinder Heads

As you may already be aware, there is a dizzying number of cylinder heads available for the Chevrolet small-block. For more than 40 years, Chevrolet has developed heads for all types of uses, including stock, high-performance, smog emissions, and over-the-counter all-out race heads. Each was designed to provide the type of service intended and reflected the technology and thinking of the times. Aftermarket head makers also have contributed to the design changes over the years. The sheer number of choices can be mind-numbing. Just keep in mind what your intentions are; that helps narrow down the selection for you.

Cast-iron heads are still cheaper than aluminum heads, but when you consider the weight savings, aluminum heads are reasonably priced. Cast-iron production heads weigh about 44 pounds each, while Corvette aluminum D-port heads each weigh 19 pounds bare.

If you are going to use unleaded pump gasoline for a street-driven machine, then the heads you build or purchase need to have hard valve seats in order to survive. Most factory heads made before 1975 had soft seats that need to be upgraded to hardened seats for today's unleaded pump gasoline. Remember that cylinder heads have different amounts of chamber volume. These volumes have a direct effect on the static compression ratio of the engine and the compression ratio, in part, depends on which head casting you use.

***The head casting number (3991493) is located in the rocker arm valley. The date code is positioned below it; "L 2 1" means December 2, 1971. These are from a 350 LT1 with 64-cc combustion chambers.***

Chevrolet has used various raised casting symbols on the ends of small-block cylinder heads, which on some heads are duplicated in the rocker arm valley. These symbols were used to indicate the type of features found on those particular heads. The same symbol can be found on different heads with different casting numbers. These symbols are helpful,

***The rocker arm valley on the 333882 head has pressed-in rocker studs. This particular head was fitted with 1.94/1.5-inch valves and had 76-cc chambers.***

***This 3927186 could be found on a 302 or 350 small-block and sports 2.02-inch intake valves. On some casting dates, Chevrolet felt that the use of the letter "I" for the month of September might be confused with a numeral "1." So sometimes they skipped the "I" in the monthly alphabetical sequence and "J" was used for the month of September and then "M" was used for the month of December.***

*Chevrolet used a variety of different casting symbols on the side of small-block heads. This helps denote their application at a glance. What jumps out immediately are the push-in rocker studs and the lack of any accessory bracket holes, making it a pre-1969 example. Casting numbers clearly identify the application. This particular head is a 3884520 that was used on 283s in 1966 to 1967.*

*The double hump or camel hump casting symbol on the end of this head indicates a performance cast-iron head used in the 1960s. Pre-1969 heads do not have accessory mounting holes. When there are no mounting holes, you need to use a short water pump with the factory brackets.*

*Not all casting symbols are equal and many have minimal visual differences. The head with the three accessory bolt holes is a 333882 casting. This is a mid- to late-1970s 197 small-block head that was fit with 1.94-inch intake valves designed to use unleaded fuel. Always research a head by its casting number and date code.*

but should not be solely relied upon to determine what type of heads you have or what features they have. For instance, the classic camel hump symbol (also called double hump) can be found on 461, 461X, 462, and 291 casting heads. The 492, 292, and 186 heads have a slightly different-looking camel hump. These heads may have come with 1.94/1.5-inch valves or they might have been made with 2.02/1.6-inch valves.

The chamber shapes found on the 461 and 461X heads are not the same as those found on the 291, 462, or 186 heads. The 461X castings are popular for racers because they actually had slightly larger port volumes as cast than the 461 and other production heads. Some of these heads had accessory mounting holes, but heads made before 1969 do not. Just to make things interesting, another casting, the 041, was basically the same as the 186 heads but did not have the camel hump casting symbol. The 041 heads have a completely different right angle symbol on their ends.

Sounds confusing, but the point is that you need to look at all of the identifiers on the head in order to know what you have. Some later head castings have the last three digits of the casting number stamped into a ledge on the ends of the head that are visible when the heads are on an engine. You may need a mirror to read them, because the ledge faces down when the head is on the block. End casting symbols give you some clues, but they don't tell you the whole story.

Small-block heads have been made since 1955 and some of these heads are still in circulation. Many things could have been done to these used heads over the decades. They might have had hard seats from the factory or had hard seat inserts installed at a machine shop or may still have the original soft seats. They may have been ported (correctly or incorrectly) or decked. They may have small-diameter valves and pressed-in rocker arm studs or bigger valves, and screw-in studs may have been installed. The heads may be cracked (not uncommon even on newer heads). Someone may have added accessory bracket bolt holes to heads that didn't originally have them (this is usually crudely and badly done). They may be in such bad shape that they are not rebuildable. Be careful. Some of these old heads are fit for use as boat anchors or to hold down a tent but not for use on any engine.

From the 1955 to 1959 model years, small-block cylinder heads had a different staggered valve cover flange bolt pattern. The top two bolt holes were closer together than the lower bolt holes. Valve covers were made with bolt holes to match. In 1959, the valve cover holes in the heads were changed so that the holes were the same distance from one another across the top when compared to the lower holes. The 1959-and-later valve cover holes were changed to match.

In 1987, the way in which valve covers were attached to the heads was

*On the left is the factory combustion chamber of a 1956 265 small-block. The head on the right is from a camel hump head from the 1960s. You can really tell the difference between the sizes of the valves.*

*The single rear exhaust manifold bolt hole is seen in this cast-iron head. Also note the position of the temperature sender. In 1968, Chevrolet started putting the boss in the head rather than the intake manifold. Some 1968 heads may have the boss not yet machined.*

*Various oil stem seals have been used on small-block heads. The most common seal used on Gen I heads is the small O-ring-style (right). The umbrella seal (middle rear) is found in many rebuild kits. The positive seals (left) slip over the valve guides and can also be used with double and triple valve springs since they fit inside the innermost spring coils.*

*When using the Gen I long water pump and its associated pulleys and accessory brackets, you need to use cylinder heads that have the necessary bolt holes in their ends. Heads cast from 1955 through 1968 don't have them, and with the early heads, you need to use the short water pump, pulleys, and accessory brackets.*

*The valve guide on the left is fit with a factory-installed PC-type valve stem seal, instead of the old O-ring that was used for decades on the small-block. The other guide is being inspected before assembly.*

*If you use a 400 block with steam holes in the deck, you need to use a 400 head gasket and cylinder heads with matching steam holes. If your heads don't have the holes, you can use a 400 head gasket as a template, mark the steam hole location, and drill the six additional holes in each head yourself.*

changed again. The covers bolt to bosses in the center of the rocker arm valley and the gasket was changed to accommodate machined valve cover rails on the heads. This was done to help eliminate, once and for all, the notorious valve cover oil leaks of previous designs. You can get an adapter that allows the use of the 1959 to 1986 flange-mounted valve covers on the center-bolt 1987-and-up heads through the aftermarket.

During the 1968 model year, head castings were changed so that a boss could be mounted in the side of the head to mount the water temperature sending unit. Prior to that, the temperature sending unit was mounted in the intake manifold and the heads did not have a boss for the temp sender. Some 1968 heads have the boss in the head, but the boss is not drilled or threaded.

In 1969, Chevrolet changed the way that engine accessory brackets were mounted. Prior to 1969, there are no holes in the ends of cylinder heads on which to bolt accessory brackets. From 1969 onward, the heads have threaded bosses and holes to mount the new-style brackets. If you need these holes to use

*This closed-chamber head is equipped with 1.94/1.5-inch valves. If the factory installed 2.02/1.6-inch valves, additional machining was done to the chamber walls to reduce valve shrouding. If you are adding larger valves to production closed-chamber heads that originally had 1.94/1.5-inch valves, make sure your machinist unshrouds the chamber walls appropriately.*

*This cast-iron head has two exhaust manifold bolts in the very back (note that the other hole has a broken bolt in it). It's odd to find both end holes threaded, as either one or the other is generally used, not both.*

*This is the chamber of a 1974 333882 head. From the factory, they had hardened seats since that was about the time for the switch to unleaded fuel at the pumps. Not high up on the performance list, but for stock rebuilds they work just fine. This set has just been freshened.*

*On many late-model heads made from 1987-on, the center two intake manifold bolt holes are at a 72-degree angle instead of the 90-degree angle found on earlier heads. Your intake manifold must accommodate these new bolt angles.*

*These types of rocker nuts with a positive-locking Allen screw require that the top of the rocker arm stud be spot faced, otherwise the Allen screw can loosen and back off.*

*This is the chamber of the popular cast-iron Vortec head. These heads are a proven performance upgrade for most small-blocks and are available from GM Performance Parts under PN 12558060. These heads are supplied completely assembled with 1.94/1.50-inch valves and 64-cc chambers. When using them, be sure to use an intake made for them due to the mounting bolts.*

your brackets, make sure the heads you plan to use have them. If they don't have accessory holes, use the earlier-style, short water pump, and pulleys with the related early style brackets for use with short-style water pumps.

From 1970 through 1980, 400-ci small-blocks were installed in various vehicles. These engine blocks were different in that the cylinder barrels were siamesed in order to enlarge the cylinder bores to 4.125 inches. In order to help the cooling system, the 400 blocks have six additional steam holes in each of the decks between cylinder bores. Heads originally installed on 400 blocks have corresponding holes in their decks so that steam and coolant can flow between the block and the heads. 400 head gaskets also have the additional matching steam holes. If you are going to use a 400 block and if you want to use heads that were not originally installed on a 400 small-block, you'll need to have the six steam holes drilled into each

## Cylinder Head Casting Numbers

| Casting Number | Model Year | Engine Size | Notes |
|---|---|---|---|
| 330545 | 1973 | 350 | 76-cc chambers, 2.02/1.60-inch valves |
| 333881 | 1974–1975 | 350 | 76-cc chambers, 2.02/1.60-inch valves |
| 333882 | 1974–1980 | 350/400 | 76-cc chambers |
| 340292 | 1970s | | Over-the-counter, angle plug, 64-cc chambers |
| 354434 | 1975–1979 | 262/267/305 | 60-cc chambers |
| 358741 | 1976–1979 | 305 | |
| 376445 | 1977–1985 | 350 | 76-cc chambers, small valves |
| 376450 | 1975–1981 | 262/267/305 | Six or seven exhaust bolt holes, 60-cc chambers |
| 462614 | 1977–1979 | 305 | 60-cc chambers |
| 462624 | 1975–1986 | 350/400 | 76-cc chambers, 1.72/1.5-, 1.94/1.5-, or 2.02/1.6-inch valves |
| 468642 | 1976-up | 350/400 | |
| 471513 | 1979 | 267/350 | |
| 517513 | 1979 | 267/350 | |
| 1816887 | 1963 | 283 | Made in Canada, GMC heavy-duty truck |
| 3636839 | 1955 | 265 | |
| 3703523 | 1955 | 265 | |
| 3713358 | 1955–1956 | 265 | |
| 3713569 | 1955–1956 | 265 | |
| 3725306 | 1956 | 265 | |
| 3731539 | 1957 | 283 | 283-hp FI |
| 3731544 | 1957–1961 | 283 | |
| 3731554 | 1957–1962 | 283 | |
| 3731556 | 1957 | 283 | Made in Canada, truck |
| 3731762 | 1956 | 265 | Vette, 2x4 carburetors |
| 3737775 | 1962–1967 | 283/327 | |
| 3740997 | 1957 | 283 | 1x4, 2x4, and FI (except 283 hp) |
| 3743056 | 1958 | 283 | |
| 3743096 | 1962–1967 | 327 | GMC truck |
| 3747363 | 1957–1961 | 283 | |
| 3747460 | 1959–1967 | 283/327 | 70-cc chambers |
| 3748770 | 1958 | 283 | |
| 3748772 | 1958–1961 | 283 | |
| 3755537 | 1957–1962 | 283 | |
| 3755539 | 1958–1962 | 283 | |
| 3755549 | 1957–1962 | 283 | |
| 3755550 | 1959 | 283 | |
| 3755585 | 1962–1967 | 327 | GMC truck |
| 3767462 | 1962–1967 | 327 | |
| 3767465 | 1959–1961 | 283 | |
| 3767754 | 1959–1961 | 283 | 60-cc chambers |
| 3767792 | 1960–1964 | 283 | |
| 3770126 | 1969 | 327 | |
| 3774682 | 1960–1964 | 283/327 | 70-cc chambers |
| 3774684 | 1962–1964 | 327 | 75-cc chambers |
| 3774692 | 1958–1964 | 283 | 60-cc chambers |
| 3782461 | 1964–1966 | 327 | Camel hump, no accessory holes, 160/62-cc port volumes, 62-cc chambers |
| 3782461X | 1960–1963 | 283/327 | Camel hump, no accessory holes, larger 172/64-cc port volumes, 62-cc chambers |
| 3795896 | 1963–1965 | 283 | 60-cc chambers |
| 3795896 | 1962–1964 | 327 | 60-cc chambers |
| 3798996 | 1963–1967 | 327 | |
| 3814480 | 1960–1967 | 283/327 | 70-cc chambers, 1.72/1.5-inch valves |
| 3814482 | 1962–1967 | 283/327/350 | 75-cc chambers |
| 3817680 | 1963–1967 | 283/327 | |
| 3817681 | 1962–1967 | 327 | |
| 3817682 | 1961–1962 | 283 | |
| 3836839 | 1955 | 265 | |
| 3836842 | 1957–1967 | 283/327 | |
| 3837064 | 1956–1962 | 265/283 | |
| 3837065 | 1955–1956 | 265 | Truck |
| 3848720 | 1957–1958 | 283 | |
| 3876775 | 1960–1967 | 283/327 | 75-cc chambers |
| 3884520 | 1960–1967 | 283 | Some marked "Made in Canada," 60-cc chambers, also used by Studebaker |
| 3884520 | 1962–1967 | 327 | Some marked "Made in Canada," 60-cc chambers, also used by Studebaker |
| 3890462 | 1966–1967 | 302/327/350 | Camel hump, no accessory holes, 64-cc chambers |
| 3901068 | 1987-up | 350 | Crate engine, 285 hp, 64-cc chambers |
| 3911032 | 1968 | 307/327 | 70-cc chambers |
| 3912264 | 1958–1962 | 283 | |
| 3912265 | 1963–1964 | 283 | |
| 3912311 | 1965–1967 | 327 | |
| 3912313 | 1965–1967 | 327 | |
| 3917290 | 1967–1968 | 307/327 | |
| 3917291 | 1967–1968 | 302/327/350 | Camel hump, no accessory holes, 64-cc chambers |
| 3917292 | 1968 | 327/350 | Camel hump, 64-cc chambers |
| 3917293 | 1968 | 307/327 | 75-cc chambers |
| 3927185 | 1969–1976 | 307/327/350 | 70-cc chambers |
| 3927186 | 1969–1970 | 302/350 | Camel hump, accessory holes, 64-cc chambers |
| 3927187 | 1969–1970 | 350 | Camel hump, accessory holes, 64-cc chambers |
| 3927188 | 1969 | 327 | 74-cc chambers |
| 3927188 | 1970 | 307 | 74-cc chambers |
| 3931633 | 1968–1973 | 307 | |
| 3931635 | 1968–1976 | 350 | |
| 3931638 | 1968 | 327 | Truck |
| 3932441 | 1969–1970 | 350 | 76-cc chambers |
| 3932441X | 1969–1970 | 350/400 | 80-cc chambers |
| 3932454 | 1969–1973 | 307 | |
| 3932454 | 1969–1979 | 350 | Truck |
| 3946812 | 1969 | 350 | |
| 3946813 | 1969–1979 | 350 | Truck |

## Cylinder Head Casting Numbers *(Continued)*

| Casting Number | Model Year | Engine Size | Notes |
|---|---|---|---|
| 3947040 | 1968 | 327 | Right-angle casting identifier, 64-cc chambers, good HP head, used in trucks, no accessory holes |
| 3947041 | 1969–1970 | 302/350 | Right-angle casting identifier, 64-cc chambers, good HP head, accessory holes |
| 3947041X | 1969–1970 | 302/350 | Right-angle casting identifier, 64-cc chambers, 165-cc intake port, good HP head, accessory holes |
| 3951598 | 1970 | 400 | 76-cc chambers |
| 3964286 | | 350 | |
| 3965742 | 1970 | 350 | Over-the-counter, angle plug |
| 3970126 | 1967–1970 | 327/350 | |
| 3973370 | 1969–1970 | 350 | Over-the-counter, 64-cc chambers, straight or angle plug |
| 3973414 | 1970 | 350 | LT1 370 hp, camel hump, 64-cc chambers |
| 3973487 | 1971–1972 | 350 | LT1, 75-cc chambers |
| 3973487X | 1971–1972 | 350 | 75-cc chambers |
| 3973493 | 1971–1972 | 400 | 76-cc chambers |
| 3986316 | 1971 | 350 | 76-cc chambers |
| 3986336 | 1971 | 350 | 76-cc chambers |
| 3986336X | 1971 | 350 | 76-cc chambers |
| 3986339 | 1971 | 307/350 | 74-cc chambers |
| 3986339X | 1971 | 307/350 | 74-cc chambers |
| 3986388 | 1968–1976 | 307/350 | |
| 3991492 | 1970 | 350 | LT1, camel hump, accessory holes, 64-cc chambers, straight plug |
| 3991492 | 1970-up | | Over-the-counter, camel hump, 64-cc chambers, straight or angle plug |
| 3998916 | 1972 | 350 | Also used with 1972 350 LT1, big valves, screw-in studs, 76-cc chambers |
| 3998920 | 1972–1973 | 350 | |
| 3998991 | 1972–1973 | 307/350 | 75-cc chambers |
| 3998993 | 1972–1973 | 307/350 | 75-cc chambers |
| 3998993 | current | 350 | Goodwrench crate engines, Made in Mexico, 75-cc chambers |
| 3998997 | 1972–1973 | 350/400 | 76-cc chambers |
| 3998997 | 1978–1984 | 305/350 | 76-cc chambers |
| 4079261 | 1975 | 350 | |
| 10033867 | | | Aluminum, over-the-counter, Pontiac 23-degree head, 62-cc chambers, angle plug, 196-cc intake port |
| 10045434 | | | Over-the-counter, Pontiac 15-degree head, 55-cc chambers, angle plug, raised runner aluminum, "roll over" head |
| 10051101 | | | Bowtie, aluminum, 55-cc chambers, angle plug, raised runner, 196-cc intake port |
| 10065202 | 1987–1995 | 350 | Truck |
| 10065203 | 1987–1995 | 350 | Truck |
| 10065204 | 1987–1995 | 350 | |
| 10065205 | 1987–1995 | 305 | |
| 10065206 | 1987–1995 | 350 | |
| 10065207 | 1987–1995 | 305 | |
| 10088113 | 1988-up | 350 | Aluminum, 58-cc chambers, angle plug, raised D-port exhaust, 1.94/1.5-inch valves |
| 10093328 | | | Over-the-counter, Pontiac 15-degree head aluminum, 224-cc ports, 61-cc chambers, "roll over" head |
| 10106178 | 1990 | 350 | LT5, ZR1, DOHC, 32-valve, passenger side, aluminum |
| 10106179 | 1990 | 350 | LT5, ZR1, DOHC, 32-valve, driver side, aluminum |
| 10110810 | 1991-up | 350 | Gen I |
| 10120928 | 1987–1995 | 350 | |
| 10125320 | 1994–1996 | 350 | Gen II LT1, cast-iron version, used on 9C1 police package, Impala SS, Cadillac Fleetwood, Buick Roadmaster, reverse-flow cooling |
| 10128374 | 1992-up | 350 | Gen II LT1, 53-cc chambers, angle plug, aluminum, reverse-flow cooling, 175/68-cc ports |
| 10134352 | | | Bowtie, 45-cc chambers, angle plug, low port, 223-cc intake port, aluminum, 18-degree race head |
| 10134363 | | | NOTE: This casting number has been used in at least six different versions of this aluminum 18- and 15-degree Bowtie race head. Variations include chamber volumes, port volumes and locations, valve sizes, etc. Check to determine which features it has. |
| 10147898 | 1995–1998 | 350 | Gen I crate engine |
| 10159550 | 1987–1995 | 350 | |
| 10159551 | 1987–1995 | 305 | |
| 10159552 | 1987–1995 | 350 | |
| 10159553 | 1987–1995 | 305 | |
| 10174389 | 1991–1994 | 350 | LT5, ZR1, DOHC, 32-valve, driver's side, aluminum |
| 10174390 | 1991–1995 | 350 | LT5, ZR1, DOHC, 32-valve, passenger's side, aluminum |
| 10185040 | | | Bowtie, aluminum, 45-cc chambers, 1st version, symmetrical ports, 263-cc intake ports, splayed valves |
| 10185040 | | | Bowtie, aluminum, 45-cc chambers, 2nd version, symmetrical ports, 240-cc intake ports, splayed valves |
| 10205245 | 1993 | 350 | Gen II LT1, aluminum, reverse-flow cooling, 175/68-cc ports |

## Cylinder Head Casting Numbers *(Continued)*

| Casting Number | Model Year | Engine Size | Notes |
|---|---|---|---|
| 10207643 | 1994–1996 | 350 | Gen II LT1, aluminum, reverse-flow cooling, 175/68-cc ports |
| 10208890 | 1994–1996 | 265 | Gen II, L99, 4.3-liter V-8, cast iron, reverse-flow cooling |
| 10225121 | 1994–1995 | 350 | LT5, ZR1, DOHC, 32-valve, driver's side, aluminum |
| 10225122 | 1995 | 350 | LT5, ZR1, DOHC, 32-valve, passenger's side, aluminum |
| 10239902 | 1996-up | 350 | Gen II LT4, aluminum, reverse-flow cooling, 195-cc port, 54.4-cc chambers, angle plug |
| 10239906 | 1996-up | 350 | Vortec 5700, L31, 64-cc chambers, 170-cc intake port, 1.94/1.5-inch valves |
| 12367712 | 1999-up | | Fast Burn, aluminum, 210-cc intake port, 2.00/1.55-inch valves, 62-cc chambers |
| 12367713 | 1999-up | | Fast Burn used on ZZ430 crate engine, aluminum, 210-cc intake port, 2.00/1.55-inch valves, 62-cc chambers |
| 12480011 | 1997-up | | Bowtie SB2.2, aluminum, 2nd version of SB2, 48-cc chambers, mirror ports, revised valve angles and plug location |
| 12480129 | | | Aluminum, SB2.2, semi-finished |
| 12480146 | | | Aluminum, splayed valve, rough-machined |
| 12480147 | | | Aluminum, splayed valve, semi-machined |
| 12480153 | | | ROX Splayed valve, aluminum |
| 12506450 | 1987–1995 | 350 | |
| 12509859 | 1987–1994 | 305 | |
| 12516852 | 1987–1995 | 350 | |
| 12551561 | 1996 | 350 | Gen II, LT1, aluminum |
| 12552520 | 1997-up | 305 | Vortec, truck |
| 12554290 | 1994–1996 | 350 | Gen II, LT1, cast-iron version, reverse-flow cooling, used on 9C1 police package, Impala SS, Cadillac Fleetwood, Buick Roadmaster |
| 12555690 | 1996 | 350 | Gen II, LT4, aluminum |
| 12558059 | 1997 | 305 | Vortec, truck, 1.84/1.5-inch valves, 64-cc chambers |
| 12558062 | 1998 | 350 | L31 Vortec, truck, 64-cc chambers, 1.94/1.5-inch valves, 170-cc intake port |
| 14008856 | 1979–1981 | 267 | |
| 14094093 | 1986–1988 | 350 | |
| 14010201 | 1982–1985 | 305 | |
| 14011034 | | | Bowtie, cast iron, 64-cc chambers, 184-cc ports, angle plug, Phase II head |
| 14011049 | | | Bowtie, aluminum, 55-cc chambers, angle plug, 180-cc ports, Phase 6 |

| Casting Number | Model Year | Engine Size | Notes |
|---|---|---|---|
| 14011083 | 1955–1986 | 350 | Crate engine for years indicated 285/300 hp, 64-cc chambers, 1.94/1.5-inch valves |
| 14014415 | 1980–1985 | 267/305 | |
| 14014416 | 1980–1986 | 305 | 1.84/1.5-inch valves, 58-cc chambers |
| 14014440 | 1980 | 305 | 1.84/1.5-inch valves |
| 14019821 | 1980–1986 | 350 | |
| 14019924 | 1979–1981 | 267 | |
| 14019926 | 1980–1986 | 350 | |
| 14010516 | 1980–1986 | 350 | |
| 14020517 | 1980 | 350 | |
| 14020555 | 1981 | 305 | |
| 14020556 | 1981 | 350 | |
| 14022056 | 1985 | 350 | |
| 14022206 | 1980 | 350 | |
| 14022301 | 1980–1986 | 305 | |
| 14022601 | 1980–1986 | 267/305 | 1.84/1.5-inch valves, 58-cc chambers |
| 14022801 | 1980–1986 | 305 | |
| 14024816 | | 350 | 76-cc chambers, 1.94/1.5-inch valves, Gen I crate engines |
| 14034806 | 1978–1982 | 267 | |
| 14034807 | 1978–1986 | 305 | |
| 14034808 | 1980–1986 | 350 | |
| 14034808 | 1996-up | 350 | 76-cc chambers, 1.94/1.5-inch valves, Gen I Goodwrench crate engines |
| 14034810 | 1980–1986 | 350 | Truck |
| 14034811 | 1980–1986 | 350 | Truck |
| 14039121 | 1981–1986 | 305 | Truck |
| 14039122 | 1981–1986 | 305 | Truck |
| 14071114 | 1980–1986 | 350 | |
| 14075381 | 1980–1986 | 350 | Truck |
| 14079261 | 1986 | 350 | |
| 14085844 | 1980–1986 | 350 | Truck |
| 14085963 | 1986 | 350 | |
| 14089119 | 1986–1988 | 350 | |
| 14094093 | 1986–1988 | 350 | |
| 14096217 | 1955–1986 | 350 | Crate motor, 285 or 300 hp, 64-cc chambers, 72- or 90-degree center intake manifold bolt angles |
| 14101081 | 1987–1995 | 305 | |
| 14101083 | 1987-up | 350 | Gen I, also used on crate engines, 285 or 300 hp, 64-cc chambers, 72-degree center manifold bolt angles |
| 14101128 | 1986–1987 | 350 | Aluminum, 58-cc chambers, angle plug |
| 14102187 | 1987–1991 | 305 | 1.84/1.5-inch valves |
| 14102191 | 1987-up | 350 | |
| 14102393 | 1987-up | 350 | |
| 19331470 | | | Iron Vortec Bowtie, 66-cc chambers, 185-cc intake, 65-cc exhaust, dual bolt pattern |

## Cylinder Head Casting Numbers *(Continued)*

| Casting Number | Model Year | Engine Size | Notes |
|---|---|---|---|
| 19331472 | | | Iron Vortec Bowtie, 65-cc chambers, 225-cc intake, 77-cc exhaust |
| 19300955 | | | Aluminum Fast Burn, 210-cc intake, 78-cc D-shaped exhaust, 62-cc chambers |
| 24502559 | 1996–1997 | | Bowtie, SB2, 1st version, mirror ports, aluminum, 196-cc port, CNC version 280-cc port, 38-cc chambers |
| 24502580 | | | Aluminum, semi-finished 18-degree, no seats or guides |
| 24502615 | | | Aluminum, semi-finished 15-degree, no seats or guides |
| 25500141 | | | Buick/Chevy aluminum 10-degree head, 42-cc chambers, symmetrical ports, 235-cc intake port volume, 2.1/1.625-inch valves |
| 25534351 | | | Iron Vortec, 185-cc port, 66-cc chambers |
| 25534371 | | | Iron Vortec, 225-cc port, 66-cc chambers |
| 33417369 | 1990-up | 350 | Gen I Goodwrench crate engine, Made in Mexico, 76-cc chambers |

head. You can use a 400 head gasket as a template to locate and drill the six holes in each head deck.

During the 1971 model year, Chevrolet changed the spark plugs used in production small-block heads. Prior to this time, the plugs used a 13/16-inch hex with a spark plug washer. During 1971, they were changed over to a peanut-style plug that used a 5/8-inch hex. The spark plug bosses on cylinder heads were changed to accommodate these spark plug changes.

Make sure you know the casting date of your heads so that you use the correct-style spark plug. Be especially careful if the engine was rebuilt using parts from different engines. Always get the plugs to match the heads. Don't rely on the casting date of the block or the model year of the vehicle. If your heads were made in the 1971 model year, you have to check the spark plug bosses to see which plug they take. It is a remote possibility that an engine with two 1971 head castings requires two different plug styles.

Depending on the vehicle and horsepower application, some production Gen I closed-chamber heads came with the 1.94/1.5-inch or the larger 2.02/1.6-inch valves and were sometimes offered in the same casting. However, you need to know that when Chevrolet installed the larger-diameter 2.02/1.6-inch valves, the chamber walls in the head received an extra machining operation that unshrouded the larger valves by moving the closed chamber wall away from the valve edges. Heads with smaller valves did not get this extra factory machining operation.

Here's why I want you to know about this: For decades folks have put 2.02/1.6-inch or even larger valves into closed-chamber heads that originally came from the factory with 1.94/1.5-inch-or-smaller valves, all in an effort to improve performance. However, the 1.94/1.5-inch closed-chamber production heads do not have the extra factory machining done to unshroud the larger 2.02/1.6-inch valves. When you add the larger valves to these 1.94/1.5-inch heads and fail to do the extra machining to unshroud the larger valves, per-

***This aluminum head assembly (from an older ZZ4 crate engine) uses screw-in rocker arm studs. Cast-iron heads can easily be modified to accept screw-in studs, which are recommended for higher lift cams, higher RPM, and increased performance.***

***The rocker arm stud on the right shows the spot facing of the top that is necessary on aftermarket rocker arm jam nuts with Allen screws (also called poly locks) so that they fit tightly and do not back off. The top surface of the production rocker arm studs often is irregular and not flat, as you can see on the stud on the left. If you are using production rocker arm jam nuts, this is not a concern.***

formance may not improve. In fact, the heads probably flow less air than when they had the 1.94/1.5-inch valves in them because the larger-diameter valve edges move closer to the chamber walls. With closed-chamber heads, always unshroud the valve edges when moving to a larger diameter valve by machining away the chamber walls.

The factory originally used an intake valve unshrouding cutter with a 2.40-inch diameter. Later, the cutter diameter was reduced to 2.34 inches with no effect on airflow when using a 2.02-inch intake valve. You can also use a head gasket to scribe the extent of the cylinder bore on the head. You can then remove chamber wall material to the gasket line to unshroud the valves. However, keep in mind that this increases total chamber volume and decreases static compression. After the unshrouding cut, you can deck the heads to reduce the chamber volume and increase the static compression ratio if necessary.

Putting larger-diameter 2.02/1.6-inch valves into large open-chamber (70- to 76-cc) heads that originally had 1.94/1.5-inch valves generally does not create a valve shrouding problem. Keep in mind that blocks with less than 4-inch bores used small-diameter valves because using larger valves causes a valve shrouding problem with the tops of the cylinder bores. You can do something about this by relieving the tops of the cylinder bores near the valve edges, if you use large-diameter valves on a small-bore engine.

Some heads may require pushrod guide plates. These guide plates may have been installed at the factory and some have been previously added by enthusiasts trying to upgrade their valvetrains. Some of the guide plates are flat, while some use a step design. Either design is okay, but the step design may limit the amount of cam lift you can use because the rocker arm tip may come close to or strike the upper part of the step.

Some guide plates are hardened and some are not. Later-model aluminum Corvette D-port heads, when used with flat-tip rocker arms, should use a GM hardened guide plate (PN 14011051) that is marked with an "05" identifier. Guide plates are also marked "up" or "down," which indicates the direction of installation. Make sure you use the correct guide plates for your application.

Beginning in 1975, some cylinder heads received an extra exhaust manifold mounting hole, making a total of seven bolt holes on the exhaust port side of the head. This extra seventh hole was required because of a change in passenger-side cast-iron exhaust manifolds required to fit some vehicles. If your stock cast-iron exhaust manifold requires this extra hole to fit, then you need a cylinder head with this seventh bolt hole; otherwise you are out of luck. However, if you use a stock cast-iron manifold that was used on a six-hole head, but your heads have the extra seventh hole, you are okay; just don't use the extra hole. Some head castings have a flat boss where the seventh hole would be drilled, but the hole isn't drilled. On these particular castings, you can drill and tap this boss for the seventh hole if you need it.

In 1974, Chevrolet started to use lighter cast-iron head castings than those used previously. These light castings are more prone to cracking than previous heavy cylinder head castings. If you have a choice, use the heavy castings. Some heavy casting heads are still being made and they are also used on the Goodwrench crate engines and under the Bowtie logo. Make sure that whichever casting you use, you have the heads magnafluxed to find any cracks. It is no fun to spend your hard-earned money rebuilding a set of heads only to find out after they are installed that they leak water.

In 1986, Chevrolet made a number of changes to cylinder heads. Some cast-iron and some aluminum heads received large ramps in the bowl section of the intake port. They are easily seen from the valve side of the port. These ramps helped promote high swirl in the incoming fuel charge and in the cylinder itself to increase fuel efficiency and a better burn of the mixture. On the downside, it makes it difficult to port this style of intake port and your bowl porting efforts can be better spent on different castings.

In 1987, cast-iron production cylinder heads and some related intake manifolds changed the way the intake manifolds bolted to the heads. The two center intake manifold bolt holes on each side of the manifold, and their respective matching holes in the heads, were changed so that the bolts entered the heads at a 72-degree angle instead of the previous 90-degree angle.

Aluminum heads do not have these bolt angle changes and continue with the 90-degree bolt holes in the heads and intake manifolds. It is possible to use a pre-1987 intake on 1987-on heads by elongating and spot facing the two 90-degree center manifold bolt holes on each side to accommodate the 72-degree bolt hole angle on the heads. Aftermarket suppliers are also making versions of their performance aluminum manifolds for the 1987-on heads that have the 72-degree center-bolt angles.

In 1992, the Gen II production heads were introduced on the Gen II

LT1 350 engines. Corvettes, Camaros, and Pontiac Firebirds received an aluminum version, while the Chevrolet Impala SS and the Caprice with the 9C1 police package received a cast-iron Gen II LT1 head. These heads were designed to work with the reverse-flow coolant designs of the Gen II blocks and also have revised intake manifolds and intake gaskets. Intake manifold bolt hole angles and spacing were changed from those found on Gen I–style heads and intakes. These Gen II production heads have small chambers and the ports flow extremely well.

Don't confuse the Gen II reverse-flow cooling motors with the reverse-rotation water pumps used with serpentine belt systems on Gen I engines. It's not the same thing. The reverse-flow cooling found on Gen II engines allows higher cylinder wall temperatures and much better, more uniform cooling of the exhaust valves and spark plugs in the head. A Gen I reverse-rotation water pump spins in a counterclockwise direction when used with a production serpentine accessory drive-belt system.

The 1990 to 1995 Corvettes could be ordered with a special 350 ZR1 engine. This engine, which was initially rated at 375 hp and then later at 405 hp, was built by engine subcontractor Mercury Marine in Oklahoma. This engine was unique in that it featured, among other changes, aluminum heads with 4 overhead camshafts and 32 valves. The heads for this engine only fit on one side or the other and are designated for the passenger's side or driver's side. Each head, depending on which side it goes on, has a different casting number than the one intended for the other side of the engine. (The RPO ZR1 code was previously used in the 1970 to 1972 model years to designate a Gen I LT1 350 engine and heavy-duty transmission and suspension components on 1970 to 1972 Corvettes.)

Because of the unique nature of the 1990 to 1995 350 LT5 ZR1, there is not much interchange with other Gen I, II, or Vortec small-blocks. Given that the LT5 ZR1 has been discontinued as a factory-installed engine (thus creating an immediately collectible Corvette series with this engine), I don't think you will see many of these engines showing up in the junkyards or swap meets. Total ZR1 Corvette production from 1990 through 1995 was just under 7,000 units.

Most Chevy production heads have 3/8-inch pressed-in rocker arm studs. Some high-performance versions received factory-installed 3/8 screw-in rocker arm studs. Other heads received factory-installed screw-in studs and guide plates. If your plans include using other than stock production valvetrain parts or the use of higher-than-stock valve spring pressures and your heads have pressed-in studs, you can have the pressed-in rocker arms studs pulled out, the stud bosses machined down in height and the stud holes tapped for screw-in studs and guide plates. This improves the strength and reliability of your setup. The 3/8-inch small-block and 7/16-inch big-block Chevy screw-in studs with matching guide plates and rocker arms are available. The 1996-on Gen II engines have non-adjustable net lash valvetrains.

Always check the combustion chamber volume by cc'ing the chambers. While a particular head may be widely known to be, say, 64 cc in volume, many things can change this figure, particularly on used heads. Sinking the valve during repeated valve jobs increases the volume, while adding larger valve diameters may decrease chamber volume. If the head has been decked to ensure the flatness of the surface, the volume is decreased. If the heads are angle milled, chamber volume is decreased. Using flat-faced or dished-faced valves affects chamber volume. If someone has ground or machined the chamber walls in an effort to unshroud valve edges, this increases the volume. Any calculation you do to determine the actual static compression ratio of your engine must take into account the actual measured chamber volume along with other dimensions.

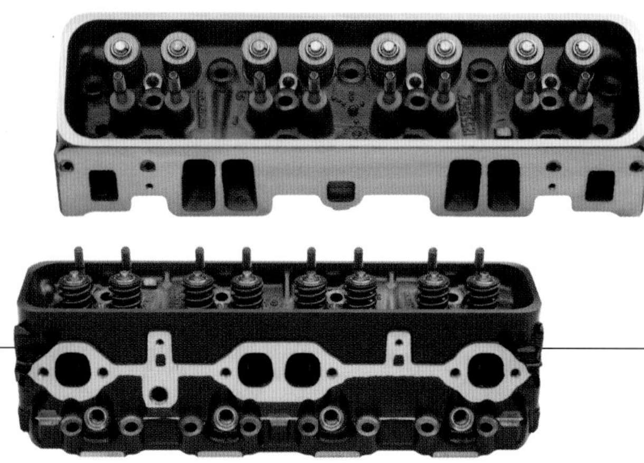

*This is the popular cast-iron Vortec cylinder head. These heads deliver high on the bang-for-your-buck scale of bolt-on performance. The heads fit 1955-on small-blocks, except the later LT1/LT4 due to the reverse cooling system, but do require a Vortec specific intake. The heads feature modified combustion chambers with GM's high-velocity port technology to outflow non-Vortec heads. They're ready to bolt on right out of the box as PN 12558060. (Photos Courtesy Chevrolet Performance)*

*LT4 heads are an important part of making a 1992-on LT1 really run. These aluminum heads feature 2.000/1.550-inch valves and the exhaust ports are raised 0.100-inch, requiring specific gaskets. The D-shaped exhaust ports increase the scavenging of the spent gasses and the chambers have a volume of 54.4 cc. (Photos Courtesy Chevrolet Performance)*

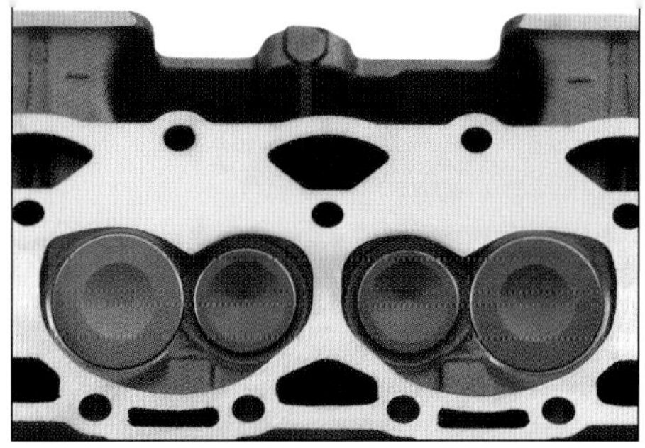

*These are the combustion chambers of the Vortec iron head (PN 12558060). The chamber measures 64 cc and features straight spark plug entrances. The valves are 1.94/1.50 inch but they can be machined to accept 2.020/1.600-inch valves. They have pushed-in rocker arm studs that could be pinned or drilled and tapped for 3/8-inch studs. (Photo Courtesy Chevrolet Performance)*

## Service Replacement Cast-Iron Heads

As you can imagine, many replacement heads have been offered by Chevrolet, but not every design is still available over the counter. Throughout this chapter, I've noted a number of different Chevrolet part numbers for specific cylinder heads for reference. Most are available as new, and some may have been obsoleted by Chevrolet, but they can still be found as new old stock (NOS) or used.

PN 93438649 is a cast-iron cylinder head for use on Gen II engines and supplied with 1.940/1.500-inch valves, straight spark plug holes, and 76-cc chambers. The head is for use on the 350/290-hp crate engine and other base 350s (PN 10067353).

PN 12558060 is an upgrade for Gen I engines, the Vortec head. The combustion chambers have been modified and feature high velocity port technology to outflow earlier OEM cast iron heads. Note that a Vortec-style intake is required. They're assembled from a casting number 10239906 or 12558062.

PN 14034808 is a bare cast-iron production head. This discontinued bare head came with hardened seats and guides and was intended for use with 1.94/1.5-inch valves. Chamber size is 76 cc. The head uses pressed-in rocker arm studs.

PN 3987376/casting number 3991492 is the same head used on the 302 Z28 and original Gen I 350 LT1, 64-cc closed chamber, 2.02/1.6-inch valves, straight plug, 3/8-inch screw-in studs and guide plates. This head has a heat riser passage. The valve seats are not heat-treated or hardened.

PN 464045/casting number 462624 was used on the low-compression 9.0:1 350 Z28, 1970 to 1972 350 LT1 and L82 Corvette, 76-cc open chamber, 2.02/1.6-inch valves. The valve seats are heat-treated, and it has screw-in studs and guide plates. It has a heat riser passage and uses straight plug angles.

PN 10125377/casting number 14101083 or 14096217 is a cast-iron 64-cc, 1.94/1.5-inch valves, 1987-and-later head, with 72-degree center bolt angles. Use with the matching intake manifold. These heads are used on the 350/285-hp crate engine. It uses center bolt valve covers and has hard seats.

PN 12356026/casting number 14011083 or 14096217 has 64-cc chambers and 1.95/1.5-inch valves but is intended for use with 1955 to 1986 intake manifolds with 90-degree bolt angles and bolt spacing. Use on the 350/300-hp CC crate engine. This head has hard seats.

PN 12529741 1994 to 1997 Gen II, cast-iron LT1 heads were used on the Impala SS and in the Caprice with the 9C1 police package version of the Gen II 350 LT1 reverse-flow coolant motor. These cast-iron heads have the same features as the aluminum LT1 versions but are less expensive. When the iron-headed LTI engines were installed in these two full-size B-Bodies, they were rated at 260 hp.

PN 12529742 or 12525578, used in natural gas conversions, is a cast-iron head used on the Gen II 265 4.3-liter V-8 L99. This Gen II reverse-flow coolant motor was used in full-size 1994 to 1996 Caprice sedans and wagons.

PN 12529093/casting number 10239906 is a 1996 Vortec 5700 L31 head. It has a heart-shaped 64-cc chamber with 1.94/1.50-inch valves and pressed-in rocker studs. Intake port volumes are 170 cc, and they are 0.080-inch taller than standard-port Gen I intake port openings. These heads use only four intake manifold bolts on each side and position the holes differently from those found on previous production Gen I heads. They have excellent airflow. Edelbrock offers an aluminum high-rise 4-barrel carb intake for the Vortec heads that match their unique bolt pattern, coolant crossover, and port openings.

## Cast-Iron Bowtie Heads

Bowtie heads are designed for higher-performance applications with a goal of 400 to 450 hp. They feature larger valves, a thicker deck surface and 66-cc chambers. PN 19331470 is a small-port Vortec design that is supplied complete and ready to install. It has 185/66-cc ports and will work with both Vortec and early design intake manifolds. A bare head is available as PN 19331471.

A larger port Bowtie head (PN 19331472) is also offered with a 225/77 port design, but still with 66-cc chambers. The bigger ports allow for greater air volume, thus more power. This head is also supplied completely assembled. Note that these Bowtie heads are limited to a valve lift of about 0.450-inch in stock form. Larger cams will require extra machining.

## Aluminum Production Heads

PN 19300955 heads, Chevy Performance's Fast Burn design, are 23-degree heads used on newer crate engines such as the ZZ6 and will bolt to Gen I blocks (with a 4.0-inch bore). The heads are CNC machined and completely assembled with 2.00/1.55-inch valves and 210-cc intake ports with 78-cc D-shaped exhaust ports. The spark plugs are positioned at an angle and the heads are machined for center-bolt valve covers and perimeter style covers. The heads use intake gasket PN 19301685 and will work with both early-style and Vortec manifolds.

PN 10185086/casting number 10088113 is a bare-aluminum head used on the 1988 to 1991 Gen I 350 TPI Corvette. It features 1.94/1.5-inch valves, has a 58-cc chamber and fits 1955 to 1991 small-blocks. Weight is 19 pounds each.

PN 10185087 was used on the 1988 to 1991 L98 350 TPI Corvette and on 350 HO ZZ3 and ZZ4 crate engines. These heads can be used on any Gen I production 4-inch bore block.

Casting number 14101128 head features 58-cc chambers, screw-in studs, and angle plugs. It was used on 1986 to 1987 350 L98 TPI Corvettes.

PN 10168448/casting number 10128374 has 53-cc chambers, used on 1992 and newer Gen II LT1 350 in the Corvette, Camaro Z28, and Pontiac Firebird. It uses a reverse-flow coolant head, screw-in studs and angle plugs, and adjustable rocker arms.

PN 12363289 is a Gen II 350 LT4 aluminum production head but has non-adjustable rocker arm studs to work with the 1996-on Corvette 350 LT4 production Crane 1.6:1 self-aligning roller rocker arms. These LT4 heads can be used on Gen II LT1 engines with the appropriate LT4 intake manifolds to fit the raised intake ports and runners. Use it with Gen II blocks; this is a reverse coolant flow head. (PN 12555689 is a Gen II LT4 bare casting.)

***Want a set of the same heads that help make 425 hp from a 383? PN 19300955 gets you a Fast Burn aluminum head that is CNC machined and features a 210-cc intake port to pack the cylinder. The heads are machined to accept perimeter or center-bolt valve covers as well as traditional or Vortec-style intake manifolds. D-shaped exhaust ports make quick work of the spent fumes. (Photos Courtesy Chevrolet Performance)***

## Aluminum Racing Heads

Chevrolet Performance has offered a number of aluminum heads designed for racing, many designed that have been proven in NASCAR and National Hot Rod Association (NHRA) competition. Many designs and configurations have been used over the years, so it is important to do your research if looking at a set of used or NOS heads.

Today, Chevy Performance offers several sets of heads made for racing that start with castings (of 355-T7 aluminum) designed with thicker decks and manifold flange areas. The combustion chambers are designed for maximum air flow, high compression, and high RPM. Extra machine work will be necessary in most applications.

### *18-Degree Heads*

PN 24502580 is a semi-finished aluminum head with combustion chambers in an "as cast 60 cc" state. It is designed for up to a 2.200-inch intake valve and 1.625-inch exhaust. The intake port is 215 cc and left unmachined as well. There is 0.080-inch extra material left on the deck face with another 0.055-inch on the intake face.

### *15-Degree Heads*

PN 24502615 is similar to the small-bore 18-degree aluminum head (PN 24502580), except the valve angle has been rolled over 3 degrees more by angle-milling the casting 2 degrees, and altering the valve guide holes 1 degree more. This head is intended for small-bore engines, especially those competing in the Competition Eliminator drag race classes. A small 35- to 37-cc combustion chamber is possible. The head is capable of supporting over 900 hp and is supply fully machined, semi-finished without seats or guides.

### *Splayed Valve Bowtie Heads*

Splayed valve heads are all-out competition heads that were never intended for street duty. The "splayed" design points both valves toward the center of the cylinder bore to increase the airflow and efficiency of the head. The heads are manufactured with extra material for custom porting and modifications. They require a custom-fabricated intake as well.

PN 24502517 is a semi-machined splayed valve head with 240-cc intake port runner volume and 45-cc chambers. Intake valve angles are at 16 degrees and tilted 4 degrees. The exhaust valves are at 11 degrees with a 4-degree cant. It will accept 2.20/1.625-inch valves that are longer than stock (5.7-inch stem length).

PN 12480147 is similar to the PN 24502517 except its main surfaces are machined and the exhaust bolt pattern, valve guides, and plug holes are all machined as well. (PN 12480146 doesn't have the valve guides or plug holes machined.) The head bolt and dowel hole locations, intake bolt holes, and pushrod holes are not machined on either of these splayed valve aluminum heads either.

Chevy Performance also offers two splayed valve heads designed for 4.500-inch bores. PN 12480153 is a semi-machined head, popular for use on NHRA competition engines with dual carbs. It has a 240-cc "peanut" intake and exhaust ports with a 40-cc combustion chamber all in an "as cast" state. This head requires 3/8-inch fasteners and there are 19 bolt holes. PN 88958684 is a "cubed" head with no seats or guides.

## Chevy Valve Specifications

| Part Number | Diameter (inches) | Stem Size | Comments |
|---|---|---|---|
| INTAKE | | | |
| 10241743 | 1.940 | 11/32 | Replacement used in some crate engines |
| 12555331 | 2.000 | 11/32 | 1996 Gen II 350 LT4, Fast Burn Heads, ZZ383 |
| 12363757 | 2.000 | 11/32 | Stainless steel, undercut stems, hardened tips |
| EXHAUST | | | |
| 12550909 | 1.500 | 11/32 | Replacement used in some crate engines |
| 12551313 | 1.55 | 1 | 1996 Gen II 350 LT4, Fast Burn Heads, ZZ383 |

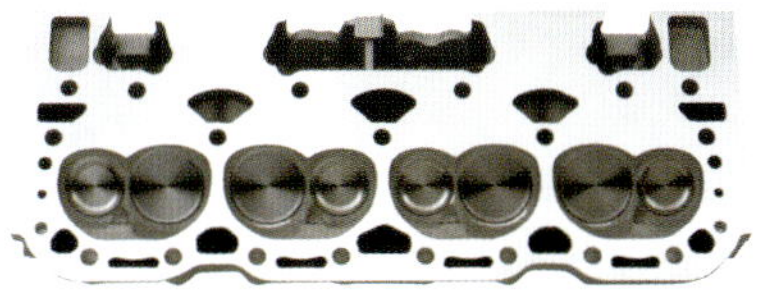

*The Fast Burn combustion chambers are 62 cc with a 0.400-inch deck to accept milling. Note that the heads can only be used on small-blocks with any 4.00-inch bore with a standard-flow coolant system. (Photo Courtesy Chevrolet Performance)*

*The bare Bowtie Vortec heads feature a closed 66-cc combustion chamber with a 0.450-inch deck thickness. The intake port holds 185 cc with a 65-cc exhaust port and hardened valve seats.*

*Angled spark plugs and 62-cc chambers coupled with 2.00/1.550-inch valves provide the details of the ZZ6 aluminum-head assembly, which is available as PN 19300955.*

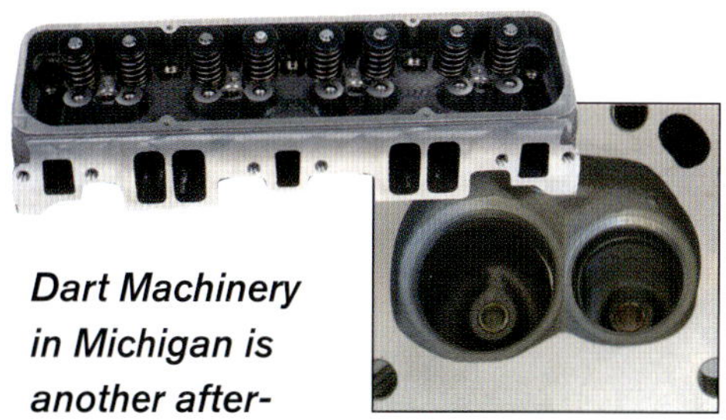

*Dart Machinery in Michigan is another aftermarket source for heads and blocks. Its Iron Eagle S/S cylinder heads are performance upgrades over OEM parts. The intake runners are 165 cc with models available with chamber sizes of 67 or 72 cc. (Photo Courtesy Dart)*

*The evenly spaced intake ports on the SB2.2 head are referred to as mirror ports because the intake runners each face the direction of the intake plenum. (Photo Courtesy Chevrolet Performance)*

*The exhaust ports on the SB2 head look somewhat similar to the conventional small-block head ports, but the spacing is different, and additional cooling is provided for the two center exhaust ports. (Photo Courtesy Chevrolet Performance)*

### *SB2 Bowtie Heads*

The SB2 cylinder head was designed for the NASCAR competition small-block of the same name. The latest heads, the SB2.2, were developed to improve durability and performance of the racing engine. The spark plug location is moved toward the center of the bore and the intake ports were also angled toward the center of the engine. The entire design was developed with a single 4-barrel carb in mind by "mirroring" the position of each intake port. Several versions of cylinder heads have been offered for the SB2 block since its launch in the late 1990s, so again, do your research before buying any used or NOS components.

PN 12480011 and PN 12480129 are both Chevy Performance SB2.2 heads that are accepted by NASCAR. The heads are supplied bare with no seats or guides installed. They feature an "as cast" 48-cc combustion chamber and peanut ports. The PN 12480011 has standard 0.500-inch guide holes, while the PN 12480129 has 0.375-inch guide holes.

## Aftermarket Cylinder Heads

Unless you're building a numbers-matching restored small-block or an engine with a nostalgic target, there's almost no reason to completely rebuild a 30-or-more-year-old cylinder head. Not only does Chevy Performance offer a number of complete heads, the aftermarket is full of options from street to race.

You can easily find a set of cast-iron or aluminum cylinder heads to fit most any budget or build style from a number of different companies such as Trick Flow, Edelbrock, World Products, Dart Machinery, Brodix, and more. Different port volumes, chamber sizes, valve angles, valve sizes, with CNC machining and porting, and other options are available to help complete an engine from mild to wild.

*Notice the valve sequence on this CNC machined version of the SB2.2 head. It is different from other small-block heads and requires, among other things, a camshaft with the proper intake and exhaust lobe sequencing to match the heads. (Photo Courtesy Chevrolet Performance)*

*Edelbrock's Performer RPM heads have 2.02/1.60-inch valves, interlocking hardened seats, and angled or straight plug entry. The chamber measures 70 cc. Port volumes are 170/60 cc. (Photo Courtesy Edelbrock)*

*Edelbrock aluminum heads have accessory holes to fit your application.*

*Racing Head Service (RHS), a division of Comp Cams, offers a line of performance replacement cast-iron heads called the Pro Torker. They feature "fast burn" 64-cc chambers and 2.020/1.600-inch valves with an intake runner of 170-cc and 67-cc for the exhaust. (Photo Courtesy RHS)*

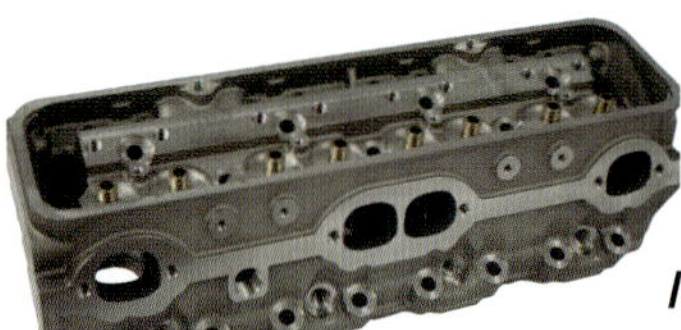

*World Products offers a long list of cast-iron and aluminum heads for the small-block. From improved replacements that are even CARB legal, to race-prepped aluminum designs. The Motown line (shown) is meant for engines over 383 ci. (Photo Courtesy World Products)*

*A high-speed grinder, carbide bits, and sanding rolls are needed to port cylinder heads. You can clean up the bowls under the valve seats and remove any excess casting slag or machining ledges. If you are planning to extensively modify a set of cylinder heads, you need experience and access to an airflow bench to ensure accurate work that actually improves the heads. You can also clean up the block to remove sharp edges and aid oil drainback in the lifter valley.*

# VALVETRAIN

Timing chain covers are interchangeable between Gen I engines. Gen II timing covers are different from Gen I covers and are not interchangeable between engine families. Also keep in mind that the timing tabs found on Gen I timing covers were either welded on or were bolted in place. It is important to note that the timing tab was also placed to match whichever diameter vibration damper the engine originally received at the factory.

In addition, the location of the timing mark on Gen I vibration dampers indicating TDC was moved in later years in relation to the damper keyway on the crank snout. So it is important when you are mixing and matching parts from Gen I engines that the timing cover and timing tab match the diameter of the front balancer and the TDC location on the damper. You need to determine this before final assembly of the engine. If you are not careful here, you may have a mismatched setup that makes it difficult to correctly set the initial ignition timing.

Two dowel pins are used to help position the timing covers on Gen I engines. If you need them, the block dowel pins are readily available through the aftermarket or your local machine shop.

There is also a small dowel pin used on the camshaft that should be available with your new cam. If the gears are not aligned properly, you can add a 0.015-inch-thick shim behind the cam sprocket. Camshaft bolts are 5/16-18 x 0.75 inch and are available individually as PN 9424877.

*Gen I timing covers came with a timing tab that was either welded or bolted in place. The position of the indicator moved to different locations over the years to match the diameter of the front vibration damper and the TDC timing mark on the damper. On this dingy example, the tab is welded to the cover.*

*If the cover does not have a timing indicator on it, Chevy Performance offers a stamped steel bolt-on version as PN 3991435.*

*Chevrolet offered many dampers and timing indicators. Always confirm TDC of the number-one cylinder when the timing mark is aligned with the indicator.*

Using a roller cam without a cam thrust plate requires an aluminum cam thrust button.

Two-piece timing cover sets are sold through the aftermarket. These enable you to remove the top half of the timing cover to access the camshaft without having to lower the oil pan and/or break the gasket seal between the oil pan and timing cover. They are very handy for cam swaps or to alter the cam timing.

## Timing Sets

A number of timing sets available today come with a crank gear that has multiple keyways. These different keyways allow you to advance or retard the cam timing in relation to the crank. Generally speaking, advancing the cam timing may increase engine power at the low end of the RPM scale, while retarding the cam timing may increase the top-end power. It depends on the rest of the engine combination.

Some aftermarket timing chain systems have adjustable cam gears that allow for cam timing changes without resorting to offset dowel pins. However, I suggest if you are unfamiliar with these types of cam timing changes and what can result to your particular engine and cam combination, use the stock "0" setting on the crank timing sprocket keyway.

A few cams are ground with a certain amount of advance when they are made. Other cams are ground straight up. Check with the manufacturer and the cam timing card you receive when you purchase the cam. Any changes you intend to make can be made when the cam is degreed in.

Some of the engine dyno simulator computer programs can help you determine whether cam advance or retard makes more power in your situation. Specific cam timing can be entered into these programs and then you can advance or retard the cam timing from the manufacturer's specs on the computer. When you actually build the engine, make sure that there is adequate clearance between the valve and piston deck. Changes to the cam timing can affect the point where the valve comes closest to the piston as it approaches and passes over TDC.

Different types of timing sets are available from Chevrolet Performance as well as the aftermarket. Chevrolet has used a stock, production silent link chain with metal gears that have plastic teeth on the large cam sprocket and metal teeth on the crank gear. These timing sets are quiet, inexpensive, and dampen crank vibrations transmitted to the cam gear. However, the chains stretch quickly with use, and cam timing then changes because of chain slack. Many racers use these chains, but they must be replaced frequently because of stretch.

Single-roller chains with metal cam and crank gears offer more durability, but chain stretch can still be a problem.

Double-roller chains offer more strength, have metal teeth on the gears, and are a little noisier, but they still stretch with use.

True roller chains have increased strength and larger solid bushing rollers that roll as they pass over the gear teeth. They do not stretch as much and provide accurate cam timing for many miles.

Aftermarket suppliers make a number of variations of three or four types of gear drives for regular-rotation camshafts. These gear drives are noisy and transmit crank vibrations to the cam. However, since there is no chain to stretch, cam timing stays relatively accurate.

Aftermarket belt-driven timing sets are the ultimate in cam timing, and this is reflected in their price. They use a flexible cog belt and matching gears to drive the cam. No crank vibrations are transmitted because the vibrations are absorbed by the belt. Cam timing adjustments can be made easily without the use of offset dowel bushings. Some of these belt-driven setups fit on the outside of a timing cover and some fit

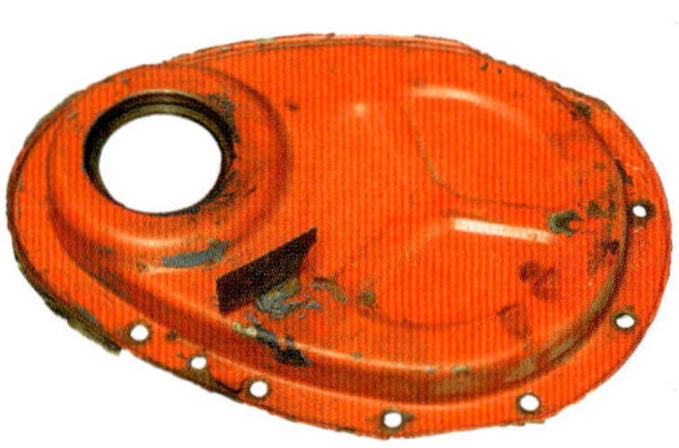

*This early timing cover has a welded-on timing indicator and is positioned for a 6-inch-diameter damper.*

*This handsome chrome timing cover is available through Chevrolet Performance as PN 12302089. Note that it requires a bolt-on timing indicator.*

*Double-roller timing chains sets are often used in street and performance applications. They give good service and, with the metal gear sets, long wear.*

under a timing cover. These sets are strictly for race applications.

No matter which type of timing set you use, make sure the cam sprocket or gear does not rub against the front face of the block or it will interfere with the rotation of the cam gear. You can use a brass shim under the cam gear for clearance or have the block cam thrust surface or cam timing gear machined for clearance. Cam thrust bearings can also be used to provide clearance and protect the cam thrust surface on the block.

The 1987-on Gen I blocks that were machined to use a factory production roller cam were made with a front cam thrust plate to control the forward movement of the cam. This requires a special cam timing gear to clear the front of the block where the thrust plate is mounted. Use crank timing gear PN 14088784, and single-roller timing chain PN 14088783 in these applications.

Adjustments in cam timing, whether it is to correct a manufacturing problem or to try advancing or retarding the cam placement for power reasons, can be accomplished a number of ways. All of these changes are made with the timing gears.

For a long time, folks would get out their degree wheel and piston stop to check the accuracy of the cam as delivered and make whatever adjustments they felt necessary. If a change in cam placement was to be done, the cam dowel pin hole on the cam timing gear was slightly enlarged, and then an offset bushing that gave the appropriate increment of change was placed in the hole. Offset crank keys were also offered to do the same thing. It is a cumbersome process.

Now many timing chain sets are available that have multiple keyways that allow you to change cam timing by choosing the appropriate keyway to get the advance or retard you may want. On many belt timing sets and some timing chain sets, very precise changes can be made quickly and easily through Vernier adjustments made on the cam gear itself. It is one of the advantages of these timing systems. You still need to check the cam timing with a degree wheel to ensure

## Valvetrain Selection Tips

It is extremely important that the valvetrain parts you select match each of their respective parts. Whichever camshaft you choose, it has a matching valve spring, retainer, locks, stem seals, spring installed height, spring diameter, and open and closed spring pressures. Some of the Gen I stock production heads have exhaust valve springs that are shorter in length than the intake valve spring. The shorter exhaust spring may use a valve rotator mounted on top of the spring.

Valvetrain clearances are critical if your assembly is to have a long, trouble-free life. Spring installed height, coil-bind, rocker arm stud clearance, retainer clearances, rocker arm geometry, piston deck to open valve clearance, valve guide, stem seal clearance, and guide plate clearances must all be checked. On a stock valvetrain, there is usually no problem; however, if you are increasing valve lift; using a higher-than-stock rocker arm ratio, non-stock valve springs, different length pushrods; or if the block has been decked considerably, the heads have been angle milled or decked, or if you have changed the cam installed timing, the clearances may have been altered. Proceed carefully if any modifications or machining have been done!

It takes time and effort to make proper part selections, so accommodate your planned changes and make these clearance checks. However, it takes more time, effort, and money to remove the heads after assembly and possibly the engine, because all of the valves were bent when you fired the engine up for the first time. Broken pistons, heads, blocks, valve springs, bent pushrods, etc., are very possible if you don't take the time to check valvetrain clearances. ■

*Double-roller timing chains are a popular choice. Many come with crank sprockets that allow you to install cam timing either straight up, 4 degrees advanced, or 4 degrees retarded. Look very carefully at the timing marks on these multiple keyway crank sprockets when you install them. It is very easy to mix up which slot you are using, and you may set the cam timing incorrectly.*

*Gear-driven timing sets are available from aftermarket suppliers, such as COMP Cams, Edelbrock, or Crower. There is no timing chain to stretch, but these gear sets are noisier than a chain setup.*

## Valvetrain Geometry

Valvetrain geometry often gets overlooked when making parts changes to improve engine performance. When you move to a higher-lift camshaft, deck the block or heads, change to a different head casting, use a different head gasket with a different compressed thickness, change valve stem length, use a different pushrod length, change installed valve spring height, or change to a different rocker arm ratio, the relationship of the rocker arm tip to the tip of the valve stem can be altered.

Remember that the rocker arm tip rotates in an arc as it pushes the valve stem down. The rocker arm tip motion is not straight up and down. It looks like it is, but it's not. It rocks on the stud, and the tip of the rocker sweeps across the face of the valve stem. If you look very closely at the motion and the actual contact point between the surface of the rocker tip and the valve stem tip, you see that as the rocker starts to open the valve, the contact point is slightly inboard of the center of the valve stem toward the outboard. As the valve is opened farther, the contact point moves toward the center of the valve stem tip. Opening the valve still farther toward full lift, the contact point now continues to move slightly inboard of the center of the valve tip.

If the geometry is okay, the rocker arm is at 90 degrees to the valve stem tip when the valve has been opened one-third of the total lift. The other two-thirds of the valve lift is accomplished by the remaining motion in the rocker arc as the contact point moves slightly inboard. Needless to say, this is very difficult to see with the naked eye. So after you look at it and can't really see anything, you start thinking that it doesn't matter and, besides, the geometry is probably okay. The problem is that if the geometry is not correct, a number of problems can occur.

Certainly, accelerated valve guide and valve stem wear is one. Side loading of the guide is worsened by improper geometry. More importantly, the rate of acceleration given to the valve opening is not optimum. This is where power can be lost by improper geometry. Keep in mind that the cam lobe has a certain amount of lift and the rate of lift and acceleration is transmitted to the cam lifters, then to the pushrod, then to the rocker arm, which also multiplies the lift and acceleration motion by its rocker arm ratio. The rocker arm ratio actually changes as the rocker arm goes through its opening motion. With some high-pressure spring combinations, deflection (bending) of the pushrod, rocker arm stud, rocker arm, or even the valve stem changes this relationship.

So what do you do next? You can use an adjustable-length pushrod checking tool (available from cam makers) to determine which length you need. Or you can get an inexpensive length checker from Manley (PN 42137 3/8-inch studs or PN 42132 7/16-inch studs) that slips on the rocker arm stud in place of the rocker arm and helps determine whether you need a different length valve stem or different length pushrod.

Generally, greatly increasing the valve lift or increasing the valve stem length to get more spring installed height requires that you use a longer pushrod. However, as indicated above, other factors are involved. Custom-length pushrods are available in off-the-shelf lengths or just about any particular length you need can be made. ■

that the cam you have purchased is in fact doing what it should and that the valve events occur when they ought to.

If you have had your block align-bored, the distance from the crank axis centerline to the camshaft bore centerline may have been decreased. Cloyes or COMP Cams make timing sets that are slightly shorter and make up for the decrease. Likewise, longer timing sets are available for blocks that feature a raised cam bore.

Gen II engines use a gear mounted to the front of the cam to drive the front-mounted Opti-Spark distributor and the Gen II specific water pump. (Note that the ignition timing is not adjustable.) A timing chain and crank timing gear complete the system.

### Camshafts

Hydraulic and mechanical flat-tappet cams have been used in the small-blocks from General Motors. Hydraulic roller cams have been used since 1987. The "Factory Cams" sidebar on page 83 gives information on current camshafts available from the factory. Keep in mind that some late-model Gen I blocks were cast with provisions to use a factory hydraulic roller cam. Earlier blocks do not have the bosses cast into the lifter valley to hold the lifter retainer bars used in factory roller cam installations. You can use a flat-tappet cam in a Gen I block that originally had a factory roller cam. Some late-model Gen I blocks are machined for roller

## Factory Cams

A number of older production and over-the-counter factory camshafts are no longer made by Chevrolet, but many of these earlier grinds are available from aftermarket cam makers as "factory blueprint cams."

Chevrolet Performance offers several cams that are designed to be similar to vintage favorites. They also offer several "hot" hydraulic rollers. ■

| Part Number | Type | Duration at 0.050 inch | Lift (inch) | LSA | Use |
|---|---|---|---|---|---|
| 10185071 | Hydraulic roller | 208/221 | 0.474/0.474 | 112 | 350/345 ZZ3 and ZZ4 crate engine |
| 19210723 | Hydraulic roller | 222/230 | 0.509/0.528 | 112 | Off-road use, lobe for mechanical fuel pump |
| 19244485 | Hydraulic roller | 232/242 | 0.539/0.558 | 112 | Off-road use, lobe for mechanical fuel pump |
| 24502586 | Hydraulic roller | 218/228 | 0.525/0.525 | | Gen II LT4 Hot Cam, 1.5 rocker |
| 14097395 | Hydraulic roller | 196/206 | 0.431/0.451 | 109 | For the HT383 truck engine with 1.5 rockers |
| 12480002 | Hydraulic roller | 218/228 | 0.525/0.525 | 112 | Same as PN 24502586 except with 1.6 rockers, springs, and retainers |
| 3896962 | Hydraulic flat tappet | 222/222 | 0.450/0.460 | 114 | 350 L46, L82 |
| 24502476 | Hydraulic flat tappet | 212/220 | 0.435/0.460 | 112.5 | 350/300 crate engine |

cams; however, some have been fitted with flat-tappet hydraulic cams for use in trucks. Gen II engines all use a factory-installed hydraulic roller camshaft.

Aftermarket cam makers produce an almost endless and sometimes confusing variety of cams for the small-block Chevy. It is impossible to list them all. The best advice I can give you is to talk with the suppliers. They will help you make the best choice for your engine. Don't choose a camshaft just because it worked well in somebody else's engine combination. The camshaft is the "brain" of the engine and has an enormous influence on how the engine performs, how it idles, and what other assorted parts it needs to operate correctly.

Cams used in the 265 engine blocks made in 1955 and 1956 (check the block casting date) need oiling flats ground in the rear cam journal and a matching rear cam bearing for the oiling system in these blocks to work properly.

You have to be careful when you make cam comparisons because cam timing may be calculated as seat-to-seat timing, SAE timing, or at 0.050 inch of tappet lift timing. In addition, with a solid lifter cam that requires additional lash made at the rocker arm, this lash has to be subtracted right off the top when comparing total valve lift figures. Finally, different cam companies use different methods and starting points when calculating cam specifications and dimensions. This complicates your ability to make comparisons between camshafts made by two or more different cam manufacturers.

Cam duration is comparatively

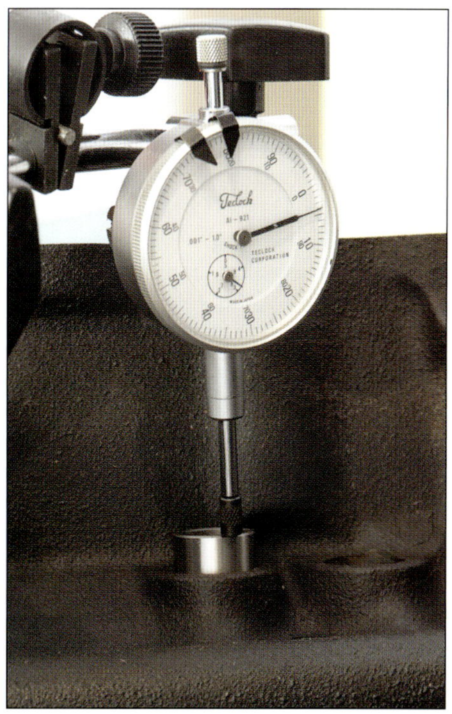

*A dial indicator has many uses when building an engine, such as when degreeing the camshaft.*

## Cam Lobe Separation Angles

Cam lobe separation angle is often ignored or misunderstood. The first thing many people look at is total valve lift or duration figures when they are making cam selections and comparisons. Part of the problem is the confusing number of terms used when folks talk about cams. So many of the words or terms used sound similar, so a person thinks he or she understands, but really doesn't.

The lobe separation angle (LSA) is the number of camshaft rotation degrees measured from the centerline of the intake lobe to the centerline of the exhaust lobe. This amount is manufactured into the cam when it is made and cannot be changed by the end user unless they have the cam lobes reground. Various LSAs can be built into a cam and the number of degrees can generally vary from 100 to 120 degrees. If the lobe separation is tighter, say from 100 to 110 degrees, the amount of time that both the intake and exhaust valves are open at the same time is increased. With a wider LSA, this overlap period is decreased.

There are a few general things to be said about LSAs. Keep in mind that this and other cam and engine factors have an effect on your particular engine. Because of the shorter overlap period, wide LSAs (112 to 120 degrees), build more low-RPM torque because more air is trapped in the cylinder at low- and mid-RPM engine speeds, give a better vacuum signal in the motor at low engine RPM, idle well at low RPM without cough and sputter, and work with vacuum-powered accessories such as power brakes. Less overlap means less raw fuel is pulled out the exhaust valve and fuel mileage is improved. Low- and mid-range-speed drivability is enhanced and the engine generally has a wider power band. However, at high RPM, these wide LSAs and valve timing may inhibit the breathing characteristics of the engine.

Narrow LSAs generally cause the opposite effects. Idle quality may be rough and lopey, power brakes may not receive enough engine vacuum to work properly, the torque peak on the engine moves upward in the RPM band, and less low-speed power is created. However, the mid- and high-RPM-speed breathing improves and power increases, but over a narrower power band.

Some of these effects can be offset by changing valve timing, duration, induction systems, use of a manual transmission, or cubic-inch displacement increases.

Talk to your cam manufacturer and get a recommendation. Make sure they understand what you intend to do with your engine. Different grinds are available for different types of street performance and racing and even different race classes in order to take into account class rules and engine limitations. If you are going to use nitrous or a blower of some sort, there are appropriate wider cam LSAs for these types of induction. ■

## Cam Duration

If you know when cam timing events occur, you can determine the amount of duration that a particular cam has. Just add the two intake events together and add 180 degrees to that figure to determine duration. The same is true for the exhaust. Just add the two exhaust events together and add 180 degrees to determine exhaust duration. If the figures for the timing events were taken at 0.050 inch, then you find duration at 0.050 inch. If the timing was calculated for seat-to-seat timing, the duration you find is advertised duration.

As an example, let's say you have a cam with the following timing at 0.050 inch:

- Intake opens at 29 degrees before top dead center (BTDC)
- Intake closes at 59 degrees after bottom dead center (ABDC)
- Exhaust opens at 67 degrees before bottom dead center (BBDC)
- Exhaust closes at 25 degrees after top dead center (ATDC)

Add the two intake events together (29 + 59 = 88), now add 180 degrees (88 + 180 = 268). So, the intake duration at 0.050 inch on this cam is 268 degrees.

On the exhaust side, add the two events (67 + 25 = 92), and then add 180, (92 + 180 = 272). The exhaust duration at 0.050 inch is 272 degrees.

If you have a cam with unknown timing specs, you can use a degree wheel and a dial indicator to figure out the timing events and then calculate duration. ■

measured by different cam makers at 0.050 inch of actual valve tappet lift by the cam. It is expressed as duration at 0.050 inch and is not the same as advertised duration measurements. This duration at 0.050 inch is an important figure to look for when you compare camshafts. A short duration figure of, say, 195 to 225 degrees at 0.050 inch of tappet lift, works with a stock torque converter in an automatic car, has a decent idle, and generally shows good street manners in terms of low and medium RPM power. Above 225 degrees of duration

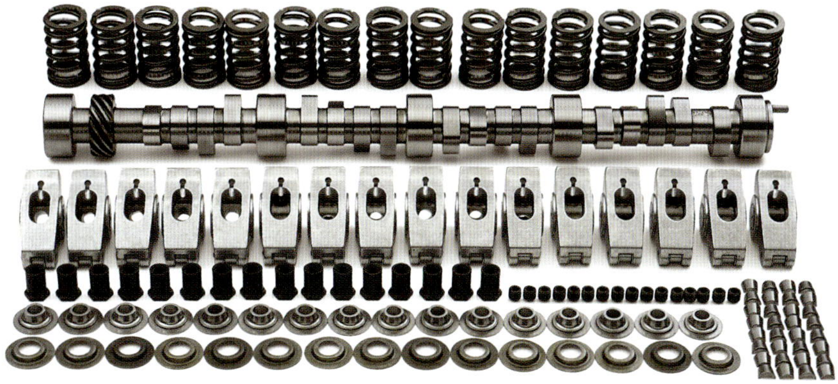

***Chevy Performance offers a number of cams designed to improve the performance of your 350-ci engine. PN 12480002 is a Gen II LT4 Hot Cam Kit that is supplied with 1.6:1 ratio aluminum rockers, springs, and retainers. (Photo Courtesy Chevrolet Performance)***

## Camshaft Lobe Intensity

When you look at the advertised duration of a cam and compare that to the duration at –0.050-inch tappet rise figures given for the same cam, they are obviously different. There are some clues to cam profile and performance that can be made by analyzing these two figures.

Some advertised duration measurements are generally made at the point where the lifter rises off of the base circle from 0.004 to 0.006 inch and begins its travel up the ramp. Some cam types use a different measurement starting point (0.020-inch lifter rise) for their advertised duration measurement farther up in lift. Solid flat-tappet and roller cams also require a certain amount of valve lash, which must be taken into account when initial tappet rise is considered. In an attempt to make comparisons somewhat easier, most cam makers also give a duration at –0.050 inch, which begins its duration calculation when the tappet has risen 0.050 inch in the tappet bore.

If you subtract the duration at 0.050 inch from the advertised duration, you get some idea of the intensity of the ramp profile of that particular cam. A cam with a more aggressive and quicker valve opening ramp has a lower intensity figure than one with a larger figure when you do the subtraction.

Let's do an example. If you have two cams, and one cam has an advertised duration of 280 degrees and a duration at 0.050 inch of 212 degrees, the intensity of the lobe ramp is 280 – 212 = 68. If you have another cam and its advertised duration is also 280, but its duration at 0.050 inch is 225 degrees, you get 280 – 225 = 55. The lower the intensity number (55), the quicker the valve starts to open or close. The higher the number (68 in this example), the more slowly a valve is opened or closed because the lobe opening and closing ramps have a gentler profile compared to the other cam.

Intensity figures around 50 to 55 or lower give you a cam that quickly opens a valve, and this adds more power to the engine. Some roller cams with very aggressive opening ramp designs have an intensity figure of 34 to 40. On the other hand, with a higher intensity figure, it may be argued that since the valve is opened at a slower rate, the life of the valvetrain is longer because the stresses made on the valvetrain are not so acute. The valvetrain is also quieter. However, modern camshaft design, manufacturing techniques, and materials, especially when used with a roller cam design, enable cam makers to produce cams with intensity figures of 34 to 60 that live just fine in a race engine, if you follow the correct cam prelubrication and break-in techniques and match the rest of the valvetrain to the cam requirements. It is possible that if you compare two cams with the same lift and duration figures but different intensity in the opening and closing ramps, the one with the lower intensity figure—and therefore the quicker opening and closing ramps—puts more lift under the curve than the slower-opening camshaft.

Roller cams have very quick opening and closing rates, and this is one of the advantages of using a roller cam. However, very quick opening flat-tappet cams are available. Try to make your comparisons within the product line offered by one manufacturer. Because of the different measuring standards used, comparing one cam made by a particular company to a cam made by another company is sometimes misleading. ■

at 0.050 inch, you need to change to a higher stall torque converter with an automatic transmission. The cam tends to make more power in a higher RPM range and may not have a smooth idle. Manual transmission vehicles or larger cubic inch engine are more forgiving of cam duration increases than an automatic tranny or a smaller cubic inch engine.

The lobe separation angle (LSA) is not to be confused with intake lobe centerline angle (LCA). The LSA is the angle of difference, measured in degrees of cam rotation between the centerline of the intake lobe and the centerline of the exhaust lobe. Narrow LSAs (104 to 112) generally make a small-block cam have a lopey idle but make more power at higher RPM and create a lower engine vacuum. Wider LSAs (112 to 117) tend to have a smoother idle, higher engine vacuum, and generally operate well at low- and medium-RPM levels. If you were to take two cams with the same lift and duration but made one with an LSA of 108 and the other an LSA of 116, then put them in the same engine one after the other, the engine would exhibit completely different ways that it idled and ran, and where it made power.

Cam duration, total lift, and lobe separation angles affect the volume of air/fuel that the engine breathes in and out. The amount of time a valve is open (duration), how much it opens (lift), the time both intake and exhaust valves are open at the same time (LSA), and how quickly a valve opens and closes (determined by the shape of the cam lobe) have a direct effect on the way the engine works. If you want an engine that idles smoothly, has enough engine vacuum to run vacuum-operated accessories such as power brakes, works with a stock stall speed torque converter, and makes its power at low- and medium-RPM levels for street driving, then use a cam that has a short duration and a wide LSA.

If you're looking for high-performance street use or want to go racing, then look at high lift, longer duration, narrow LSA cams. But be warned! You may have to increase the engine's static compression ratio, use a lower gear ratio in your rear end, change the stall speed of your torque converter, upgrade your valvetrain, and use a separate vacuum reservoir container to make your power brakes and other vacuum-assisted accessories work correctly. Blower, turbo, or some large-displacement, maximum-effort racing engines can use wider LSAs to help prevent incoming fuel and air from being pushed right out the exhaust port.

In 1987, Chevrolet began to use hydraulic roller cams in small-block engines. Aftermarket roller cams and roller lifters, both hydraulic and solid, are available that reduce internal friction and open and close valves more quickly in the engine. Roller cams can provide large performance gains, but they are more expensive than solid or hydraulic flat-tappet valvetrains and cams. You have to purchase roller lifters, different pushrods, matching springs, retainers, roller rockers, a cam thrust bumper, and possibly a bronze distributor gear to install a steel billet roller cam. Depending on how radical a roller cam you purchase, you may also need a rev kit, stud girdle, and tall valve covers.

However, because the roller lifter can follow a cam lobe more closely, much more aggressive lobe opening and closing ramp and flank profiles

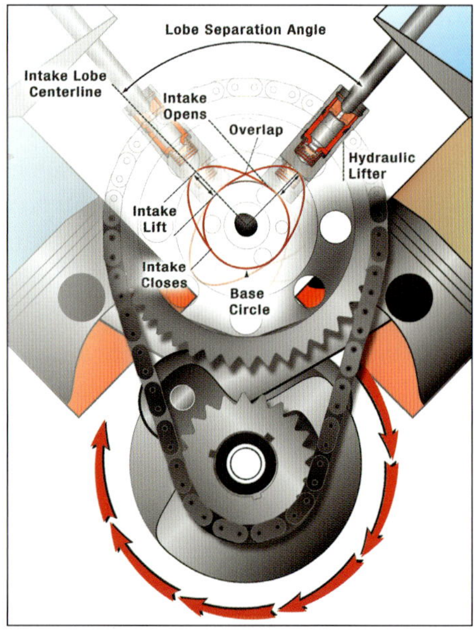


*The lobe separation angle (LSA), shown at the top of this illustration, is the angle difference between the centerline of the intake lobe and the exhaust lobe. (Illustration Courtesy Comp Cams)*

can be used. Valve opening and closing can be made to happen more quickly when compared with a cam using a flat tappet. The valves stay open longer in the cam rotation. Because the roller lifter must stay directly on the cam lobe, the springs used on a roller cam are much stiffer. If the roller on the cam follower loses contact with the cam lobe, the lifter quickly self-destructs.

These stiffer valve springs may be taller or larger in diameter than a stock spring, so additional changes may be necessary. These changes can include widening the valve spring pocket on the head to accommodate a wider-diameter spring or increasing the valve stem length to fit a spring with a taller installed height. Keep in mind that most factory stock distributor drive gears are compatible with the stock cast-iron camshaft gear. If you change to a steel roller cam, you may need to change the distributor

## Gen II Timing Chains and Gears

The timing chain and gear sets found on Gen II L99, LTI, and LT4 engines are different from those found on earlier Gen I engines. This is due to the fact that the front-mounted Opti-Spark distributors and the water pumps used on Gen II engines are driven by the cam timing gear. There are small differences in this setup for the L99, LTI, and 1996 LT4.

The cam gear has a step, found at the front cam journal, to accommodate the cam thrust plate used with the hydraulic roller camshaft. The cam gear used on 1992 to 1994 LTI engines used a splined shaft mounted in the center of the cam timing gear to drive the front-mounted distributor. The 1995-and-later L99 and LTIs and the 1996-on LT4s dropped this splined distributor driveshaft in the cam gear and switched to a longer drive pin dowel. This new dowel pin fits much the same as all previous cam/cam gear dowel locating pins, except that it protrudes above the face of the cam gear after installation and the protruding end of the dowel then drives the 1995-on front-mounted distributors. The 1995-on camshafts also have a larger pilot hole in the front of the camshaft to help locate the new dowel pin drive distributors. Changes were also made in the 1995-on later timing chain covers.

The timing set in production L99s and LT1s is a silent link with powdered metal gears. The production LT4 uses steel gears and an 8-mm-pitch roller chain.

Chevrolet offers a heavy-duty timing set over the counter for the 1995-on Gen II engines. The chain (PN 12370835) uses steel timing gears and a 1/2-inch-pitch roller chain. It is noisier than the previous timing sets, but it has much increased strength and durability. However, this heavy-duty timing set uses the long dowel pin setup found on 1995-on Gen II engines.

If you use this heavy-duty timing set on the earlier 1992-to-1994 Gen II block, you need to order the timing set and the additional parts required to change over to the new long dowel pin distributor drive system, including the proper cam, front mount distributor, timing chain cover, vacuum line harness, and vacuum fitting. ■

gear to a bronze gear. Bronze gears are designed more for racing applications and will wear when used on the street. Some roller camshaft makers are now producing steel roller camshafts with a cam/distributor drive gear manufactured with a different material that is compatible with the stock gear found on most distributors. Talk to the manufacturer about the recommended distributor gear.

As with any cam change, you need to check the rocker arm geometry to see if any changes in pushrod length are also required. It is a little more involved and certainly more expensive, but changing to a well-thought-out roller cam can provide a substantial increase in power when compared to a flat-tappet-style camshaft and lifters.

Some late-model stock production small-block engines come with a non-adjustable net lash valvetrain. If you change cams and substitute a cam with less or more lift, it may not work with the non-adjustable valvetrain. Be careful, and check with your cam supplier.

Keep something else in mind: A number of available Chevrolet factory cams for the small-block are designs that are decades old. Now, this does not mean that the cams are unsatisfactory. In the right combination they do just fine. You may even be required to use them under certain class race rules. The point is that many changes in camshaft design have taken place over the years. Chevrolet Performance offers a variety of cams modeled after original "hot" cams and the aftermarket is ripe with cams of all grinds and characteristics for stock engines or full-on race-built small-blocks.

Manufacturing techniques and tooling, materials, ramp designs, and the use of computer-assisted design have made significant advances possible. This means more camshaft for your dollar. You may ask yourself, why didn't Chevrolet offer these types of performance cams in the first place? The main reasons are parts longevity and production cost. A more conservative approach is taken when you want a mass-production street cam that needs to last 100,000 miles. A street-driven vehicle needs a decent idle and must work well with an automatic transmission and vacuum-operated accessories. Hydraulic cams and lifters don't usually require lash adjustment, so maintenance is low.

If you are looking for greater performance in a race engine, you must be prepared to periodically check valve springs, valve lash, and to replace worn parts. You are asking the race parts to take more abuse and

## Cams and Computers

If you have a late 1980s to 1990s computer-controlled engine and you wish to keep the computer controls but want to upgrade the engine performance with a cam change, keep in mind that you cannot just put any cam you want into this type of engine. Make sure that when you speak to cam companies they understand that you wish to maintain the stock computer controller.

Most cam companies offer grinds designed to work with stock controllers and their calibrations, are emissions-legal, improve street performance, and work with pump gasoline and low static compression levels. Of course if you can move to a custom calibration, more camshaft possibilities become available. However, you have to consider whatever emissions regulations you are required to meet in your state. ■

to make more power. The tradeoff for that increased power is more vigilance required on your part. With higher lifts and more aggressive profiles, stiffer valve springs are required to control the lifters. These increased pressures reduce the life of the camshaft and lifters, especially flat-tappet varieties. The roller cams give you more life because the roller lifter can handle the increased spring pressures up to a point. Some of the 600- to 800-psi spring pressures required on the most aggressive drag-race-style roller cams require that you constantly check for broken valve springs, rocker arms, and lifters, as well as pushrod deflection. It's part of the price you pay to keep a race engine running at extreme levels.

Still unsure of what you need in a cam? I remind you to call the cam makers directly. They have made these types of choices thousands of times and can help you get the right cam, the first time.

### Static Compression Versus Dynamic Compression and Cam Selection

There are two types of compression measurements: static and dynamic. The static compression ratio is a measurement that takes into account the bore and stroke of the engine, combustion chamber volume, head gasket volume and thickness, the piston-deck-to-block deck height, and the piston dome or dish volume. In other words, static compression is a measurement that includes the total volume inside a particular cylinder and cylinder head chamber combination. This is a very useful measurement. Remember, if you change any of the above items, the static compression ratio changes.

For example, if you changed from a head gasket that was 0.022-inch thick to one that was 0.038-inch thick, the total cylinder volume increases and the static compression decreases. If you changed from a domed piston to a flat-top piston, the static compression decreases, because the total volume above the piston increases. These are all measurements of total cylinder volume made while the engine is static and not running.

Dynamic compression is the measurement of compression while the engine and its particular combination of parts are running. What you must understand is that the parts you choose for your engine have a direct effect on the dynamic compression of the running engine. One of the most important part selections is the cam timing. Remember that the cam does not instantly open or instantly close the valve when the piston is at the top or bottom of the stroke. It physically can't be done. Most camshafts start to open the intake valve before the piston actually reaches TDC on the exhaust stroke.

The piston then swings over and starts down the cylinder on the intake stroke; and since the intake valve is open, air and fuel are pulled into the cylinder. When the piston reaches BDC and actually starts to move up on the compression stroke, the intake valve is starting to close, but it is still open a little way. On the compression stroke, the piston goes up the cylinder wall a little before the intake valve actually closes and the piston starts to compress whatever volume is in the cylinder. This means that at lower RPM, while the intake valve is open on the upward compression stroke, part of the air/fuel mixture and residual exhaust gases may get pushed back out of the intake valve toward the intake manifold. At higher RPM, there is not enough time for this to happen. After the intake valve closes, the piston keeps going up on the compression stroke and the spark occurs a little before the piston reaches TDC. The cylinder fires and the piston heads back down the cylinder on the power stroke.

Here's an example: You might have noticed that when a high-lift, long-duration camshaft is put into an otherwise stock low-compression engine, the engine runs differently. The engine may not want to idle at a low speed, say 750 rpm. It coughs and spits or just dies when you try to set the idle speed under 1,000 rpm. You blip open the throttle and as the RPM increases, the engine seems to smooth out and then really jumps right up on the tach. You find out that you have to set the idle around 1,500 rpm before the engine sits there and idles, but it still may idle roughly with a distinctive lope and *rump-rump* sound from the exhaust.

You probably heard that putting a bigger, longer duration cam into an engine would make it run better, but now that the change has been made, it seems that the performance isn't what was expected. It's hard to pull away from a traffic light, the engine wants to stall when put it in gear, and you have to coax it along until the RPM increases, then the engine pulls smoothly, until the next traffic light and the fight to keep the engine going starts all over again. You start to think there has been a mistake made with the cam, but it's not the camshaft, it is the parts combination that isn't working well.

Now, let's go back to that intake valve closing point. You figured out the static compression ratio, but a cam with a very late intake valve closing point was installed. The static compression measurements told you that you had a certain amount of volume in the cylinder, but because the intake valve was open during part of the compression stroke, the actual volume trapped in the running engine is less than what you calculated when you used your static compression ratio formula.

The piston had already moved up part of the cylinder before the intake valve closed. This pushed some of the incoming air/fuel mixture back through the still-open intake valve and back up the intake passages toward the carb. The air/fuel mix in the intake passages doesn't know whether it's coming or going. More to the point, the actual volume that the piston compresses is less than what you thought it would be because dynamic compression is not the same as static compression. You may have an engine with a static compression of 8.5:1, but if you chose incorrect parts, the dynamic compression of the engine may be as little as 3.0:1. That's why the engine pulls so badly. There's hardly any dynamic compression or cylinder pressure on the example engine when it runs at lower RPM. The engine picked up at higher RPM because there was not enough time for much of the mixture to be pushed out of the intake valve.

The cylinder pressure, developed when the piston reached TDC on the compression stroke and the mixture was fired, was lower because it had less total volume to compress. Cylinder pressure is also a way of thinking about torque. The more cylinder pressure, the more torque the engine has. The less cylinder pressure, the less torque the engine puts out. Increases in cam duration necessitate increases in the static compression of the engine to keep the cylinder pressures where they should be. The way to do this is to increase the piston dome or use a smaller combustion chamber volume in the head, or both.

When you choose a camshaft, take a look at the information supplied by the cam maker. When does the intake valve close in relation to BDC? The cam makers show this measurement in degrees of crank rotation. When the piston is at BDC, it's at 180 degrees; when the piston is at 0 degrees, it's at TDC. For example, a cam card may show that the intake valve closes at 82 degrees ABDC. That means that the piston is on its way up on the compression stroke and is almost halfway up the cylinder before the intake valve is totally closed. Halfway up the cylinder would be 90 degrees ABDC.

In this example, the volume in the cylinder bore that is actually compressed by the piston is almost one-half of what was in the cylinder when the piston was all the way down (BDC). If you had installed a different cam with an intake valve that closed 35 degrees ABDC, the piston would compress more cylinder volume because the piston would barely have moved up when the intake valve closed. Dynamic compression and cylinder pressure increases and the engine makes more power.

The idea is to get the best combination possible. Generally, if you build a stock, carbureted, street engine with 8.25 to 9.0:1 static compression, you need a cam with an intake closing point that is compatible with this static compression. That means a short-duration cam with an intake closing point that occurs quickly after the piston reaches BDC. This traps more volume in the cylinder to be compressed, and the cylinder pressures increase to where they should be.

Now you should understand why sticking a long-duration cam into an otherwise stock, low static compression engine doesn't usually work out. The stock static compression of the engine may be 8.25:1, but with a long-duration cam, the intake valve closes much later, not enough volume gets trapped in the cylinder, and the dynamic compression of the engine decreases so much that the engine no longer runs well. Cylinder pressure and dynamic compression are so low that the engine can't get out of its own way until the RPM of the engine reaches a point where there isn't enough time to bleed off as much cylinder pressure.

The faster you spin an engine, the less time is available for everything to work properly. At higher RPM, say above 4,000, the valves are open for less time, air and fuel have less time to move down the intake passages, and the piston is moving up and down in the cylinder much more quickly. There is less time for the exhaust to be pushed out of the engine. In order for the engine to make more power, you have to figure out a way to get more air/fuel into and out of the engine at these high-RPM speeds.

You also want to develop as much cylinder pressure as your parts combination allows while avoiding detonation. So now you can keep the valves open longer by increasing the cam duration (this is the amount of crank rotation that the valves are open). You can also increase how far the valve opens, so you use a cam with a higher lift. You can also increase the speed of the valve opening and closing by using a roller cam.

Now, something else is going on. In a performance engine with a good intake and a properly set up induction, the air/fuel mix has a certain velocity, mass, and momentum. On the compression stroke, at higher RPM, the mixture can continue to pack into the cylinder while the intake valve is open, even though the piston has started to move up. This is one of those small things that happens and will increase the power of an engine parts combination setup to take advantage of it.

Now you realize why the dynamic compression of the engine can be too low if the intake valve closes later. You must increase the static compression on the engine in order to make up for this by adding domed pistons or decrease the chamber volume by installing cylinder heads that have smaller combustion chambers. The cylinder holds less total volume now, but the cylinder volume you still have is squeezed into an even smaller space. The static compression is higher, as are the dynamic compression and cylinder pressure.

Add tube exhaust headers so the exhaust flows out more quickly. Also add better heads and a better designed intake manifold. Even though there is less time to pull air into the cylinder, the superior heads and better intake ports on the manifold allow you to get more air and fuel in the engine more quickly at higher RPM by taking into account the inertia of a fast-moving column of intake charge. The longer-duration cam combination starts to work and produces more power than the stock combination but at higher RPM.

However, you must still consider the static compression that your engine develops. If you plan on using unleaded pump gasoline, the static compression should be 9.5:1 or less. Race fuels with higher octane ratings (105 and above) resist detonation at higher compression and cylinder pressure levels. Using aluminum heads allows more static compression because they transfer heat more quickly and help resist detonation.

Think about an engine with a supercharger or a turbocharger. When you check the static compression on many of these engines, it might be as low as 7.0:1. These two types of blowers push more air/fuel into the engine so the cylinder volume is artificially and mechanically increased. Dynamic compression is increased when the blower or turbo engine is running. Cylinder pressures increase; more power and torque are made. Nitrous-oxide injected engines do the same thing, but instead of mechanically increasing cylinder volume, nitrous engines do it with chemistry, by making the air/fuel mixture cooler and denser and providing additional oxygen molecules to burn additional fuel.

Along these lines, blower or nitrous engines need different cam timing. Because of the artificially increased cylinder volume created, more exhaust cam timing and a bigger exhaust valve may be beneficial, along with a larger exhaust system. Cam lobe separation angles on a blower engine should also be wider.

This is why cam makers ask so many questions when you talk to them about cam selection. They want to know what kind of vehicle you have, how big the engine is, how much the car weighs, what kind of transmission you are going to use, and what rear end ratio you have. What is the static compression of your engine, what kind of heads, intake, carb, exhaust system, and most importantly, what do you want to do with the engine? Drive it on the street and use pump gasoline? Pull a trailer? Get better mileage? Go drag racing, stock car racing, or road racing and use higher octane racing fuels? Do you want a smooth idle? Do you want to make power at low RPM? Or do you want an engine that makes power at high RPM?

## Valve Lifters

If you are rebuilding an engine and intend to use the old cam and lifters again, there are some things to keep in mind. First, it's easier and safer to simply replace the cam and lifters during the rebuild. Unless the engine has very low miles or wear, while the engine is that far apart, in most cases it's time for a new cam and lifters. Which reminds me, putting used lifters on a new cam is definitely not something you should contemplate or do.

If you do plan to reuse the cam and lifters, start by visually inspecting and measuring the cam lobes to make sure they are not worn out. If they pass inspection and are okay to reuse, then check the lifters for wear. If each lifter still has a crown on the foot of the lifter, they can be reused. During disassembly, you must take the lifters out of the engine and sort them according to which lifter bore they came out of because they must be installed in the same lifter bore and on the same cam lobe. Otherwise, you run the risk of the cam lobe or lifter quickly self-destructing and spreading small metal particles all around your engine.

## Hydraulic Flat Tappets

Chevrolet Performance offers a set of hydraulic flat tappets as PN 12371044, which includes 16 PN 5232720 lifters. These can be used on 1986-and-older Gen 1 and II blocks. The lifters are designed for use with standard length pushrod kit (PN 12495491).

## Factory Production Hydraulic Roller Tappets

Production hydraulic roller lifters (such as PN 17120735) do not need periodic lifter adjustment, similar to their flat-tappet hydraulic cousins. Chevy Performance offers PN 12371042, which is a set of 16 lifters designed for 1986-and-newer Gen I blocks. This kit is also supplied with eight valve lifter guides, the retainer, and its retainer bolts and washers.

The stock GM production hydraulic roller lifters are longer than a flat-tappet lifter and need shorter pushrods (7.122 inches) which are available as PN 12371041 in a complete set or PN 10241740 as a single.

## Aftermarket Roller Tappets

A number of aftermarket cam makers produce hydraulic or mechanical roller cams for Chevy small-block engines. Generally, if you are using an aftermarket roller cam, you should follow suit with the company's roller lifters, as well as its pushrods, both of which may be different lengths than Chevy production hydraulic lifters. Likewise, the pushrod length required may be different.

As an upgrade, aftermarket roller cams and roller lifters are also available to fit Gen I blocks that were originally fitted with flat-tappet cams. If you plan to upgrade from a flat tappet cam to a roller tappet cam and lifters, it is best to source a complete kit from a single manufacturer. A complete kit will be engineered to work together and eliminate any guesswork when it comes to spring rates, pushrod guide plates, lifter retainers, and such.

## Vacuum Storage Tanks and Electric Vacuum Pumps

If you are using a lumpy camshaft on the street and are having trouble producing enough engine vacuum to run your power-assisted brakes or other vacuum-operated accessories, there are some choices to solve your problem. A number of aftermarket companies offer an inexpensive vacuum storage tank. These tanks build up and store the necessary amount of vacuum to operate your power brakes and other vacuum-operated accessories.

There is also the option of running an electric vacuum pump. An electric vacuum pump, available through the aftermarket, can be used to help operate power brakes or other vacuum-operated accessories if you are using a lumpy cam that results in lowered engine vacuum.

*Inside a hydraulic lifter reveals several different components.*

*Chevrolet has used hydraulic and hydraulic roller lifters and cams in most of its engines (a small number of high-horsepower models in the 1960s used solid lifters). The hydraulic roller lifters are on the left with a conventional flat-tappet hydraulic lifter on the right.*

## Pushrods

Chevrolet Performance and aftermarket suppliers offer a number of pushrod lengths, wall thicknesses, and metal alloys. Remember to use the correct length needed to maintain pushrod geometry. If you are building a stock engine, there generally is not much to concern yourself with on pushrod length. Just make sure they are clean, straight, and show no signs of damage or wear to the tips or the shafts. Some pushrods are marked "up" to indicate the hardened end that points toward the rocker arm. This is usually found on a pushrod that is intended for use with a guide plate and has a hardened section on one end to fit inside a guide plate. Most other non-hardened pushrods can be used with either end toward the rocker arm.

PN 14044874 is a 5/16-inch diameter pushrod for a flat tappet lifter and measures 7.724 inches. Another pushrod is available that is 0.100-inch longer as PN 366277. A set of 16 standard length (7.122-inch) pushrods for hydraulic rollers is available as PN 12371041. These are for use in second design ZZ-series engines without guide plates.

If the deck surfaces of the block or heads have been milled extensively or if you are using a high-lift cam, changing the rocker arm ratio or using a longer or shorter valve stem may require a different length pushrod. Roller cams require different pushrod lengths because the roller lifters are at different lengths than a flat-tappet-style lifter.

Most pushrods for small-blocks are 5/16 inch in diameter; however, other diameters are available through the aftermarket. Beefy diameter pushrods will be needed if you are building a race engine and your valve spring pressures require a larger diameter to avoid pushrod deflection. Note that the pushrods found in 1987-on Gen I engines with factory hydraulic roller cams and lifters are 0.630-inch shorter than the factory pushrods used with flat-tappet cams.

## Roller Lifter Guideplates

Hydraulic roller tappets need to be secured through the use of lifter retainer bars used on factory roller cam applications. On late-model blocks that were equipped with roller lifters, there is a roller lifter retainer plate that bolts to the block in the lifter valley. This retainer, sometimes referred to as the "valley spider," places a small load on the cast retainers that fit over the hydraulic roller tappets.

Chevy Performance offers a complete kit with hydraulic roller tappets (PN 17120735), lifter guides, the lifter retainer, and hardware for 1986-and-newer Gen I blocks as PN 12371042 designed for roller tappets. This kit takes a cue from the now popular Gen III engine and provides the ability to change the cam without removing the intake and lifters.

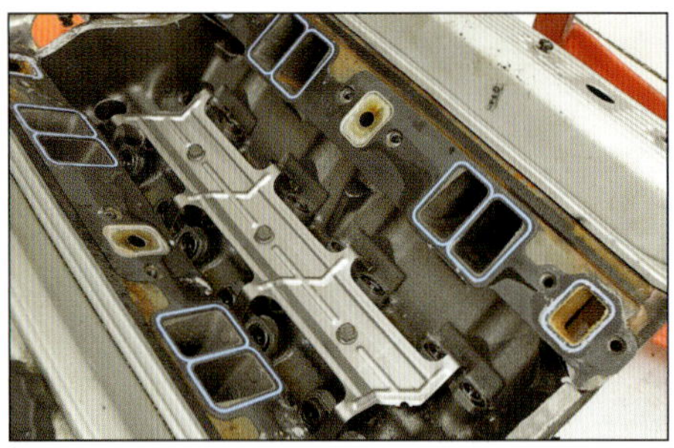

***The roller lifter retainer plate is bolted to three bosses that are cast into the block lifter valley. Also note the revised 72-degree intake manifold center bolt angles found on these late-model Gen I heads.***

***The valley spider keeps the roller lifter locating bars from moving in this production roller engine. The pushrods used with the production roller cam and roller lifters are slightly shorter than the pushrods used with flat-tappet cams.***

## Pushrod Guideplates

Pushrod guideplates are used with heads that have screw-in rocker arm studs. Cylinder heads that have pressed-in rocker arm studs do not use guideplates. Guideplates are marked "up" or "down"; make sure they are installed in the proper direction.

For production and Bowtie cast-iron heads with screw-in studs, Chevy Performance offers PN 3973418. These are for screw-in studs and should be used with self-aligning rockers. The slots are 0.0325 inch, and four are required per head.

***In many higher-RPM applications, it is good to run a pushrod guideplate. Chevrolet used these with standard rocker arms and screw-in rocker studs on production cast-iron and Bowtie 23-degree cast-iron heads. Corvette aluminum heads, Bowtie aluminum heads, and heads using self-aligning rail type rocker arms use different guideplates. This example is from Manley, an aftermarket leader in valvetrains.***

## Pushrod Part Numbers

Production standard pushrod length for factory non-roller cams is 7.794 inches overall. Pushrods for factory hydraulic roller cams are 0.630-inch shorter (7.164 inches) to accommodate the longer factory hydraulic roller lifters. If you have installed a high-lift cam, longer stem valves, or are using nonproduction block deck heights, you may need to use a different-length pushrod in order to maintain accurate valvetrain geometry.

Heavy-duty Chevy pushrods are case hardened to work with hardened guide plates. They have thicker walls and are very stiff to prevent deflection. ■

| Part Number | Specs |
|---|---|
| 366277 | Flat tappet, 5/16-inch diameter, +0.100-inch length, heavy-duty, 1010 steel 0.075-inch wall, hardened tip inserts |
| 14044874 | Flat tappet, 5/16-inch diameter, 7.724-inch length, heavy-duty, 1010 steel 0.075-inch wall, hardened tip inserts |
| 10046173 | Hydraulic roller, 5/16-inch diameter, for use with Gen I hydraulic roller cam, guide plate (PN 10111771) and guided 1.5:1 stamped rocker arms (PN 10066063 or 10089648). |
| 10241740 | Hydraulic roller, 5/16-inch diameter, for use in second design ZZ-series engines without guide plates, heavy-duty, 1010 steel 0.600-inch wall, 7.122-inch length |
| 12371041 | Set of 16 PN 10241740 |
| Custom pushrod lengths and diameters are available from aftermarket suppliers. | |

Hardened pushrod guideplates (PN 14011051) with narrow pushrod slots can be used with aluminum Bowtie heads with flat-tip rocker arms and screw-in rocker arm studs. These aluminum Bowtie head guideplates are stamped with the number "05" and have the correct pushrod spacing for the aluminum Bowtie heads.

Stock applications using a self-aligning rocker arm do not need a pushrod guideplate.

### Rocker Arms

The small-block Chevy has used a number of different production rocker arms and rocker arm ratios over the years. Some were adjustable and some late-model rocker arm assemblies are not.

From 1955 through 1987, Chevrolet used a stamped nonguided flat-tip rocker arm (obsolete PN 3974290) with a nominal rocker ratio of 1.5:1. This rocker arm gives excellent service and reliability in street-operated engines with valve lifts up to 0.510 inch. At higher valve lifts, use a long slot rocker.

Long slot, stamped, and non-guided rocker arms are available through the aftermarket. If you put non-guided flat-tip rocker arms on 1987-on heads, you must switch to a hardened guideplate to align the pushrods.

In 1988, production Gen I small-block V-8 stamped rocker arms were changed from a flat-surface tip to a guided (also called a rail or self-aligning) tip over the valve stem. These stamped self-aligning rocker arms (PN 10089648) have the same 1.5:1 nominal rocker ratio as earlier designs and are interchangeable. Chevy Performance offers a set of 16 of these rockers that includes pivot balls and nuts for 3/8-inch studs.

The use of self-aligning rocker arms also requires that the valve stem be slightly longer so that it protrudes farther above the spring retainer. Valve stems intended for use with earlier-style non-guided rocker arms are slightly shorter. Don't mix this up because without enough valve stem protruding above the retainer, the bumps or rails on the sides of the self-aligning rocker arm can touch the retainer. Use the correct retainers and valve stem lengths.

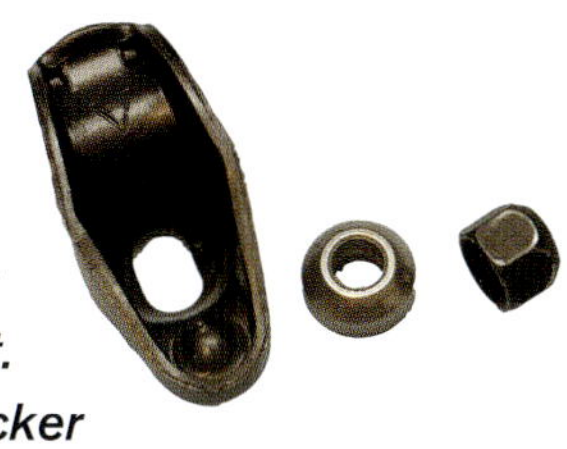

*A stamped production rocker arm, rocker arm ball, and nut allow rocker arm lash adjustment. Some late-model rocker arm assemblies are non-adjustable net lash setups.*

*These inexpensive, small, aluminum rocker arm clips fit onto stamped production rocker arms and help keep hot oil from splashing all over your engine compartment when you are adjusting valve lash on a running motor.*

***Self-aligning stamped rocker arms have been used since 1988 on small-block V-8s.***

***Kit PN 12495490 is supplied with 1.5:1 ratio self-aligning stamped rockers, pivot balls, and nuts. (Photo Courtesy Chevrolet Performance)***

***Most aftermarket roller tip rocker arms are self-aligning as well. Notice how the valve stem rides up and into the rocker arm while the rocker assembly surrounds the roller and valve tip.***

***Chevy Performance offers a set of aluminum self-aligning roller rocker arms. They're available in a 1.5:1 ratio (PN 19210728) and a 1.6:1 ratio (PN 19210729).***

Several cam manufacturers offer 1.52:1- and 1.6:1-ratio aluminum roller rockers, (1.6:1-ratio self-aligning roller rockers from Crane Cams were used on the production 1996 LT4 350s). These roller rockers have the self-aligning feature of the stamped production guided rocker arms. Crane's self-aligning rocker arms have narrow bodies that clear the production center-bolt valve-cover-bolt bosses on heads that use them and fit under factory valve covers. The self-aligning roller rockers are offered by Chevrolet Performance as a set of 16 under PN 12495490/1.5:1 ratio and PN 12370839/1.6:1 ratio. Guideplates are not recommended with these roller rocker arms. These two part numbers are designed to use the standard 3/8 rocker studs. The production 1996 LT4s use a stepped nonadjustable rocker stud. These LT4 1.6:1 ratio roller rockers are not the same as the 1.6:1 ratio Bowtie roller rockers.

Aftermarket suppliers can provide rocker arms with different rocker ratios.

Keep in mind that if you are changing from the stock 1.5:1 rocker ratio to a higher 1.6:1 ratio, you need to check the clearance between the valve spring and retainer and the fulcrum of the rocker arm. Also check that you have enough clearance between the open valve and the piston deck, both before TDC and after. Altering the rocker ratio may be beneficial in some engines. Some engines respond to changing all of the rockers to a higher ratio, while other engines may respond to only adding higher ratios on the intake or exhaust valves. Some engines may not experience an improvement at all. It depends on a number of factors.

The stock stamped rocker arms can accommodate valve lifts up to about 0.510 inch, but if you use a cam with higher than stock valve lifts, you really should use a rocker arm with a long slot in order to provide enough clearance to the rocker arm stud.

## Rocker Arm Studs and Bolts, Balls, and Nuts

Since the small-block has been in production, things have changed over the years in this area, too. Rocker arm studs have been both pressed-in (on low- and medium-performance heads) and others are screw-in studs (on high-performance heads).

In later years, such as in the Gen II LT4, nonadjustable net lash production valvetrains were incorporated. The LT4s use a special stud, roller rocker arm, nut, and ball that only require that the nut be tightened to specifications to give a net lash setting when using the production hydraulic

## Rocker Arm Studs

Over the years, various methods have been used to position the rocker arms on small-block Chevy heads.

### *Pressed-In Rocker Studs*

Gen I heads from 1955-on used 3/8-inch-diameter pressed-in rocker arm studs on low- and mid-performance engines. These give excellent service for their respective applications. Issues will occur when a high-lift camshaft is used with higher-than-stock valve spring pressures as the pressed-in stud could be pulled out of its socket. Early racers tried to solve this problem by drilling a small hole in the rocker arm stud boss, then through the pressed-in stud. A pin was then pressed into this hole to lock the pressed-in stud in place. This was cumbersome and still not a great solution.

### *Screw-In Rocker Studs*

In an effort to improve valvetrain stability at high RPM and higher valve spring open pressures, the pressed-in stud would be pulled out. Then the bosses were cut down and the existing holes were drilled and threaded to accept a screw-in stud. Commonly 3/8-inch-diameter screw-in studs were used; however, 7/16-inch screw-in studs have also been used to further increase strength and prevent rocker arm stud deflection in race situations. Chevrolet itself installed 3/8-inch screw-in studs in many high-performance cast-iron and aluminum heads.

| Part Number | Specs |
|---|---|
| 10168410 | 3/8-inch screw-in stud for Gen I-style heads |
| 3921912 | 7/16-inch screw-in stud for Gen I-style heads, use with small-block Bowtie rocker arms with provision for 7/16-inch stud |
| 12552126 | 3/8-inch screw-in stud for Gen II 1995 to 1996 LT1 and aluminum service replacement LT4 head (PN 12363287), which is intended for use on 1992-and-up LT1 motors |

The 1996 Gen II 350 LT4 production heads use a screw-in stud also, but this bolt has a shoulder and a long, unthreaded portion. These LT4 production studs hold 1.6:1 aluminum roller rockers, which are not adjustable. Tightening the LT4's rocker arm nuts and bringing them down onto the shoulder of the stud results in a nonadjustable net lash valvetrain. ■

roller cam. Since production hydraulic roller cams are used with these "0" or net lash engines, no valve lash adjustment is anticipated or possible.

## Valves

Depending on the head casting that you use, a number of valve diameters are available. Some Gen I low-performance heads received 1.72-inch intakes and 1.5-inch exhaust, partly because the small-bore engines had cylinder barrels and head combustion chamber volumes that would shroud a larger valve diameter as it opened.

Other common sizes are 1.84-, 1.94-, 2.00-, 2.02-, and 2.05-inch-diameter intake valves. Exhaust valves of 1.50-, 1.55-, and 1.60-inch-diameter have been used, depending on the head casting and application. Stainless steel, sodium-filled, flat-faced, dish-faced, and undercut stem valves are available.

Physically, some heads do not have room for the larger valve diameters. There may be clearance or valve shrouding problems with small-bore engines that have large valve combinations. Check for any valve clearance or shrouding problems, both in the combustion chamber and with the tops of the cylinder barrels. The Gen I Corvette aluminum 113 casting, for instance, comes with 1.94/1.50-inch valves and it is limited to a 2.00/1.55-inch valve-diameter enlargement.

Remember, if you are adding larger diameter valves, you may have to unshroud the combustion chamber walls to improve airflow. The larger diameter valve edges come closer to the existing chamber walls. If you do not unshroud the larger valves by removing the appropriate amounts from the chamber walls, there may not be an improvement in airflow.

## Valve Springs

It is very important that the valve springs match the cam requirements. A valve spring's installed height should also be adjusted correctly. If you are building a high-performance or race engine, the valve spring pressures must be checked in both the closed and open positions to ensure that the springs are delivering the pressures they are supposed to.

If you are using a non-stock combination with a wider-than-stock spring diameter, you may have to cut the valve spring pockets on the heads to get things to fit. Some head

*Valve springs are vital to the performance and longevity of the valvetrain. Ensure that you are using the correct springs to match the range of the camshaft and retainer. (Photo Courtesy Chevrolet Performance)*

castings are very thin near the spring pocket. Water jackets are located nearby. Determine whether the pocket can be deepened or widened in diameter before you start cutting the spring pocket. Some aftermarket performance springs are tapered or barrel-shaped. These springs were designed to fit a stock-diameter spring pocket, yet deliver increased spring pressures.

Recently, Chevrolet adapted beehive valve springs on its Fast Burn heads (PN 19300955), which are installed on several crate engines including the SP350, ZZ5, ZZ6, SP383, and others. The form of the beehive valve spring, as expected, is the shape of a beehive, which provides better high RPM valvetrain stability. Chevy offers a conversion kit (PN 19300952), which includes the springs (PN 12625033), cap (PN 19301708), seats (PN 19301707), and keepers (PN 19301709). This kit is intended only for Fast Burn heads and not compatible with Vortec heads.

Don't fall into the trap that more is better. If a cam calls for 300 pounds open spring pressure; 500 pounds open spring pressure with that cam is not necessarily better. In fact, it is a sure way of ruining the cam lobes.

The opposite is also true. Don't try to save money buying a performance or race cam and skipping new springs. The new cam may require a spring with completely different characteristics from your old valve springs. Buy the cam, lifters, springs, stem seals, retainers, and locks to match.

## Oil Seals

For years, Chevrolet used a valve stem that had two grooves cut into it near the valve stem tip. The upper groove was used to hold the retainer split keys, while the lower groove held an O-ring-style oil seal. The valve springs had oil splash caps that reduced the amount of oil going down the valve stem, so the small stem O-rings took care of the rest.

Umbrella-type stem seals have also been used with the stock springs and some dual springs as long as there was room inside the spring coils to fit an umbrella seal.

PC-type seals are smaller in diameter and slide onto the valve guides. They do a good job of oil sealing, and they fit inside just about any spring combination, including triple spring race setups. If the cylinder head you use did not originally come with PC-type oil seals, you can have your machinist cut down the top of valve guides to a smaller diameter so the PC seals slide on.

In the late 1980s, Chevrolet started using a one-groove valve stem. It dropped the valve stem O-rings on some engines and went with either a PC-type oil seal or an umbrella seal with a splash cap or both.

PN 460483 is a PC-type oil seal used on ZZ-series 350 crate engine aluminum heads.

PN 12511890 is an O-ring-style oil seal used on 11/32-inch valve stems.

PN 10212810 is a PC-stem oil seal used on a number of Gen II 350 LT4, ZZ4 heads, and several other Chevy Performance head assemblies.

If you are going to use a high-lift cam, make sure that the stem seals have enough clearance when the valve is at full lift.

## Retainers

Valve retainers must match the valve spring. Most Chevy valves have 11/32-inch-diameter valve stems and use 7-degree retainers and matching locks. Be careful if you decide to use Chevy's aluminum retainers or aftermarket aluminum varieties. At higher valve spring pressures, the spring can cut into the bottom of an aluminum retainer. If you want to use a lightweight retainer, Chevrolet has a number of reduced-weight steel retainers available.

If you are building a serious race engine, you can use an aftermarket titanium version for the ultimate in reduced weight and increased strength.

Each GM retainer is intended to be used with a particular valve spring. Be careful as the valve springs must match the cam requirements, and the retainers must match the spring and valve stem diameters. Ten-degree retainers and matching 10-degree locks are available from aftermarket suppliers if your race engine requires more retainer strength.

## Valve Stem Locks

The production 11/32-inch valve stem locks or split keys are PN 24503856. These valve stem locks are 7-degree keepers and a set of 32 is available as PN 12495503.

Ten-degree locks and matching 10-degree retainers are available from aftermarket suppliers if you use a high-performance or race cam with high spring pressures and you need a high-strength setup that reduce the chances of a valve lock failure.

## Stamped Rocker Arm Ratios

Gen I and II Chevy small-block stamped production rocker arms have a theoretical rocker arm ratio of 1.52:1. The term theoretical or nominal is used because the blueprints call for a 1.52:1 ratio, but the actual stamped factory rocker arms may not achieve this ratio. It is very difficult to mass-produce a stamped rocker that produces the ratio in every part made. When actually measured, the rocker arm may only operate at a ratio of 1.45:1 or another may measure out at 1.49:1.

For a daily driven, stock engine, the fact that some of the rocker arm ratios are off is of no consequence and does not affect the way in which the engine runs or its longevity. However, if you are using a performance camshaft or plan to race an engine, keep the rocker arm ratio in mind. If the Gen I measured ratio is less than 1.52:1, the amount of lift to the valve is less than you expected. Some valves may open more or less than others, which will affect the overall performance. It is important to use a set of rocker arms that provide a true and consistent measured ratio.

In 1988, Chevrolet small-blocks began using a self-aligning or rail-type stamped rocker arm (PN 10066063). These rocker arms have a bump on either side of the valve stem end. These bumps keep the push-rod's side-to-side movement under control and center the valve tip on the rocker arm. This rocker arm is available with a ball and nut under PN 10089648.

Keep in mind that the 1996 350 LT4 Gen II engine uses a 1.6:1 ratio self-aligning roller rocker arm. These roller rockers fit under the production valve covers and clear the center mounted valve cover hold down bolts. Not all roller rockers do this. ■

### Valve Covers

Besides the production valve covers, Chevrolet Performance and aftermarket suppliers offer a vast array of valve covers for the Gen I or II small-block. If you have installed a high-lift cam, nonproduction roller rocker, or a stud girdle, you probably have to use tall valve covers to ensure valvetrain clearance. Tall covers may not fit in some applications if you intend to use stock A/C brackets or if there is a clearance problem with the power brake vacuum boosters or A/C and heater core boxes.

Early valve covers were bolted onto the heads at the flange edges, while late-model covers use bolts that enter the center of the cover. Make sure you determine which of these systems your heads require and match the covers to the heads. Some aftermarket heads are being produced that allow you to use either style of valve cover.

With the advent of higher, machined gasket rails on heads made after 1986 combined with the use of a better gasket and valve cover gasket surface, leaks from small-block valve covers are a thing of the past. Plus, these later valve covers use center bolt hold-down locations.

Chevrolet Performance offers a number of different valve covers from stamped to cast with perimeter bolts or center bolts. Many other styles of short and tall valve covers are offered through the aftermarket as well.

*The valve cover on top is for use on a 1955 to 1958 head due to the staggered bolt holes on the top. Both top bolt holes are inward of the bottom holes. In 1959, the holes were aligned as shown in the bottom example and lasted like that until Chevrolet moved to the center bolt design.*

*Gen I valve covers made before 1986 tended to leak if everything wasn't perfectly straight or flat. The bars (PN 14082321 and 14044820, chrome) under the valve cover bolt shown here are available to increase the hold down force and keep your older small-block oil leak free.*

*The Gen II LT1 has center bolt valve covers. With the raised rail heads introduced in 1986 and better cover gaskets, the center bolt valve covers cured the problem of leaky valve covers.*

## Chevrolet Valve Springs

It is extremely important that you use a valve spring that matches the operating range of your camshaft and the retainer. Check for correct installed height and that there is no coil bind at full valve lift and there is clearance for the retainers, valve rotators (if you are using them), oil seals, rocker arm slots, and the tops of the valve guides. If you use an aftermarket camshaft, use the matching valves and retainers and install the springs at the recommended installed height. Do not use more or less valve spring pressure than your cam requires. ■

| Part Number | Spring Type | Outside Diameter (inches) | Pressure at Installed Height (pounds) | Retainer Part Number | Valve Seal Kit | Technical Notes |
|---|---|---|---|---|---|---|
| 94666580 | Single with damper | 1.241 | 80 at 1.700 inches | 14003715 | 10132715 | Production spring for 350/290 hp engines |
| 10134358 | Single with damper | 1.273 | 110 at 1.700 inches | 14003974 | 10132715 | Chrome silicon steel; use with aluminum heads PN 12556463; orange color code |
| 330585 | Dual | 1.379 | 140 at 1.750 inches | NA | 10132715 | Use with cam PN 3927140, and all moderate lift racing cams |
| 10206040 | Single spring | 1.300 | 85 at 1.780 inches | 10168424 | N/A | 1992–1993 LT1 production Corvette engine |
| 12625033 | Single spring | 1.320 | 101 at 1.780 inches | 19301708 | N/A | CT400, ZZ5, ZZ6, ZZ383, SP383 (Beehive Spring) |
| 12499224 | Spring kit | 1.320 | 101 at 1.780 inches | 19301708 | N/A | Kit of 16 springs PN 12625033 (Beehive Spring) |
| 10212811 | Single spring | 1.250 | 80 at 1.700 inches | 10241744 | N/A | CT350/350, 350 HO engines |
| 19154761 | Spring kit | 1.250 | 80 at 1.700 inches | 10241744 | N/A | Kit of 16 springs PN 10212811 |

## Checking Installed Spring Height

Here's a tip for checking installed height on valve springs. You can use a dial indicator caliper or a spring height micrometer specially made for this task or you can use a piece of very stiff wire or rod to make the measurement. Determine what the correct installed height of the spring should be. Most, but not all, Chevy small-block springs install at 1.70, 1.75, or 1.78 inches (follow the manufacturer's suggested installed spring heights).

The installed spring height is the distance from the surface of the spring pocket on the head to the bottom of the spring retainer. So put a valve in the head and put on the retainer and locks that you are going to use.

Let's assume that the installed spring height you need is 1.70 inches. Cut the wire or rod to that length plus a little extra and double-check it with a dial caliper. Make sure that the ends of the wire or rod are flat. If you have to grind or file the wire or rod, make sure the length is still correct. Keep removing material until the length is exactly 1.70 inches.

Now use the rod or wire to check the distance between the head and the retainer. If the retainer has a step on the bottom surface, measure the retainer surface farthest from the head, near the side edge of the retainer. How is it? If there is additional space, you can use spring shims to reduce the distance. Shims come in various thicknesses: 0.015, 0.030, and 0.060 inch. If the distance is shorter or less than the 1.70 inches required, make sure that the retainer is pulled up tight against the locks. If you are still short, there are other types of aftermarket retainers that sit slightly higher so that you can get the necessary installed spring height. On some combinations, you may have to use a valve stem that is longer than stock in order to get the installed height you need. Also, if you have removed the exhaust valve rotators from above the exhaust valve springs, the rotators should be replaced with a matching spring and retainer combination that gives the correct installed height.

Remember to check the valvetrain geometry, no matter what combination of parts you use. If you are going to be using the stock-style O-ring valve stem seal, remember to install the spring and compress it and the retainer before you install the O-ring on the valve stem. Also, it is a good idea to use a steel shim under the valve springs as used with aluminum heads. The shim keeps the spring ends from digging into the aluminum. Make allowances for the shim thickness when determining spring installed height on aluminum heads. ■

## Piston-to-Open-Valve Clearance

There are many clearances to check when you build an engine, and they are all important. There is one area that is often overlooked, however, especially by folks who don't build engines often. It's the piston-to-open-valve clearance. I want to talk about this because many enthusiasts aren't building a complete engine and in an effort to increase their engine performance replace the stock cam with another grind.

Too many times I have talked with people who have spent their hard-earned money on a replacement performance cam, taken the time to install it, fired the engine up, and then bent every valve in the heads. And in bad situations, broken pistons and ruined cylinder heads. They are disappointed, angry, frustrated, and embarrassed. Their hopes of doing something that would increase performance and their pride in doing the work themselves was shattered. The money they spent for the camshaft was wasted, and if they decide to fix the damage, the amount of time and money needed is far more.

All of this could have been avoided. You have to buy a cam that works with the other parts in the engine. Don't fall into the trap that you can put the highest lift cam you can find, install it, and everything is fine. Talk to the cam manufacturer before you make a decision on a particular grind. If your engine has stock production pistons, the amount of piston valve relief limits how much cam lift fits. Even if your engine has aftermarket pistons with generous valve relief, there still may be a clearance problem with particular cams. Piston-to-valve clearance can be affected by other factors, such as rocker arm ratio, how much the heads or block have been decked, head gasket compressed thickness, piston-deck-to-block-deck height, valve spring pressures, and their effect on valve float. Have you advanced or retarded the cam timing? Does the timing chain have too much slack? Are the lifters, pushrods, or valve stems the correct length? Did you install bigger valve diameters?

You may be able to install a high lift cam and even turn the engine over by hand without feeling anything hit. The problem is the valve edges may be just clearing the piston deck by a couple of thousandths of an inch or may even be just kissing the piston by a few thousandths. You won't know until the engine is revved or you float the valves the first time.

The only way to be sure is to check the open-valve-to-piston clearance. Believe me when I say that it is less expensive, less time-consuming, and less aggravating to check the clearance, than not to check it and have a valve hit the piston.

With the head off, you can use modeling clay to measure the clearance. Place a layer of clay on the piston deck over the valve reliefs. Put the head back on, with the same head gasket thickness that you intend to use, adjust the valves and turn the engine over through a number of full revolutions. Turn it over slowly and stop if you feel any hesitation or obstruction. Take the head off and measure the thickness of the clay. On a performance or race engine, there should be 0.080-inch intake clearance and 0.100 inch on the exhaust valve. The valve edge may come closest to the piston before or after TDC depending on cam timing. If you need more clearance, the piston valve reliefs can be deepened the appropriate amount or perhaps you can use a thicker head gasket.

Another method works with the heads on. Switch the valve springs with a checking spring. Use a degree wheel and dial indicator to measure the valve lift and locate the piston position. With the piston at TDC and the cam at full lift, you see how much farther the valve opens until it touches the piston deck. Check the clearance from 20 degrees BTDC through 20 degrees ATDC. If the minimum clearances are not found, deepen the valve reliefs appropriately or use a cam with less total lift or duration.

A stock production cam is usually not going to be a problem. Most cam makers know which of their performance grinds work without having to deepen valve reliefs. At some lift point, however, you need to check the clearances, and the bigger the cam lift, the more you need to check and confirm these clearances. ■

CHAPTER 7

# INDUCTION SYSTEM

Gen I and II intake manifolds were offered in cast iron or aluminum. The 1996-on Vortec small-blocks used an aluminum base with a composite plastic upper intake manifold with fuel injection. Over the years, Chevrolet used single 2-barrel and single 4-barrel carburetors made by Carter (WCFB, AFB, and Quadrajet), Rochester (4-Jet 4GC and 4MV Quadrajet), and Holley 4-barrel carburetors. Chevy also used 2x4 inline 4-barrels, 2x4 cross rams, Rochester mechanical fuel injection, single-unit Throttle Body Injection (TBI), 2xTBI crossfire throttle body injection, and tuned-port and multi-port electronic-fuel-injection intake manifolds. There was even a twin turbocharged, electronic-fuel-injected 350 Callaway Corvette engine option (RPO B2K) that was available from 1987 to 1991.

*For those of you craving simplicity in an engine compartment, here is what a 283 in a restored early Nova looks like. "Hey, where's the computer and fuel injection?"*

No tri-power (3x2) manifolds were factory installed on small-blocks (only big-block Corvettes from 1967 to 1969 were available with tri-power). If you must have a 3x2 intake or other intake manifold exotica, there are many shapes and sizes available through the aftermarket.

Most production aluminum intakes were used for high-performance applications, but some aluminum intakes on later-model small-blocks were designed for low and moderate performance. These moderate performers mostly are designed with a spreadbore carb pad to accept a Quadrajet carb. Many of the aluminum intakes were cast by the Winters Foundry, a long-time outside contractor for Chevrolet (it also made aluminum heads and water pumps for Chevrolet). These aluminum manifolds carry the Winters Foundry "snowflake" and "W" logo.

Beginning in 1987, most production intakes and cylinder heads had center intake manifold mounting bolt holes that were inclined 72 degrees instead of the former 90 degrees. These intakes and heads must be matched together, or as an alternative, you can elongate and spot face the two center bolt holes on each side of the intake to work with the later-style head bolt angles.

Vortec 5000 305s and Vortec 5700 350s, introduced in 1996, have only four bolts holding down each side of the intake manifold, and thus the Vortec cylinder heads, intake gaskets,

*Craving electronic fuel injection (EFI) without the hassle? Chevrolet Performance offers its Ram Jet intake manifold separately (or as a complete crate engine, PN 19417619). This intake assembly (PN 12498032) provides a cool-looking EFI system that is easy to adapt onto many small-blocks using Vortec cylinder heads.*

*This aluminum dual-plane intake is machined for a Carter carb as identified by the four equal-size holes.*

*This cast-iron 2-barrel intake features two heat-riser passages on the sides. It is important to use the correct carburetor gasket in this application. These types of passages were also used on 4-barrel intakes, such as with a Quadrajet, so make sure to use the correct gasket set and carb for the application.*

*Though Chevrolet never offered a tri-power setup on a small-block (big-block Corvettes used them), that didn't stop hot rodders! Aftermarket tri-carb intakes, similar to this one, are still available from companies such as Edelbrock.*

and intakes must be used together. The coolant passages between the Vortec heads and the intake are also unique. Vortec and Gen II engines have unique head/intake manifold bolt spacing and intake gaskets that must be matched.

Whichever intake manifold you use, make sure there is enough room to close the stock hood. Many hood heights do not allow the use of a high-rise aluminum intake, carb, and air cleaner. Chevrolet has many shorter aluminum intake designs that provide the necessary stock hood clearance.

Over the years, intake manifolds have had various features that you may or may not need for your interchange installations. Such features include EGR valve mounting bosses, oil filler tube mounting holes, various choke spring and choke hot air tube mounting bosses, heat riser channels cut into the carb mounting pads, heat riser holes in the carb pad, coil mounting bosses, heater hose nipple bosses, A/C mounting bracket bolt bosses, vacuum takeoff bosses, power brake vacuum takeoff bosses, fuel injector nozzle port locating bosses, and carb mounting pads for different types of carbs or multiple carbs. Make sure the intake manifold you use has the features, mounting bosses, and threaded holes you need for your application.

## Plenums

Generally, 4-barrel intakes have two types of plenums: split or open. A split, dual-plane, or divided plenum, is so-called because a divider splits it in half. This type of manifold works well on the street because it helps create low- and mid-RPM power, as well as generate a strong vacuum signal to the carb boosters at low RPM. Carb size on these manifolds can cover a larger CFM range because each cylinder pulls from only one-half of the total plenum volume.

An open plenum manifold has no center divider, and consequently, each cylinder has a much larger plenum volume from which to draw. These manifolds enable the cylinders to receive more volume at high RPM, but they lose some of

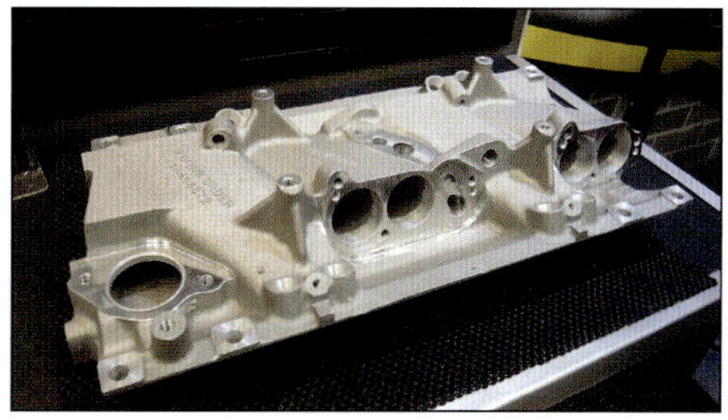

*Tuned Port Injection (TPI) was first offered in the mid 1980s and is still a popular upgrade from carburetors. Scoggin-Dickey Parts Center offers a TPI intake (PN SD3816) that bolts to the new-style raised-port Vortec heads (PN 12558060).*

*This grungy cast-iron 2-barrel intake is from a 283 out of a 1966 Nova. Notice the oil fill tube on the front of the manifold, which was used on all small-block intakes through 1968.*

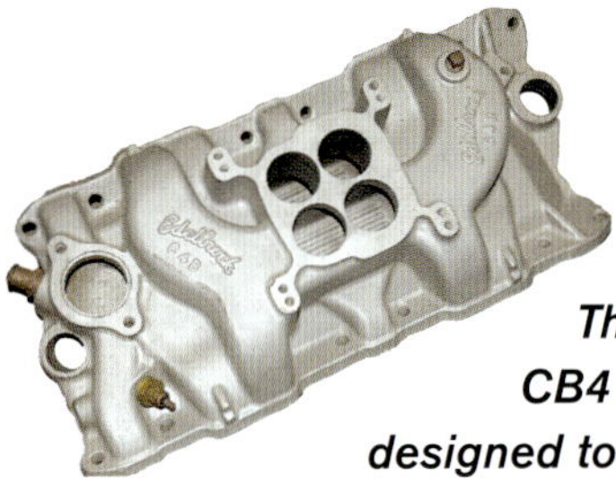

*This Edelbrock CB4 manifold was designed to install on mid-1960s small-blocks. It is set up for a Carter AFB carb and features the front oil fill tube.*

*Make sure the intake you use has the features you require. This Edelbrock manifold has provisions for both an EGR valve and a choke hot-air tube.*

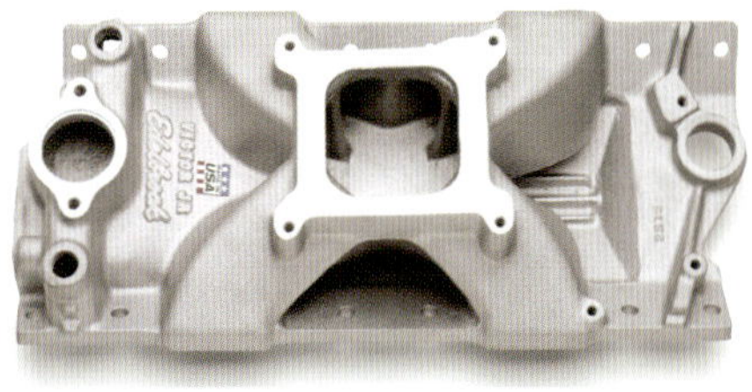

*The Edelbrock Victor Jr. aluminum, open-plenum intake is one of the most popular performance and racing intakes for small-block Chevys. (Photo Courtesy Edelbrock)*

*The intake casting number and casting date are found at the rear section of Chevrolet intakes. This example "C 20 8" means it was cast in the third month, March, on the 20th day in 1968.*

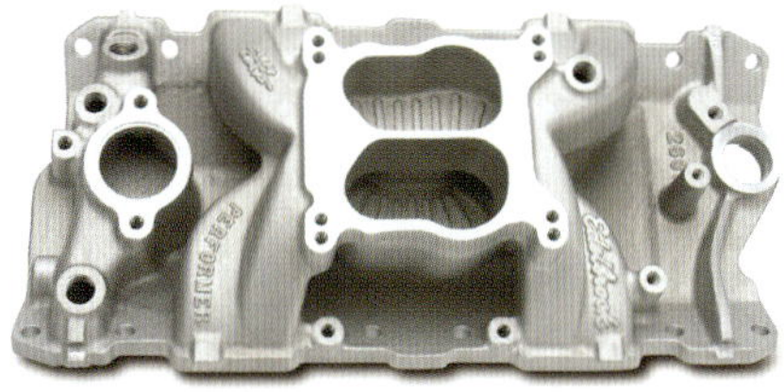

*Edelbrock offers several versions of its popular Air-Gap manifolds. This is the Performer Air-Gap, which is identified by the space between the bottom of the carb runners and the base of the intake. This air gap keeps the fuel charge cooler. (Photo Courtesy Edelbrock)*

their low-RPM power and response. Open plenum manifolds are more sensitive to carb CFM size, and they tend to work best within a narrower range of carb CFM sizes. Extending the port divider walls in an open plenum manifold and bringing them closer to the center of the plenum seems to add power.

Extending the divider walls used to be a hand-fabricated project, but a number of race intakes are now manufactured with this detail. Brodix offers aluminum, high-rise, open-plenum race manifolds with various features to fit various heads, and standard square flange or Dominator-style carbs. Brodix also offers an intake with a Dittmer-style round plenum/carb opening that uses a Holley Dominator carb. It can also have a "turtle" installed in the plenum floor, which helps direct fuel to the individual port runners.

A split plenum manifold allows the use of a carb CFM that is substantially larger than what might be considered minimum. A split plenum generally keeps engine vacuum higher at low- and mid-RPM power, and therefore, the carb booster signal and throttle response are crisp at low and middle RPM. However, as RPM increases, the split plenum manifold's smaller plenum volume becomes too small to feed the high-RPM airflow demand of the engine. Power falls off. A larger-than-normal-CFM carb may help the engine in this situation by providing additional volume and less restriction. Notching the plenum center divider wall can extend the RPM range of these manifolds.

The open-plenum-style manifold generally has the opposite characteristics of the split plenum. The engine has a large plenum volume to pull from, so at low-engine RPM the vacuum signal to the carb is not as strong as a split plenum, but as engine RPM increases (above 6,000 rpm), the open plenum starts to show some advantages. It's better able to meet the demands of a high winding or large cubic engine because the open plenum provides more volume for the individual cylinders to draw from.

Modern intake manifold design and advanced casting technologies have eliminated some of the characteristics found in early designs. Split-plenum, dual-plane manifolds have been created that work better at higher RPM than the old designs by improving intake runner and plenum design. The same can be said for open-plenum styles. Better design has made them more tractable at low- and mid-RPM ranges. In older manifolds, the angle at which the intake manifold runners met the intake ports on the head was too sharp. Modern single 4-barrel designs call for the intake manifold runners to curve more and meet the head port at a better angle, which improves flow.

Many of the newer manifolds are cast with a floor that isolates the hot oil that is found in the lifter valley from the intake manifold. This air gap passage above the manifold

*Two 4-barrel carbs on a tunnel ram intake make quite a show on a street rod, but performance is generally poor in the low- and mid-RPM ranges. These manifolds perform best on high-RPM race engines that have the other engine components properly matched to take advantage of the large airflow volume these manifold setups can produce.*

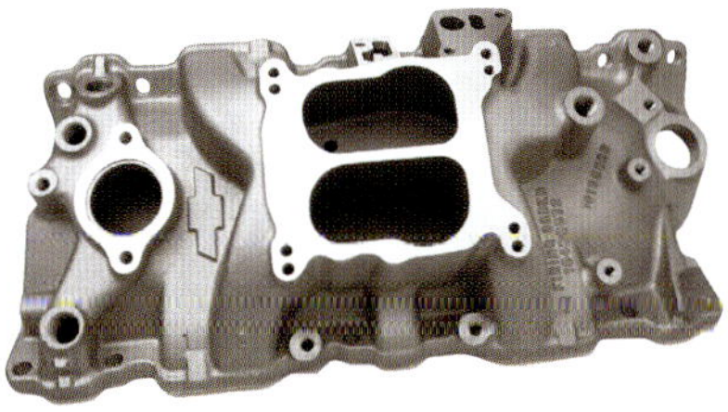

*Chevrolet offers aluminum intakes that have dual-bolt pattern carb flanges to fit square flange or spread-bore carbs. This is the ZZ-series intake (PN 10185063). (Photo Courtesy Chevrolet Performance)*

base floor helps reduce the temperature of the manifold runners and surface. Edelbrock offers a number of Air-Gap intakes for the small-block ranging from split-plenum Performer RPM designs to the Super Victor Jr. with an open plenum. Chevrolet Performance also offers aluminum intakes with this feature, primarily for racing applications.

Maximum-effort race engines that operate in the 6,500- to 10,000-rpm range are another story. Engines with race-prepared heads, efficient large tube race exhaust headers, and high RPM can use large Holley Dominator carbs, and open-plenum race manifolds, tunnel rams, or mechanical fuel injection. Whatever you do, don't put a tunnel ram manifold on top of a street-driven engine with stock heads unless you want to drive a dog. These types of manifolds are meant for high-RPM race engines that can effectively use the volume of air made available by tunnel rams. It might look cool, but this combination kills bottom-end torque, which is just what you need in a street-driven vehicle. Stick with a

## Intake Manifold Casting Numbers

| Casting Number | Model Year | Engine/Application |
|---|---|---|
| 340261 | 1974–1976 | 350/160, 185, 195, 245, 250 hp Pass, Vette, Nova, Chevelle, Monte Carlo, Camaro, CI, 4MV |
| | 1974–1976 | 400/180 Pass, Chevelle, Monte Carlo, CI, 4MV |
| 340281 | 1982–1985 | 305, 350, CI, 4MV |
| 346249 | 1975 | 350/155, 165, 205 hp, Pass, Vette, Nova, Chevelle, Monte Carlo, Camaro, CI, 4MV, EGR |
| | 1975 | 400/175, Pass, Chevelle, Monte Carlo, CI, 4MV, EGR |
| 346250 | | 305,350, CI, 4MV |
| 458520 | | 305, 350, AL, 4MV |
| 1403372 | 1980–1982 | 350 Camaro, Vette, "Cross Fire" 2xTBI injection |
| 3711348 | 1955 | 265, Pass, Vette, CI, 4GC |
| 3728725 | 1956 | 265/225, Vette, AL, 2X4, WCFB, 1st design |
| 3731394 | 1956 | 265/225, Vette, Pass, AL, 2X4, WCFB, 2nd design |
| 3731398 | 1957 | 283/220, Pass, Vette, CI, 4GC |
| 3735448 | 1956 | 265/210, Vette, CI, 4GC |
| 3737109 | 1956 | 265 Pass, CI, 4GC |
| 3739653 | 1957 | 283/245, 270 hp, Pass, AL, 2X4, WCFB |
| | 1957–1961 | 283 Vette, AL, 2X4, WCFB |

| Casting Number | Model Year | Engine/Application |
|---|---|---|
| 3741193 | 1957 | 283 Pass, AL, FI |
| 3746829 | 1957–1961 | 283/230 Pass, CI, 4GC, WCFB |
| | 1958–1961 | 283/230 Vette, CI, WCFB |
| 3783244 | 1962–1963 | 283, 327 Pass, Chevy II (service), CI, 4GC, WCFB |
| 3783244 | 1962–1963 | 327/250 Vette, CI, WCFB |
| 3794129 | 1963 | 327/340, Vette, AL, AFB |
| 3795397 | 1962 | 327/340, Vette, AL, AFB |
| 3799349 | 1962–1964 | 327/300, Pass, Vette, CI, Carter AFB |
| 3826810 | 1963–1965 | 327 Vette, AL, FI |
| 3837109 | 1956 | 265/210 Vette, CI, 4GC |
| | 1956–1957 | 265, 283 Pass, CI, 4GC |
| 3844457 | 1964–1965 | 283/220, 327/250 Pass, Chevelle, Chevy II, Vette, CI, WCFB, 4GC, also used as service replacement |
| 3844459 | 1963–1965 | 327/300 Pass, Chevelle, Chevy II, Vette, CI, AFB, also used as service replacement |
| 3844461 | 1964–1965 | 327/350 and 365 Corvette, Chevelle, AL, Hi-rise, Holley |
| 3866922 | 1962–1965 | 283/220 Pass, Chevelle, Chevy II, 327/250 Pass, Chevelle, Chevy II, Vette, CI, 4GC, marine replacement |
| 3872783 | 1966 | 327/275 without A.I.R., Pass, Chevelle, Chevy II, CI, Holley, service replacement |

## Intake Manifold Casting Numbers *(Continued)*

| Casting Number | Model Year | Engine/Application |
|---|---|---|
| | 1966–1967 | 327/300 Pass, Vette, Holley, CI, service replacement |
| | 1966–1968 | 327, Truck, CI, Holley |
| 3875954 | 1966 | 327/275 with A.I.R., Pass, Chevelle, Chevy II, CI, 4MV |
| 3877656 | 1966–1967 | 327/350 AL, Hi-rise, Holley |
| 3882858 | 1966 | 283/220 Pass, Chevelle, Chevy II, CI, 4GC |
| 3890490 | 1966–1967 | 327/350 Corvette, Chevy II, Chevelle AL, Hi-rise, Holley |
| 3905393 | 1967 | 327/275 Pass, Chevelle, Chevy II, Camaro, CI, 4MV |
| | 1967 | 350/295 Camaro, CI, 4MV |
| 3917610 | 1967–1968 | Z28 302 Camaro, AL, Hi-rise, Holley |
| 3919803 | 1968 | 327/250, 275, 325, 350 hp, Pass, Chevy II, |
| | | Chevelle, Vette, CI, 4MV |
| | 1968 | 350/295 Camaro, CI, 4MV |
| 3927184 | 1969 | 350/255, 300, 350 hp, Pass, Chevelle, Chevy II, Camaro, Vette, CI, 4MV, service replacement |
| 3932472 | 1969 | Z28 302 Camaro, AL, Hi-rise, Holley |
| 3941126 | 1968–1969 | Z28 302 Camaro, 2X4 Holley, AL, bottom half of cross ram intake |
| 3941130 | 1968–1969 | Z28 302 Camaro, 2X4 Holley, AL, top half of cross ram intake, Winter Foundry "snowflake" logo |
| 3959594 | 1971 | 350/330 LT1 Corvette, Z28, AL, Hi-rise, Holley |
| | 1972 | 350/255 LT1 Corvette, Z28, AL, Hi-rise, Holley |
| 3965577 | 1970 | 350/300, 350 hp, Pass, Corvette, Nova, Chevelle, Monte Carlo, Camaro, CI, 4MV |
| 3972110 | 1970 | 350/360, 370 hp Camaro, LT1 Corvette, AL, Hi-rise, Holley |
| 3972114 | 1972 | 350, Z-28 Camaro AL, Hi-rise, Holley |
| 3972116 | | AL, Hi-rise, Holley, Service replacement for 1970 LT1 350 |
| 3972361 | 1970–1971 | 350 Z28 Camaro, AL, Holley |
| 3973469 | 1971 | 350/270, Pass, Chevelle, Corvette, Camaro, Monte Carlo, Nova, CI, 4MV |
| 3997771 | 1973 | 350/175, 190, 245, 250 hp, Pass, Corvette, Nova, Chevelle, Monte Carlo, Camaro, CI, 4MV |

| Casting Number | Model Year | Engine/Application |
|---|---|---|
| 6263751 | 1972 | 350/175, 200 hp, Vette, Camaro, Chevelle, Monte Carlo, Nova, CI, 4MV |
| 10051103 | | Bowtie, AL, 23-degree heads, Raised Runner, Holley same casting is also used to make standard runner Bowtie intake for 23-degree heads. |
| 10068015 | | 305, 350, AL, TPI base, EGR, 72-degree center bolt angles |
| 10185063 | | ZZ-series 350 HO crate engine, AL, dual-carb pattern, EGR, medium height, 90-degree center bolt angles |
| 12366573 | | 283–400 engines using Vortec heads, square bore |
| 12498620 | | Dual-bolt pattern for square or spread bore carb, Vortec heads |
| 12496821 | | Throttle body intake for Vortec heads on pre-1996 engines |
| 12496822 | | Vortec heads, open-plenum design for racing |
| 12676887 | | Vortec heads, dual-plane, square-bore carb |
| 14057053 | 1980–1985 | 305, 350 Pass, Camaro, Truck, AL, 4MV |
| 14081005 | 1986 | Lower, 305-350, AL, TPI, Z28 Camaro |
| 14081006 | 1986 | Upper, 305-350, AL, TPI, Z28 Camaro |
| 14096242 | | Bowtie, CI, dual-carb pattern, No EGR, 72-degree center bolt angles |
| 24502592 | | Converts an 1999–1996 Gen II to a carburetor |
| 24502481 | | Open plenum for 18-degree head competition |
| 24502654 | | Valley plate for 18-degree cylinder heads |
| 12480096 | | SB2.2, restricted spider design, use with valley plate 12370840 |
| 88958617 | | SB2.2, spider design, use with valley plate 12370840 |

Note: Single 2-barrel carb intakes are not listed.
AL = aluminum
CI = cast-iron
4GC = Rochester 4-Jet square bore 4-barrel, 400 to 450 cfm
4MV = Carter or Rochester made Quadrajet spreadbore 4-barrel
AFB = Carter AFB 4-barrel, 500 or 600 cfm
WCFB = Carter WCFB 4-barrel, 400 cfm

Other carbureted intake manifolds were made for Gen I engines, 18-degree or 15-degree Bowtie cylinder heads and the EFI units found on Gen I and II engines. Chevrolet Performance and Edelbrock offered aluminum intakes for Gen II LT1 and LT4 engines to accept a carburetor. ■

single 4-barrel split plenum manifold on the street, with a 4-barrel carb that has vacuum secondaries, and you are much happier with the results.

## Cast-Iron Intakes

PN 14057060 is a 2-barrel, high-rise intake that is suitable for those racing in restricted 2-barrel carb classes. This manifold was originally installed on truck applications.

PN 14088675 is another 2-barrel intake that was used with TBI, but it fits a 2-barrel carburetor for restricted class racing.

PN 14096011 is a cast-iron, high-rise, split-plenum, marine intake with a dual-pattern carb flange to fit either square or spreadbore 4-barrel carbs. This intake is similar to the original Z28 aluminum intake, but is made of cast iron; non-EGR.

PN 14097494 is a cast-iron, high-rise intake that fits 1987-on later 305 and 350 Gen I heads that have revised 72-degree center bolt angles. The carb flange fits square or spreadbore flange carbs. Otherwise, it is similar to the original Z28 high-rise intake; no EGR boss; split plenum.

PN 14096241 is a split-plenum, cast-iron, high-rise intake with a dual-pattern carb flange. The two center manifold bolt holes on each side are cut at the newer 72-degree angle to fit the new bolt angles found in 1987-on Gen I heads. The port runners are similar to original Z28 aluminum intake; no EGR.

## Aluminum 4-Barrel Intakes

Gen I and II aluminum 4-barrel intakes from Chevrolet Performance come in the form of 23-degree and 18-degree high-port and for the SB2 engine. Chevrolet still offers a number of the following intakes, though several can only be found used or NOS.

### *23-Degree Intake*

PN 10185063 is a low-rise, split-plenum, aluminum intake with a dual-pattern carb flange that fits Holley or Quadrajet 4-barrel carbs. The top of the carb mounting flange is 1/2 inch shorter than the height found on the 1970 LT1 350 high-rise manifold, which provides additional hood clearance. This manifold has provisions for EGR and hot air chokes, if you need them, and can be used with 1955 to 1986 small-block engines. It is also used on the ZZ series of crate engines.

PN 14007377 gets you a low-profile, dual-plane, production aluminum intake. This manifold uses a spreadbore Quadrajet 4-barrel and fits under most hood lines; EGR and choke tube bosses.

PN 10185024 is an aluminum high-rise, dual-plane intake for Gen I heads that has a square carb flange for Holley carbs. It is similar to the original Z28 intake. There are bolt bosses for A/C brackets, however, there are no bolt holes drilled for the choke stove, nor is the boss drilled for an oil filler tube. The manifold flanges that meet the cylinder heads have been chamfered to fit without interference to the machined valve cover gasket rails that are found on late-model Gen I aluminum Corvette heads; no EGR.

PN 24502592 is an aluminum high-rise, 4-barrel intake for Gen II LT1 reverse-coolant-flow aluminum heads that fits square or spreadbore carbs. It has a rear distributor mounting hole for conventional distributors or it can be used with Gen II Opti-Spark distributors. There are no heat riser or water crossover passages, so these manifolds can only be used on Gen II LT1 heads. The manifold bolt holes fit the new Gen II manifold bolt hole spacing and 72-degree bolt angles, which are different than Gen I heads and intakes. A machined plug is included with this manifold to close off the rear distributor hole if you are using a front-mounted distributor. If you use a rear-mounted distributor with this intake, you need to change the oil pump drive stub shaft to a longer conventional intermediate driveshaft (found in Gen I engines), to drive the distributor. This manifold does not work with the 1996-on LT4 heads because they have raised intake port openings.

PN 24502574 is an aluminum high-rise, 4-barrel intake for use with raised runner (+0.100-inch) 1996 LT4 Gen II aluminum heads. It has a mounting flange for square or spreadbore carbs. No water

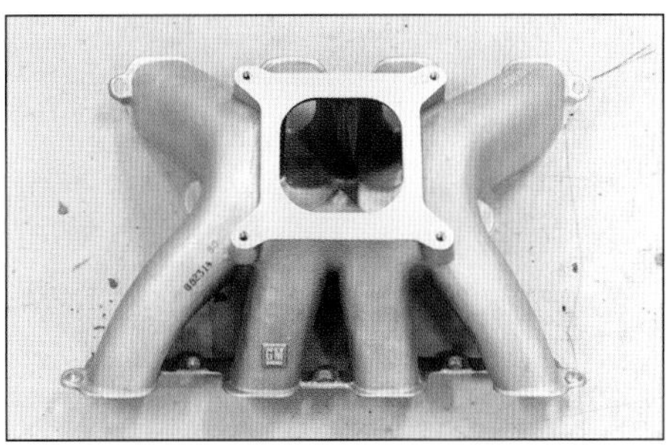

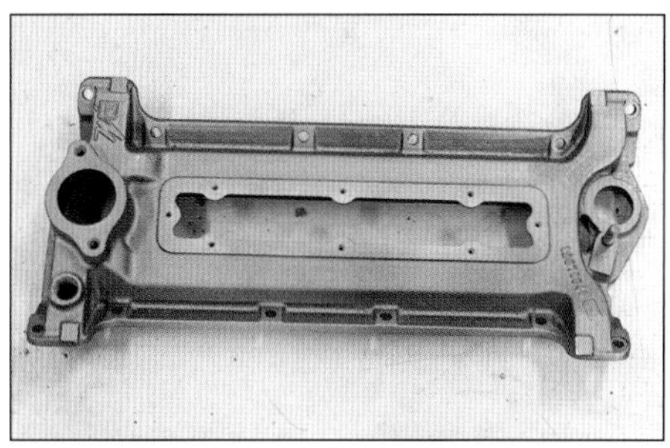

***The SB2 intake uses a unique upper intake plenum and runner that can be unbolted from the lower portion of the intake without removing the distributor or disconnecting water lines.***

crossover or thermostat housing is in the manifold casting, so it must be used with reverse-flow cooling heads and an LT4-style water pump. This intake manifold does have a boss and hole to mount a standard HEI or point distributor in the rear, or it can be used with the front-mounted, cam-driven, Opti-Spark LT4 distributor, and electronic ignition. A machined plug is included to plug the rear distributor hole if you use a front-mounted, optical-triggered GM distributor. If you use a rear-mounted distributor with this intake, you'll need to change the oil pump drive stub shaft to a longer conventional intermediate driveshaft (found in Gen I engines), to drive the distributor. Do not use this manifold with Gen II LT1 heads; the LT1 head has lower intake port openings.

#### *18-Degree High-Port Intake*

PN 24502481 is a Bowtie aluminum, high-rise intake. This open-plenum race intake is for 18-degree, high-port aluminum heads (PN 10134363 and 24502482). It has a smaller plenum volume and smaller cross-section runners for increased mid-range torque, when compared to Bowtie intake (PN 10185053) for 18-degree heads. It weighs 22.5 pounds and fits a square Holley carb flange, squared plenum opening.

The PN 24502653 is a two-piece dry manifold. It must be used with valley plate PN 24502654. It is designed for use with Bowtie aluminum 18-degree high-port heads that were made after June 1996.

#### *SB2 Intake*

The SB2 mirror port head (introduced in 1996) requires a unique intake and valley plate. The 12480096 intake is for restrictor plate NASCAR racing and is used with valley plate PN 1237080. Another intake (PN 88958617) is for nonrestricted racing and can be used with the prior valley plate or PN 88958659, which features an updated water passage for improved coolant flow from front to the rear of the cylinder heads.

### Intake Manifold Gaskets

There have been many changes to small-blocks in recent years, and the intake manifold and intake manifold gaskets must match the type of cylinder heads you are using. Gen I heads interchange within the Gen I family of engines from 1955 to 1996. The 1996-and-later Vortec 5000 and Vortec 5700 heads require a 1996-or-later Vortec intake gasket that has the revised coolant crossover holes, larger port openings, and only four manifold mounting bolts on each side. The Gen II LT1, LT4, and L99 265 V-8 engines with reverse-coolant-flow heads require intakes and intake gaskets that match their revised head bolt angles, port openings, and manifold bolt spacing, as well as the raised intake ports on the LT4.

PN 10147994 fits all 1971 to 1986 Gen I 262 to 400 small-blocks with standard port locations, intake manifold bolt spacing, and port sizes.

PN 19301685 is designed for Vortec Fast Burn aluminum heads. The gaskets have both the early six-bolt and four-bolt patterns.

PN 89017465 is the production gasket for all Vortec design heads with the four-bolt design. It requires the use of attachment bolt PN 12550027.

For LT4 engines, use PN 12528884. If you're doing an LT1 to carburetor swap using intake PN 24502592, use intake gasket set PN 12524653.

Intake manifold gasket PN 10185007 is used with 18-degree, high-port Bowtie heads. This gasket is not recommended for the 18-degree, low-port Bowtie heads.

Intake manifold gaskets for the SB2 heads are available from Fel-Pro.

### Fuel Injection

Fuel injection (FI), in the form a mechanical design, made its appearance on the small-block in 1957 as an option on 283 ci Corvettes as well as a few full-size passenger vehicles. These fuel injection units, made by Rochester, were performance engine options through 1965, when they ceased to be available as factory installations on 327 Corvettes.

The Rochester setup was quite advanced for its time and racers who understood the unit and its intricacies would fare well. However, for daily

***Before there was EFI, there was mechanical fuel injection. Chevrolet offered a very trick, yet finicky, fuel injection setup beginning in 1957 before being discontinued after the 1965 model year. Today, these systems are rare and sought after, yet still very finicky.***

## "Dry" Fuel Injection Runners

With the advent of electronic port fuel injection in the mid-1980s, Chevrolet began to use intake manifolds that incorporated individual port injectors that shoot fuel directly into the intake ports of the cylinder heads. The rest of the intake manifold, the throttle body, plenum, and tube runners, deliver the air to the cylinder heads. Consequently, these intakes are referred to as dry intakes, since no gasoline flows through them. Unlike carbureted engines that mix air and fuel at the beginning of the intake tract, these engines mix the gasoline and air at the end of the intake tract.

The L98 350s and some of the 305s used a long tube runner design that delivered excellent low-RPM torque and good throttle response, but it has rather small tube runner dimensions and the manifold base also has small port dimensions. These dimensions limit the Gen I engine's power output above 4,500 rpm. Chevrolet and aftermarket suppliers have a number of over-the-counter intakes, which feature larger intake tube runners and manifold bases that have larger port dimensions to help these engines breathe better at engine speeds well over 4,500 rpm.

The 1996-on Vortec engines and the 1992-on Gen II L99, LT1, and LT4 all use variations of the dry intake system, along with electronically controlled port fuel injection. The Vortec engines made use of heat resistant, composite plastic materials that easily handle the induction of air only. The Gen II engines used a short runner and plenum design that increased power above that found on L98 Gen I engines and were able to easily pull to 6,000 rpm.

Remember intake manifold bolt patterns and water passages are different between the Gen I, Vortec, and Gen II engines. Consequently, they are not interchangeable between engine platforms. ■

*When Chevrolet introduced fuel injection on the small-block, it was in the form of a throttle body bolted on top of an intake, similar to a carb. The throttle body had two injectors to introduce fuel above the throttle plates.*

*FAST, the fuel injection division of Comp Cams, offers a complete retrofit EFI system called EZ EFI. The self-learning kit is based on a throttle body system and is available with everything you need to upgrade to EFI in place of your carb. (Photo Courtesy FAST)*

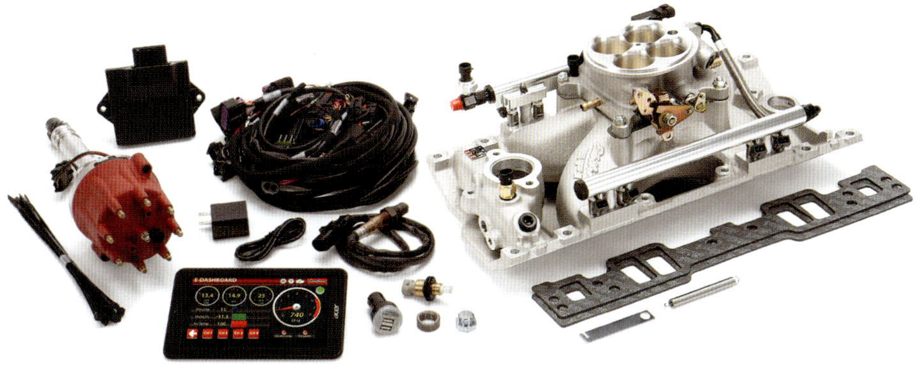

*Edelbrock can set you up with an aluminum intake with throttle body injectors machined in the intake runners with fuel rails, wiring harness, and computer for your small-block. (Photo Courtesy Edelbrock)*

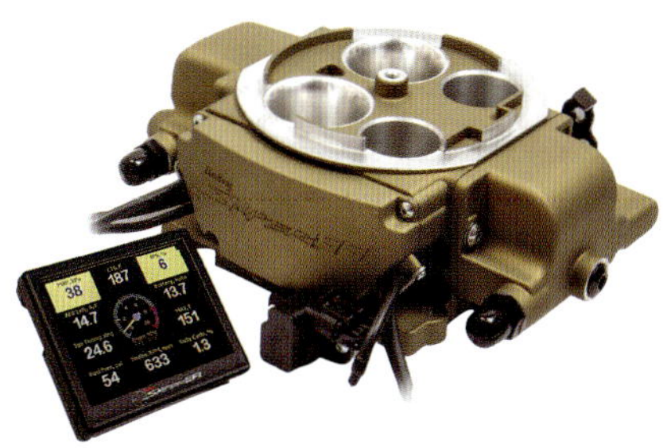

*Holley offers a throttle body that bolts in place of a Rochester Quadrajet carb. This means you can leave the original intake manifold in place and upgrade to fuel injection. (Photo Courtesy Holley)*

***Mechanical fuel injection systems are also available for small-block race applications and are commonly used with alcohol-fed engines. Throttle response is awesome.***

***Hilborn, one of the original mechanical fuel injection systems, now offers a system with the looks of an original mechanical system but with the driveability and control from electronic fuel injection.***

drivers, the units were typically pulled off in favor of a carb, though this swap was usually due to a mechanic or owner not being familiar with the inner workings or tuning of the system. Today, these early Rochester FI inductions are rare, highly sought after, and expensive. If you're doing a high-end restoration on a classic Corvette or early Chevy, it would be the crown jewel of the engine, though be ready for driveability challenges. If you're looking for great cold starts and smooth all-around performance, it would be best to look at modern electronic fuel injection (EFI) options.

EFI systems have been in use for more than three decades, and complete systems can be sourced from Chevy Performance, the aftermarket, and even your local pick-a-part junkyard. The modern systems from the aftermarket have eased the learning curve of fuel injection with less wiring, self-learning technology, as well as simplified programming (no laptops or electrical degree required).

If you decide to go in search of a used EFI system, there are two main OEM designs to choose: throttle body injection (similar to a carburetor and traditional intake) or port fuel injection (where there is an injector in each intake runner). There is now direct port injection on the Gen IV small-block where the fuel is delivered at extremely high pressure straight into the combustion chamber. This technology hasn't reached the Gen I and II small-block engine system, yet.

When EFI was first introduced on production vehicles in the mid to late 1980s, Chevrolet began by mating throttle body injection to intake manifolds similar to those previously used with carburetors. These throttle bodies bolted onto the intake just like a carburetor and had rudimentary engine computer controls. These early EFI systems can be found in donor vehicles, but you would need to take the wiring harness, electronic control unit, the different sensors and also plumb your vehicle for a high-pressure fuel pump and lines.

Several aftermarket companies offer throttle body EFI systems that can easily be installed on a standard single 4-barrel carburetor intake manifold. Holley, MSD, FAST, and FiTech all have designed TBI upgrade systems that are supplied with all of the sensors, wiring, and components you need to adapt a small-block in an older vehicle to electronic fuel injection.

These systems each have their differences; however, their installation and operation are very similar. To provide engine data to the engine control unit (ECU), these systems use a number of sensors: coolant temperature, throttle position, manifold pressure, a wideband oxygen sensor, intake air temperature, and fuel pressure. Also, upgrading to fuel injection means having to install a high-pressure fuel pump (45–60 psi) with the supporting lines, fittings, and filter.

The next revision in electronic fuel injection came with the introduction of the Gen I tuned port injection systems. These inductions used a throttle body that mounted on the front of an aluminum intake, which incorporated individual port runner tubes and a plenum. Fuel was supplied through port-mounted injectors.

*The L98 350 Corvette with tuned port injection has long intake runners to boost low- and mid-range power. The stock runners run out of breath above 4,500 rpm.*

*This is the intake assembly from an LT1 engine used on the Gen II small-block in passenger cars.*

*Shown is a Gen II LT1 350 in a 1996 Impala SS. The low-profile intake and the swap of the distributor to the front of the engine (behind the water pump) make this engine ideal for street rod swaps.*

The Gen I TPI units used on the L98 350 had long, curved intake runners that run out of breath at about 4,500 to 5,000 rpm. This worked out okay for street-driven units and provided good amounts of torque in the low-RPM range, where most unmodified street engines operate.

Chevy Performance used to offer a set of aluminum siamesed replacement intake runners for Gen I TPI manifolds for 1985 to 1992 Camaros. These dyno-tested runners increase engine power by 18 hp and 18 ft-lbs of torque over the stock aluminum runners. PN 12341415 fits 1985 to 1988 TPI units, while PN 12341416 fits 1989 to 1992 units. Several aftermarket companies offer similar intake setups for these early TPI engines.

Electronic fuel injection systems require higher fuel pressures, which mean you must use the appropriate electric fuel pump and adjustable fuel pressure regulator. Most applications also require a fuel bypass/return line to circulate the fuel back to the tank. You'll also need to run high-pressure fuel hose or lines and fittings as well as a filter rated for EFI. The aftermarket EFI companies offer all of these parts with the EFI systems and can answer any questions you may have about your specific application and best installation practices.

Mechanical fuel injection systems are still available for hardcore racing applications. These systems feature individual runners for each cylinder with old-style port fuel injection nozzles. Hilborn and Kinsler are companies that specialize in mechanical setups and can provide entire gasoline or alcohol mechanical injection systems for Chevy small-blocks, and they know what works and what doesn't.

Another interesting thing happening with mechanical fuel injection units is the marriage of a mechanical unit with modern EFI units. The old-style port fuel injection nozzles are replaced with electronically controlled injectors, and the engine needs to be fitted with the required sensors to provide feedback to an ECU. Hilborn and Borla offer a number of intake setups with the appearance of mechanical injection with the functionality of modern EFI. Vintage looks with modern driveability, that's today's hot rodding!

## Carb Spacers

Carb spacers add volume to a plenum and may help air flow through the plenum when it makes the turn into individual port runners. However, you must experiment with these spacers. Some engine and intake manifold combinations like them and some do not. Try different-size spacers or no spacer at all to see what happens. Also, since you are changing

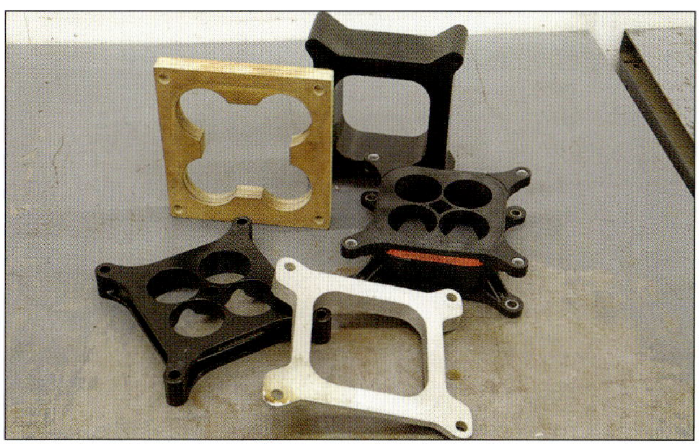

*Carb spacers come in all shapes, sizes, and materials. Some engine combinations like them; some don't. You have to experiment to see which combination works best on your engine.*

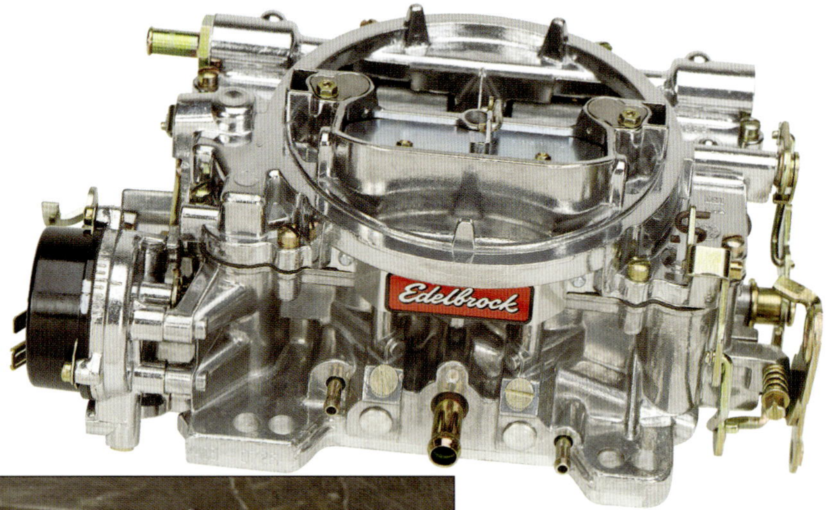

***Edelbrock offers a line of carburetors that resemble and replace the Carter AFB-style carbs. They bolt in place on the original GM AFB intakes as well and have four equal-size bores. Many CFM sizes are offered along with small parts to fine-tune them.***

the total plenum space when you use a spacer, the metering signal to the carb may be altered. You might need to change jet sizes and accelerator pump cams and shooter sizes to get things dialed in.

Spacers are made from aluminum, laminated wood, or plastic, and they have one, two, or four holes. The wood or plastic models seem to conduct less heat to the carburetor. They are available from aftermarket suppliers.

## Carb Sizes

Selecting the right size carb for your drivetrain is very important. It's easy to over-carburate any engine by thinking that the bigger the carb, the more fuel and the faster the car will go. It simply is not true. The carb must match the air/fuel requirements of your particular engine and how you plan to use your vehicle.

The 262- to 400-ci street engines should limit carburetor size to 600 to 750 cfm. Street engines should use a carb with vacuum-operated secondaries and a split plenum intake manifold. Mileage is decent and throttle response is also excellent.

Race engines, which are never driven on the street, can use from 600- to 1,450-cfm carbs and open plenum single- or dual-carb intakes depending on the fuel volume needs of the engine. Double Pumper, mechanical secondary-style Holley carbs are strictly for racing, and if they are used on a street engine, they do not get decent gas mileage and throttle response may not be sharp and crisp. Those who plan on using tunnel ram manifolds on a race engine should know that these manifolds, using two carbs, only start to work at around 4,500 rpm and then can give some benefit to 8,500 rpm or more. Low-speed drivability is poor. The dual-carb tunnel ram setup does reduce intake restrictions in a very-high-RPM engine, but you need an engine parts combination that is suited for this type of intake and high RPM to gain any advantage.

A properly set up high-RPM race engine with a tunnel ram makes power, but it is at the expense of low-speed (below 4,500 rpm) torque, power, and drivability. There isn't enough signal at the carbs to get the main circuits working properly at low RPM. This loss of low-engine-speed power and manners is one of the reasons many of these tunnel-rammed race cars get pushed to the starting line and towed back to the pits after a run. Check the formula for figuring out minimum carb CFM size with a particular volumetric efficiency.

Chevy Performance offers three different Holley carbs that all feature a square-bore "4150" style mount. PN 19170097 is a 650-cfm carb with a manual choke and mechanical secondaries. PN 19170092 is a 670-cfm model with dual feed bowls, vacuum secondaries, and electric choke. PN 19170093 is a 770-cfm carb with an electric choke, and vacuum secondaries with center-hung floats in dual fed bowls.

All aftermarket carburetor makers also offer numerous parts to dial in your carburetor for your particular combination. You should know that most carburetors are very close to what you need right out of the box. If you find that you need to make a wide range of changes to the calibration of the carb to get it right for your engine, chances are you have the wrong carburetor. For instance, I have seen people who have put a carb on that is too large for their engine, falling into the trap of thinking that bigger is better. The engine now runs too rich. They try putting in smaller jets in order to reduce the amount of

## Different Holley Carburetors

Holley's 750-cfm vacuum secondary 4-barrel (PN 3310C) is one of the most-popular carburetors chosen for street performance. This carb has vacuum secondaries that provide a crisp transition and can be tailored to suit the unique requirements of nearly any application. It also has a manual choke. (Photo Courtesy Holley)

For racing applications and serious street machines, the Holley Double Pumper is the leading contender. Available in sizes ranging from 600 to 1,000 cfm, Double Pumpers feature an accelerator pump on both the primary and the secondary metering circuits. They can be configured with adjustable four-corner idle circuits for precise tuning. (Photo Courtesy Holley)

Holley Dominators are pure racing carburetors designed to flow massive amounts of air. Most of them feature an intermediate idle circuit in addition to the two or three standard metering circuits. The Ultra line features aluminum construction, saving racers 3.8 pounds. (Photo Courtesy Holley)

A Holley 750-cfm Double Pumper carb is an excellent 4-barrel for performance or race use with a small-block. However on the street, a vacuum secondary Holley carb with a split-plenum intake may be a better choice.

The Holley List Number is found on the choke horn on most models. The carb build date is also stamped there. If it was originally installed by General Motors at the factory, there is also a GM part number. This one is List Number 4779-6, which is a 750-cfm Double Pumper with manual choke and the third (-6) design changes.

fuel. Sometimes reducing by 10 jet sizes! It's a mistake. Think in terms of which carb size is best for your parts combination and usage. What RPM range is your engine going to run in? What type of intake manifold are you planning to use? What are the pros and cons of that particular setup? If you are using a Holley 4-barrel, make sure that you get the proper power valves in the carb.

## Carb Tuning

If you have picked the correct carb size for your engine size and volumetric efficiency, there isn't much that needs to be done. For a Holley carb, you need to know that Holley calibrates its carbs for sea level operation at 59 degrees Fahrenheit. This means that if you are at a different altitude or air temperature, the air/fuel calibration of the carb can be changed to your conditions for maximum performance. Since there is less air density as you increase altitude, you can decrease the main jet sizes one jet size for every 2,000 feet in altitude above sea level. This keeps the air/fuel ratio where it should be.

Likewise, for each 35-degree temperature increase above 59 degrees you can decrease one jet size. Power valve changes can also compensate for altitude increases. For every 3,000-foot increase in altitude, the power valve opening point can be reduced 1.0 to 2.0 sizes. According to Holley, the best way to select a power valve on modified engines is as follows:

1) Hook a vacuum gauge to an intake manifold vacuum port.
2) Warm up the engine and note the vacuum reading at idle. Automatic transmission vehicles need to be in the Drive position, while manual transmission vehicles can be in Neutral.
3) Divide the vacuum reading in half. The number will determine the correct power valve.

Each power valve is stamped with a number that indicates the correct vacuum opening point. For example, a power valve with the number 65 stamped on it will open at 6.5 inches of engine vacuum. As an example, a vacuum reading at idle of 13 inches is divided by two and results in 6.5 inches of vacuum. Therefore, you should have a #65 Holley Power Valve installed in the carburetor.

If you divide the vacuum reading and it falls on an even number, you should select the next lowest power valve number. For example, a vacuum reading of 8 inches is divided by two, and you come up 4 inches. In this case, you would use a #35 power valve.

Finally, if your engine produces 13 inches of vacuum or more, the stock power valve that the carburetor is equipped with from the factory is sufficient.

As you can imagine, a 350 engine in a T-bucket will have different power valve needs than the same engine in a motor home. A more precise and thorough way of determining power valve sizing would be to follow the same procedures above except measure vacuum readings under load typical to how the vehicle is normally used, although the above procedure gets you very close for most applications.

Don't take the power valve out and then plug it. If you do this, it throws the fuel metering way off and you have to increase the main jet size 6 to 10 sizes to compensate. Part throttle mileage decreases if you remove the power valve and plug it, and at idle or part throttle the air/fuel ratio is too rich. Spark plug fouling can become a problem at low RPM when the power valve is removed.

Racers can also experiment with the accelerator pump cams and shooter size to improve the engine's performance off the line or out of corners. If you are using a vacuum-operated secondary-style carb, you can use different springs in the secondary vacuum canister to change the way the secondaries are actuated. Make sure, however, that you begin any experimentation with the stock calibrations and that you note what they are so you can go back to the original setting if

***The Rochester Quadrajet 4-barrel was installed on many factory small-blocks. Small primaries helped throttle response and fuel economy at low RPM, while huge secondaries open when the pedal is floored, giving excellent performance.***

## 4-Barrel Carb Casting Dates

The following is a guide to Carter, Holley, and Rochester casting dates.

### *Carter*

Carter WCFB, AFB, and Quadrajet 4-barrel carbs were used on early small-blocks from 1955 to 1967. These carbs have a small metal tag under an air-horn screw, which gives its part number and a date code. The date code uses a letter followed by a digit for the year of the decade. It might look like this, "F8" for June 1958. Some AFBs have the date code and part or model number stamped into the base of the carburetor.

### *Holley*

Holley carbs have a List Number, such as "List# 4781" stamped into the front of the choke horn, which tells you what type, model, and CFM size of the carburetor. If there have been changes made to that model over the years, the particular version has a number added to the List Number. It looks like this: List# 4777-2. There is also a date code, which tells you when the carburetor was made. The date code usually is three digits. It might look like this: "743." The first number is the year of decade (7). The second digit or letter is the month of the year (4). Holley used a month sequence of 1-2-3-4-5-6-7-8-9-0-A-B for January through December. The last digit stands for the week of the month (1 through 5). So our example of "743" translates to a carb made in the third week of April, in the seventh year of the decade.

You might have to look at the other features of the carb to give you clues as to which decade it was made. From 1973, the coding was changed. Four digits were used with the first three digits representing the day of the year in numerical order 1 through 365 (366 is used during leap years) and the fourth digit is the year of the decade. It might look like this: "0187," which decodes to January 18, 1977 (or 1987 or 1997).

Finally, on GM factory-installed Holley carbs made between 1964 and 1972, a GM part number is stamped in the same choke horn area. These part numbers were assigned depending on what type of vehicle, engine/carb size, and transmission combination was used. If the Holley carb was bought on the aftermarket, there isn't a GM part number stamped into the choke horn.

### *Rochester*

The Rochester 4G and 4GC were 4-barrel square-flange carbs, also referred to as Four Jets. They were used from 1956 to 1967. The 4G had a manual choke, while the 4GC had an automatic choke. Date codes used a letter and a digit to indicate the month and year of the decade. Part numbers and carb model numbers were also used. They can be found on a metal tag bolted onto the carb body or on a round tag that was then pressed into the carb body.

Spreadbore 4MV and 4MC Quadrajet 4-barrel carbs were made also by Rochester, but some early Quadrajets were built for General Motors by the Carter Carburetor Company. The ones built by Carter, for General Motors, are marked Carter. Both makers put part numbers and manufacture dates, either on small aluminum tags attached to a bowl screw or on a round tag pressed into the carb body or they were stamped into the driver's side of the carb. The stamped date codes are usually a letter and a single digit, for month and year of the decade. Later models used four digits with the first three digits the sequential day of the year and the last digit the year of the decade. It might look like, "2349," which means the 234th day of the year, in 1969 or 1979.

The stamped part ID numbers indicate the application used by General Motors, and these carbs were the most common factory-installed 4-barrel carb. They found their way onto passenger cars and trucks from 1965 through 1985 when throttle body fuel injection (TBI) units began to make their appearance. Some Canadian-sold vehicles continued to use the Quadrajet until 1988. ■

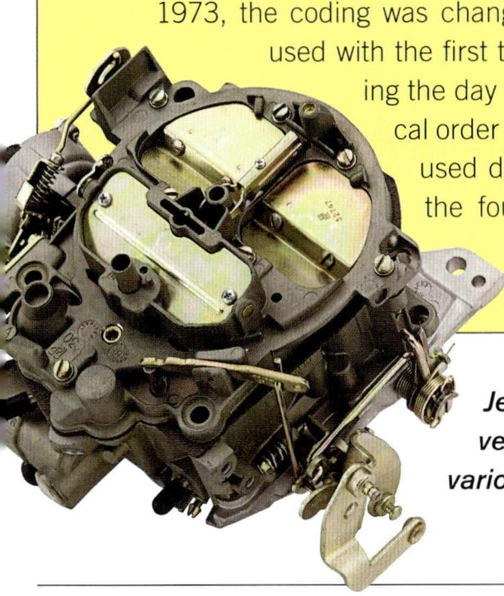

***Jet Performance not only offers computer upgrades and calibrations for late-model vehicles but also has a line of performance-enhanced Quadrajets and other carbs in various flow levels. (Photo Courtesy Jet Performance)***

## Required Carb CFM Size

There is an equation that takes into account the cubic inches of an engine, the maximum RPM that you are going to run the engine, and the volumetric efficiency (VE) of the engine combination. On most street-driven engines with stock, low-performance parts combinations, volumetric efficiency of the engine runs from 75 to 85 percent. Engines that have some performance parts, such as performance intakes, increased compression, tube headers, and performance cylinder heads, have higher VEs in the 85- to 95-percent range. Well thought out small-block race engines can actually have VEs higher than 100 percent.

Be realistic when you use this equation. Does your engine parts combination have a VE of 100 percent or is it really around 85 percent? The only way to tell exactly is to use an engine dynamometer and measure the amount of air inhaled by the engine when it is running. Since most of us don't have a dyno, this formula can help get your carb size in the ballpark.

Required Carb CFM = VE% x [(CID x MAX RPM) / 3,456]
CFM = 85% VE x [(355 ci x 6,500 rpm) / 3,456]
CFM = 85% x [2,307,500 / 3,456]
CFM = 0.85 x 667.67939
Required Carb CFM = 567.52748

A 585- or 600-cfm Holley or 650-cfm Rochester Quadrajet 4-barrel would work just fine on this street engine. Now, this doesn't mean a larger carb wouldn't work. All this shows is what the minimum carb CFM requirements are for this application.

If VE and RPM go up, let's see what happens.

CFM = 95% VE x [(355 ci x 7,000 rpm) / 3,456]
CFM = 95% x [2,485,000 / 3,456]
CFM = 0.95 x 719.03935
Required Carb CFM = 683.08738

Since no one makes a 683-cfm carb, you would choose either a 650-cfm carb or one of the 700-cfm units. ■

necessary. If your vehicle leaves the line very quickly, you may need main jet tube extensions on the secondary main jets. These extensions keep the main jets covered by fuel under hard acceleration. Using secondary jet extension tubes may require you to use a different float assembly in the secondary fuel bowl so the float clears the main jet extensions.

If you are going to run a used carburetor that you don't know the history of, I suggest you take it apart and check to see what main jet sizes are in it. Check the power valve, the gaskets, the adjustment on the accelerator pump lever, etc. Often the previous owner(s) of the carb experimented or used inferior parts, and a used carb can be far away from its original calibrations and settings. Holley has a listing of all of its carbs, their List Numbers, CFM sizes, and their respective calibrations, stock jet, and power valve sizes, which can be very helpful in reestablishing the baseline calibrations of a used carb.

For those who are using a lumpy camshaft, it often causes trouble getting the carb's idle mixture circuit to work properly. One fix is to drill small holes in the throttle plates to let in more air at idle and still have the throttle plates properly positioned near the idle transfer slots in the throttle bores. If you are uncomfortable drilling, another way of accomplishing this is to adjust the secondary throttle plate set screw off of the base setting so that it lets additional air in at idle. It performs the same function as drilling holes in the primary throttle plates but is considerably less permanent. Holley also has a number of carbs in various CFM sizes that have an adjustable secondary idle circuit built in. These "four-corner idle" carbs make it easy to adjust the idle mixture in both the primary and secondary bores and usually solves the idling problem when using a race-style, long-duration cam. Some of these Holley carbs have holes drilled in the throttle plates in addition to the four-corner idle system.

One of the problems that occasionally arises with vintage Holley carbs is the possible failure of the power valve if there was an engine backfire through the carb. When the power valve failed, the carb would run rich and the power valve would have to be replaced. However, in the early 1990s, Holley incorporated backfire protection into the power valve circuit on a number of its performance carbs and has eliminated this problem. In addition, a number of aftermarket kits are available that allow you to update older carbs that did not come with this provision.

## Mechanical Fuel Pumps

General Motors offers a number of mechanical and electric fuel pumps for the small-block Chevrolet. These high-performance mechanical pumps provide enough fuel volume to feed carbureted engine sizes from 262 to 400 ci and fit most chassis applications. The mechanical pumps listed all have rotatable lower housings, which can be very helpful in making them fit your application. Keep in mind that Gen II production engine blocks do not have a provision for mounting a mechanical fuel pump, so an electric pump must be used.

PN 12355612 is a high-capacity (110-gph) mechanical fuel pump that meets the requirements of a street-driven small-block. It does not require the use of a separate fuel pressure regulator. This pump has 3/8-inch ports and provides 7 pounds of fuel pressure.

PN 12355617 is a street-use chrome mechanical fuel pump with a free-flow volume of 70 gph and a pressure of 8.5 psi. It works with engine sizes of 262 to 400.

PN 12355613 is a high-capacity, competition mechanical pump. Pressure is set at 7 psi and it flows 115 gph. It has 1/2-inch inlet and outlet ports. It does not require an additional fuel pressure regulator.

The fuel pump pushrod used in Chevy small-block engines with a mechanical fuel pump is PN 3704817. The same fuel pump pushrod is used in the Mark IV big-block Chevy engine and is interchangeable.

When using a fuel pressure regulator with a carburetor, the pressure should be set so that a maximum of 6 or 7 psi is at the carburetor inlet ports and that the pressure does not fall below 4 psi at wide open throttle. Any pressure regulator should be mounted as close as possible to the carburetor and after any fuel filters, which can clog and restrict fuel flow.

Chevrolet offers two styles of electric fuel pumps. PN 25115899 is a 12-volt pump that free-flows 72 gph at 6 to 8 psi. This pump should be mounted in the fuel line near the gas tank to push the fuel to the engine. PN 25116279 is a late-model in-tank electric fuel pump. It provides 14 psi and should be used with a fuel pressure regulator.

Adjustable fuel pressure regulators can be used to increase the fuel flow to late-model electronically controlled injectors. Generally 10 to 20 percent more fuel flow can be had with the stock injector sizes merely by turning up the fuel pressure, if you have an adjustable fuel pressure regulator. If you still need even more fuel, you can increase the size and delivery rate (pounds per hour) of the injectors.

Holley makes a number of mechanical and electrical fuel pumps that give excellent service for all types of applications, whether they are used on the street or for racing. These pumps are rated to provide various amounts of gallons per hour and at different amounts of fuel pressure, depending on the intended uses and requirements.

The electric "Red" pump (Holley PN 12-801) delivers 97 gph, while the "Blue" pump (Holley PN 12-802) gives a free-flow volume of 110 gph and must be used with a pressure regulator. Get a pump that provides the amount of fuel you need at the pressures required and use a fuel pressure regulator (Holley PN 12-803, 12-704, or 12-707 for dual carbs). Use a fuel filter and fuel line sizes that handle the volume of fuel you plan to use. Don't forget that if you are going to use nitrous or a blower, additional fuel volume is required. Electronic fuel injection requires higher fuel pressures.

Fuel lines in any application should be steel tubing and/or braided steel hose. You should try to use the minimum amount of neoprene rubber fuel hose when making connections. The NHRA rules, as an example, only allow a total maximum of 1 foot of neoprene fuel line to be used on the entire fuel system from tank to carb. I know, you are saying to yourself that braided steel hose is expensive, especially the fittings. But the fact is that an engine fire is much more expensive.

Never use copper tubing to make fuel connections, they don't last. Make sure that fuel lines stay as far as possible from exhaust pipes and manifolds, fan blades, and other rotating parts.

*Small-blocks use a mechanical fuel pump that is operated through a pushrod activated by a lobe on the camshaft. A number of inlet and outlet positions were used over the years. When EFI was introduced in the late 1980s, a block-off plate was installed and an electric pump was added.*

## Fuels

Which type of fuel to use depends on what type of engine you are building and the uses it is intended for. Fuel-octane ratings give you an idea of the fuel's ability to resist detonation. When you increase cylinder pressures and cylinder temperatures, fuel has a tendency to self-ignite, or detonate. Fuels can be chemically formulated to resist pressure-related self-detonation and this resistance is given as its octane rating.

As static compression ratios go up, you need a higher octane rated fuel. An 8.0:1 to 9.2:1 engine can use pump gasoline that has ratings from 86 to 92 octane. Ratios of 9.5:1, with iron heads, need premium unleaded fuels of 90 to 92 octane. Above 9.5:1, pump fuels and iron cylinder heads may not provide protection from detonation, and that leaves you with octane-boosting additives or race fuels. Some engine combinations with aluminum heads and flat-top pistons have stock compression ratios of up to 10.8:1 and run on premium pump fuels. The cans of octane-boost additives can provide some increased octane levels to the fuel (6 to 8 additional octane points), but they still may not be enough, depending on the static compression ratio of your engine.

Engines with high compression ratios are going to need octane levels only currently available with race fuels. These fuels are expensive, so be sure that you consider this when planning what type of engine to build. If the vehicle is solely used to race, then race fuel costs are just one

*If power levels in your engine are increasing, remember that you need additional fuel. Using nitrous, blowers, or operating the engine at very high RPM requires a larger fuel volume that is dependable. It may be time to consider an electronic fuel pump such as Holley's HP In-Line Billet Pumps. (Photo Courtesy Holley)*

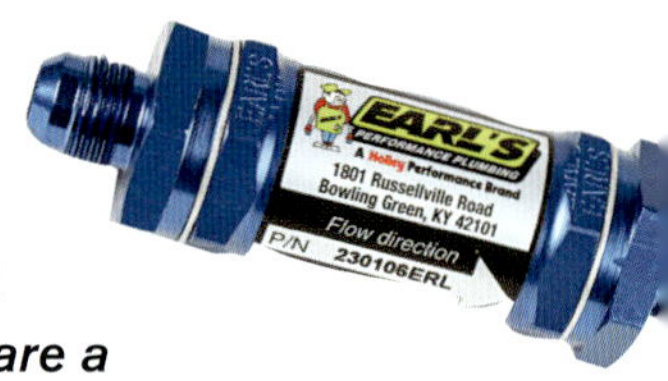


*The fuel you use needs to be filtered, and there are a number of filters available depending on your application. Filters should be plumbed into the line before any pressure regulators. (Photo Courtesy Holley)*

### Fuel System Requirements

*High-performance fuel systems are essential for any application with increased fuel demands. The old tried-and-true Holley Blue pump and regulator are still a top choice for basic bracket racing applications. (Photo Courtesy Holley)*

*Mechanical fuel pumps provide plenty of fuel in most carbureted street applications. Companies such as Holley and Edelbrock offer higher-output mechanical pumps to reach increased power numbers.*

*When you add a high-volume electric fuel pump, you also need an adjustable regulator to help keep the pressure at a fixed amount throughout the operating range of the engine. Holley offers a number of regulators for low-pressure carbs through high-pressure EFI systems. (Photo Courtesy Holley)*

of the additional expenses to go racing. However, if the vehicle is used mainly on the street, with weekend passes at the racetrack, then you are better off building an engine with a compression ratio that can use unleaded pump gasoline, and generally, this means an iron-headed engine with a static compression ratio of 10.0:1 or less.

In a related matter, since leaded fuels are not offered at pumps any more, make sure that the cylinder heads you use have hardened valve seats that survive the use of unleaded fuels. Early small-block heads made from 1955 to about 1974 and designed for leaded gasoline did not originally come with hardened seats. Hardened seat inserts can be installed in your heads by any competent machine shop.

Full-time race engines with compression ratios that are at very high levels, say 13.0:1 and higher, may get some benefits from using alcohol-based race fuels (methanol). There are pros and cons to using methanol as a race fuel. On the pro side, a well set up methanol engine can make upward of 10 percent more mid-range torque than an engine run on gasoline fuel. The engine runs cooler, provides a denser air/fuel mixture, and shows less tendency toward detonation, even at high cylinder pressures. Because of this cooling effect, the engines seem to be more consistent in terms of various outside temperatures and atmospheric conditions at a racetrack.

Since the engines run cooler, cool downs between races are reduced. If you are using a filled block or solid heads, methanol can help keep engine temperatures under control. There are a number of large-CFM Holley carbs that have been manufactured and calibrated for use with methanol. A tunnel ram intake with two Holley alcohol carbs or a mechanical fuel injection setup may be an easier solution to the increased alcohol fuel volume requirements.

Methanol fuels are cheaper per gallon than other race fuels; however, you need twice as much fuel volume than when you use gasoline. Some of the other cons relate to fuel delivery costs. Since a methanol-fueled engine needs a lot of fuel, you need a fuel delivery and induction system that can deliver that kind of volume from the tank through the carb. Everything has to have a larger fuel delivery capacity (fuel pumps, fuel lines, filters, and carbs or fuel injection). One of the major cons of using methanol is that it is extremely corrosive and demands more maintenance.

The fuel system needs to be flushed and drained of remaining methanol fuel if the engine was not run for a while. Careful attention must be given to using fresh methanol fuel, since methanol is very susceptible to water contamination. Water is absorbed by methanol from air, so keep fuel cans or barrels well-sealed. Also, the use of a top lube mixed with the methanol can help lubricate fuel system parts.

A more common alternative fuel that most of us run in some form already is ethanol. Ethanol is made from renewable sources such as corn, sugarcane, and other agricultural crops. Though engines can be run with 100-percent ethanol, the most common use is a blend with petroleum-based fuel to produce E85, which is 15-percent ethanol.

Like methanol fuels, ethanol has a higher octane level, making it a favorite for performance enthusiasts, yet more fuel is required to achieve improved performance. Other benefits include improved efficiency and emissions, as well as a less expensive fuel. Many new vehicles are designed to accept flexible fuels while our old small-blocks are able to run with E85. However, E85 absorbs water vapor which can lead to contamination of not only the fuel, but to the fuel lines, seals, and even the carburetor. There are fuel additives to help offset this contamination (to an extent), but it is something to consider when looking at alternative fuels.

## Nitrous Oxide, Superchargers, and Turbochargers

A number of nitrous and blower systems are designed for street use with a stock production engine. The amount of nitrous used in these street systems is smaller, in the range of 100 to 150 hp, and when used properly, will work well with stock parts.

Problems occur when the end user gets comfortable with the increased power and decides he or she needs more. Then the amount of nitrous used goes up or the boost from the turbo or blower system gets increased in an effort to make more power. At some point, a stock engine will decide that enough is enough.

All of these forced-induction systems have one goal: to artificially increase the amount of volume in the cylinder. In carbureted or injected systems, normal atmospheric air pressures fill the cylinders. With nitrous or blowers, the cylinders are more densely packed, cylinder pressures are increased, and power goes up in the engine. If you are contemplating such induction upgrade while building an engine, make sure you use the strongest engine parts available.

You should use a four-bolt block, forged crank, forged pistons, and heavy-duty connecting rods with quality rod bolts. Replace the stock vibration dampers with a high-quality unit, such as one sold by Fluidampr, ATI, or Chevy Performance. High-quality engine studs, instead of bolts, in conjunction with high-quality head gaskets, may be required because of their superior clamping power and resistance to high cylinder pressures.

***Nothing makes a statement like a big Roots blower standing tall over a small-block. Street cars and race engines alike take advantage of packing the cylinders with air and fuel from a blower.***

### *Nitrous Oxide*

Nitrous oxide is an interesting fuel additive because of its chemical properties. It has two nitrogen atoms and one oxygen atom, which form the nitrous oxide molecule. Inside a running engine, temperatures are high enough to break down the molecule and free the atoms adding additional oxygen to burn additional fuel.

The percentage of oxygen in nitrous is larger than the percentage of oxygen in the regular air available to a normally aspirated engine. Also, when nitrous is stored in the bottle, it is in a liquid state. When the nitrous is injected into the engine, it immediately begins to turn from a liquid to a gaseous state. When it does, the temperature of the intake charge drops tremendously. This helps deliver a much denser and cooler charge to the cylinders. So you get more oxygen, more volume, and a cooler charge.

The key, though, is to provide the additional volume of fuel so that the correct fuel ratios are maintained. In fact, it doesn't hurt to run a nitrous engine a little on the rich side when the nitrous is on, in order to further cool cylinder temperatures and keep them under control to avoid detonation. Not providing enough additional fuel results in a lean mixture and big trouble.

A number of nitrous delivery systems are on the market. One type uses a plate that fits between the carb and the intake manifold and has spray bars, which direct additional fuel and nitrous into the plenum. Another system plumbs nitrous and supplementary fuel lines to nozzles mounted directly in individual intake manifold port runners. Electric solenoids control the flow of nitrous and additional fuel.

With nitrous oxide, the travel speed of the flame front across the piston is quicker than with gasoline alone. This means that the total ignition timing is not as advanced as when the engine is run on gasoline alone. As nitrous is mixed with the gas, the ignition advance timing should be retarded. If you have multiple stages of nitrous, the timing advance should be retarded as each stage comes in. MSD makes an add-on ignition module that retards the total timing on the engine as the nitrous is switched on. The amount of ignition retard is adjustable and can be activated by each solenoid.

As you increase the amount of nitrous, you must also introduce additional fuel. This requires upgrades to the entire fuel delivery system. Most of the nitrous delivery systems provide a constant amount of additional fuel and nitrous, no matter at what RPM the engine is running. On any engine running at low RPM, the amount of time that an intake valve is open is longer than when the engine is at high RPM. With a nitrous-assisted engine, this means that if you were to activate the system at low RPM, more nitrous and fuel would be ingested by each cylinder than is ingested at high RPM. This can cause a real problem with low-RPM speed detonation because too much nitrous is present in the cylinder. Most manufacturers advise that you not activate the nitrous until the engine RPM is in the mid-range.

On a performance engine, the increases in power can be very large and, for the money, properly set up nitrous systems seem to give you the most power per dollar of almost anything currently out there. Cylinder pressures are raised substantially and this results in more engine torque. But this must be tempered with thoughts about the increased costs of building a stronger engine and drivetrain if the intended power increase is large.

### Superchargers

Superchargers increase power on an engine by forcing additional volume into each cylinder at pressures that are above the normal atmospheric pressure. The intake charge is denser and cylinder pressures go up along with increases in torque. However, as the blower vanes compress the air, the temperature of the compressed air and fuel goes up. In addition, the faster the blower is turned, the more power it takes to turn it, and the hotter the incoming air is made.

At some point, the additional power the supercharger makes is offset by the amount of power it takes to turn the blower over. There is a point with each blower system at which the amount of boost given generates the most power. At boost levels above that, power may decline. The idea is to strike a balance where the blower engine runs best, consistent with what your intentions are as far as engine use and power band. Keeping boost to 5 pounds or less enables you to use fairly stock parts if you wish to. At boost levels above this, you need premium rotating parts capable of withstanding higher engine output.

There are a couple of different supercharger types. A centrifugal blower compresses air only by using an impeller spun at very high RPM. The compressed air is then sent through a carburetor or port fuel injection system where fuel is introduced to the system. Generally, these types of blowers are compact and can be mounted in different positions as long as they can be driven by a belt. This makes them very useful in a vehicle that retains a stock hood. They can be hooked up to various types of intercoolers in order to drop the temperature of air being introduced to the impellers, which allows for cooler impellers, a denser charge, and more power. ATI, Paxton, Vortech, and others make centrifugal systems along with all of the plumbing pieces you need.

Roots-type blowers use a pair of two- or three-lobe rotors that compress air and fuel between the spinning lobes. Carburetors or fuel injection, mounted on top of these blowers, provide fuel and air to the rotors. These are considered wet systems and the fuel has a cooling effect on this type of supercharger. However, this makes for a tall assembly and holes through the hood are often required. There are some systems that can use side-mounted carbs and this lowers the overall induction system height. Roots-type blowers have many different blower-displacement sizes. A screw-type supercharger has a blower case similar to the roots type, but the rotors are screw-shaped and push the compressed mixture from front to back in the blower case.

Different drive systems for blowers are available along with various pulleys sizes. Changing the pulley diameters alters the amount of boost and the drive ratios that are required to get that boost. To find the pulley ratio, divide the number of teeth in the bottom pulley by the number of teeth in the top pulley. Keep in mind that the size of the blower displacement determines how fast it must be driven to give the boost you require.

For instance, a 4-71- or 6-71-style can give X amount of boost volume at a certain RPM, but an 8-71 with

## Ring End Gaps for Nitrous and Blown Engines

The increased heat and cylinder pressures generated by the use of nitrous oxide or when using a blower can cause the top and second piston rings to expand more. You can allow for this increased heat when you gap the rings for these engines. Speed-Pro makes the following recommendations for end gaps with iron rings.

These are recommendations only! Check with your piston and ring maker for their recommendations when using these types of fuels and inductions. When an engine is freshened or pulled down, always check to see if the ring ends have been butting together. If they have, you have to open the gaps farther. If there is no evidence of ring end butting, then you can think of reducing the gap. This requires that you keep accurate records of what the end gaps were at the time the engine was built. Be careful. There is some power to be found by getting the ring end gaps just right for your particular combination. However, the engine can be damaged if the gaps are too tight or if the ends butt together. ■

***Top Ring End Gap (ductile iron)***

Nitrous Oxide, Street: 0.006 inch per inch of bore diameter
Nitrous Oxide, Drag Race: 0.008 inch per inch of bore diameter
Supercharged: 0.006 inch per inch of bore diameter

***Second Ring End Gap (cast-iron)***

Nitrous Oxide, Street: 0.005 inch per inch of bore diameter
Nitrous Oxide, Drag Race: 0.0065 inch per inch of bore diameter
Supercharged: 0.005 inch per inch of bore diameter.

a larger volume capacity gives the same amount of boost at a lower blower RPM and with a reduction in blower-generated heat because of its increased volume. But since the engine gods have decreed that there is no free lunch, at higher RPM, the larger the blower capacity, the more power it takes to turn it over. So you are back to doing your balancing act again.

Careful attention needs to be given to how fast the engine and blower spin, the cylinder volume, the volume of the blower, the amount of boost, and the point where the law of diminishing returns come into play with regard to the amount of power generated versus the amount of power to drive the blower. How much heat is being added to the air/fuel mix? How much boost and cylinder pressure can your parts take before they start thinking about giving up? Alcohol-based fuels can help with mixture temperatures by helping to cool things down. So would nitrous oxide. When you work these things out, the engine torque can be ground shaking, instantaneous, and off idle with a supercharger.

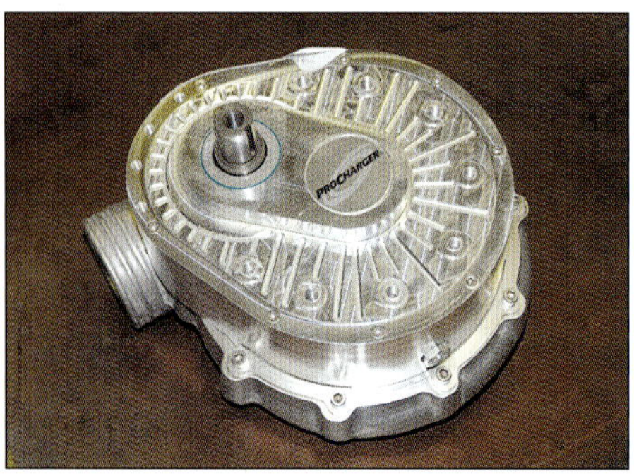

***Another type of supercharger is known as a centrifugal design. This design is popular because it can be fit under OEM hoods and work with carbs or EFI systems. A pulley that is driven from the crankshaft spins an impeller that forces air into the engine.***

Don't forget the exhaust side of engines with these types of induction systems. Because more air and fuel are sent to the cylinders, you can get additional power benefits from larger exhaust valves in the heads and more exhaust cam timing so that this increased exhaust volume can also get out of the engine. This also requires a larger exhaust system capable of handling more volume, whether it is larger diameter header tubes or larger diameter exhaust pipes and mufflers. Pistons need lower static compression ratios, and camshafts are designed differently for an engine that uses these systems. Cams with wide LSAs of about 114 degrees help keep the blower from pushing the intake charge right on past the open exhaust valve during the valve overlap period.

Most engine damage with these systems seems to be caused by incorrect engine parts combinations, inadequate fuel delivery systems, and air/fuel ratio problems that result in very lean conditions. Detonation is the enemy to avoid. Total timing advance needs to be kept to a maximum of 32 degrees with a blower. MSD makes a number of ignition boxes and ignition retard accessories that control ignition timing and help avoid detonation on a blown or nitrous engine.

***Roots blowers have been providing boost to small-blocks for decades and still look great—and perform just as well. This small blower wakes up any small-block and the entire induction fit nicely under the stock hood of a 1957 Chevy.***

Systems that provide boost above 5 psi may require forged blower pistons with thicker piston decks, forged cranks, and high-quality rods. Make sure that your fuel delivery system has increased flow capacity to match the increase in air volume made possible by these systems.

Also check that there is room to install water lines and the distributor and cap you intend to use. With some blower intake manifolds, you may have to use a different water neck or distributor to get the clearance necessary to install them.

### *Turbochargers*

Turbochargers, in a way, are similar to centrifugal blowers except that the power to run them is generated by the pressure of the outgoing engine exhaust flow. Pressure from the exhaust is routed to a finned turbine that in turn spins another turbine

***In this extreme example, you can see the impeller of the Vortech centrifugal supercharger. This spins at extremely high RPM and forces the compressed air into the engine to mix with the fuel mixture.***

*Turbos also use impellers to force air into the cylinders, except a turbo uses exhaust gases to spin them rather than a belt drive system.*

*This highly detailed engine compartment features a well-built small-block that is force-fed by a turbocharger through a carburetor. The carb needs to be modified specifically to handle the rush of air that is pushed through by the turbo's boost pressure.*

*What if one turbo just isn't enough? How about two? Since turbos are turned by the exhaust gasses, it's feasible to have two. Advances in electronic fuel control have made turbos a popular choice as a power adder.*

impeller. A wastegate in the system controls the amount of exhaust pressure driving the impeller and controls the amount of boost on the system. Compressed air can be blown through a carburetor, introduced after the carburetor or used with a fuel injection system. Turbo installations can be done without altering the hood, and intercooler systems lower incoming air temperature and help produce more power.

Be careful! Talk to your aftermarket supplier and follow their recommendations carefully and completely. Weiand, the Blower Shop, B&M, and Blower Drive Service (BDS) are good places to shop for supercharger systems. Nitrous Oxide Systems (NOS), Nitrous Works, and Zex can provide nitrous oxide systems of many different sizes and power levels. Precision Turbo, Turbonetics, and Banks provide turbocharged systems for many different applications and can provide a wealth of knowledge.

## Air Filters

Chevrolet has used metal canisters with various inlet snorkels to hold the air filter. Some high-performance engines used a 14-inch open-element-style with a 3-inch-tall air filter element along with a chrome metal top and bottom. Chevy Performance offers a number of different air cleaner assemblies. These open element filter assemblies are less restrictive than the canister-type air filter assemblies and fit over Holley or Quadrajet 4-barrel carburetors.

Some of the best air filters on the aftermarket are sold by K&N. They are free flowing and can be easily cleaned and reused. Make sure that your hood closes with the taller filter elements. Some vehicles with combinations of high-rise intake manifold, carb, and air filter won't allow you to close the stock hood. You may have to cut a hole in the hood and add a scoop or use a different intake, carb, and air filter combination in order to use the stock hood. Make sure everything fits before you make your parts selections.

Cowl-induction cold-air systems are also available on many different Chevy vehicles. Some vehicles could be ordered with a special cowl air induction system that used a screen and a foam-sealed metal base for cold-air induction. Other Chevy models used similar cold-air packages. Some passenger cars and trucks use a flexible plastic hose that is mounted to holes in the radiator support to bring cold air to the air cleaner canister.

Using cold outside air makes more power, but you must use some sort of filter to make sure that no dirt or foreign objects get into the engine. In fact, most dyno tests have shown that an engine makes more power with a properly designed air filter assembly in place, when compared to an engine running with no filter assembly at all. This is because the filter canisters and bases help to smooth out and channel the airflow into the engine. If there is room under the hood, you can add a taller filter element or stack two filter elements on top of one another to increase the total filter surface area and lower air restrictions.

Racers can use a bell-mouthed velocity stack or one of K&N's Stubstacks to smooth out the airflow into the engine. Once again, there is power to be gained by using some sort of device to smooth the air entry into a carburetor as opposed to not using anything at all. The Stubstack can be used inside a normal paper air filter, and different versions are made to fit 2-barrel and 4-barrel Holley carbs.

Certainly, if you are racing a mud bogger or off-road vehicle, a high-flow capacity, low-restriction air filter assembly is required.

A number of companies make replacement free-flowing cold-air inductions for TPI engines. These aftermarket assemblies add some power to late-model computer-controlled engines, and they don't affect the computer or emissions.

There is one other important aspect concerning air filters and air cleaner canisters: fire. If the engine belches back through the carb, it's very easy to light off the small amounts of fuel that are almost always found in the venturis and the floor of the intake plenum. Usually, it's no big deal and the fire is easily put out if the hood is up and you see it. Air cleaner assemblies usually contain it and the fire quickly goes out itself, either because it runs out of fuel or there is not enough air to sustain it. However, without any filter device on the carb, the flames have more access to air and can continue to burn. If the hood is closed, any hood insulation or paint on the underside of the hood (especially a fiberglass hood or scoop assembly) can catch fire, and things can go from a minor inconvenience to a major disaster very quickly.

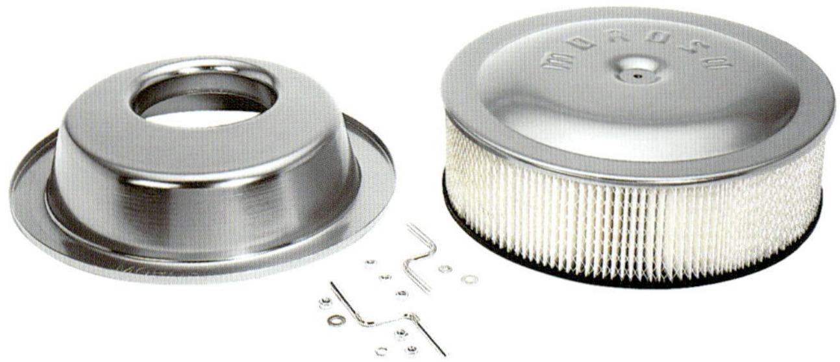


*A good air cleaner keeps dirt out of the engine, diffuses the airflow for smooth entry into the carb, and helps contain a fire if your engine belches or coughs on a bad day. Many size elements are available. (Photo Courtesy Moroso)*

*K&N has a line of air filters that have excellent flow and can be cleaned easily and then reused. They even offer a filter that acts as an air cleaner lid. This combination flows some CFM!*

*The 302 Z28 Camaro with cowl induction is a prized collector model. This small-displacement engine had all the right pieces: forged-steel 3-inch-stroke crank, heavy-duty rods, 11.0:1 pistons, small chamber heads with 2.02/1.60-inch valves, aluminum high-rise intake, and Holley carb. The air cleaner assembly seals to the hood, which helps direct the cool air going over the car into the engine.*

# IGNITION SYSTEMS

This is an area of automotive development that has seen an avalanche of new products and applications and continues to see expansion of available choices. The number of ignition devices designed to increase engine power and flexibility continues to grow. The computer and electronics age has caught up with ignition systems and made many things possible, such as electronically controlled timing curves, rev limiters, and more. It is impossible to cover everything that is currently being offered by aftermarket companies. Keep your eyes open for new developments and materials that fit your goal and application.

Small-block Chevy V-8 distributors are interchangeable with distributors found on Chevy big-block, short deck engines, and that opens a lot of interchange possibilities because so many different types of ignitions and distributors were offered for the small-block and big-block Chevy. Single-point, dual-point, high energy ignition (HEI), magnetic pulse, transistor, capacitive discharge (CD), the OptiSpark, and multiple spark discharge ignitions with rev limiters have been offered through Chevrolet Performance over the years.

If you are doing a restoration, the distributor housings are date coded and stamped with casting numbers that coincide with their respective engine/vehicle applications. The numbers were either stamped into an aluminum ring that was wrapped around the upper part of the distributor shaft housing, had a stamped plate riveted to the housing, or were stamped into the housing itself.

The date codes are in a slightly different order than other casting date codes. You might see a distributor date code such as "9B13," which translates into the ninth year of the decade (9), February (B), 13th day (13). If you are restoring a numbers-matching classic that originally had a point-style distributor, then use the correct point distributor. If you are building a stock engine that is used for everyday driving, a stock production single point or HEI electronic, noncomputer distributor is more than adequate and will provide trouble-free service for many miles. The HEI distributors work well up to 5,500 rpm and the HEI has no points to wear out or replace.

## Distributor Advance

One single ignition timing set point does not work well for the variety of engine RPM requirements and loads that an engine experiences. Engineers developed two different ways for a stock, noncomputer-controlled distributor to alter the ignition timing as parameters change: centrifugal advance and vacuum advance.

The centrifugal advance assembly of a distributor uses springs and weights that are located under the rotor. These weights are spun out centrifugally as engine RPM go up, which in turn advances the ignition timing. The spring tension regulates how fast the weights spin out and the rate of timing advance.

Another part of the advance system is a vacuum diaphragm canister that is hooked up to the point plate. The canister on the distributor

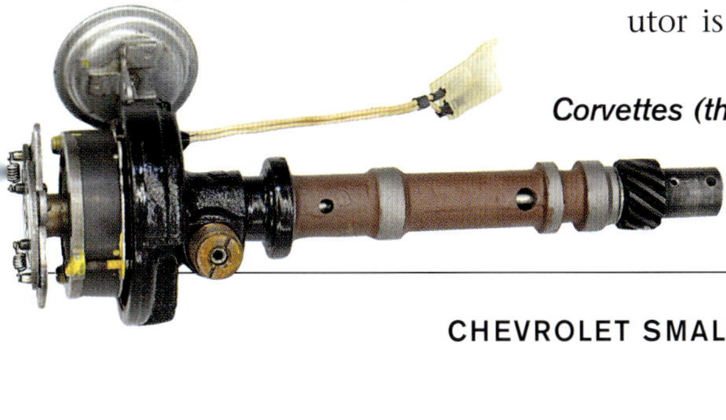

*Corvettes (through the 1974 models) received a special cable-driven tachometer that was driven off a gear assembly mounted on the distributor. Factory Chevrolet "tach drive" distributors are rare, but aftermarket units are available.*

***Single-point distributors were used extensively, and early models had cast-iron bodies while most later styles used an aluminum body.***

***Chevy distributors have casting numbers and casting dates, which can be useful while doing restorations or if you are trying to find out the original application the distributor was used in. This version is from a 1969 Nova.***

***Dual-point distributors were offered by Chevrolet on high-performance applications and are still available from aftermarket manufacturers such as Mallory or Accel.***

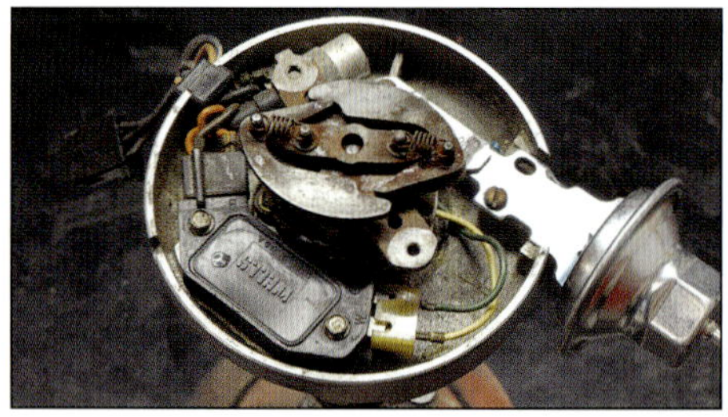

***The springs and weights for the mechanical ignition advance are seen in this noncomputer HEI. They control the amount of total ignition advance and the rate that the advance occurs.***

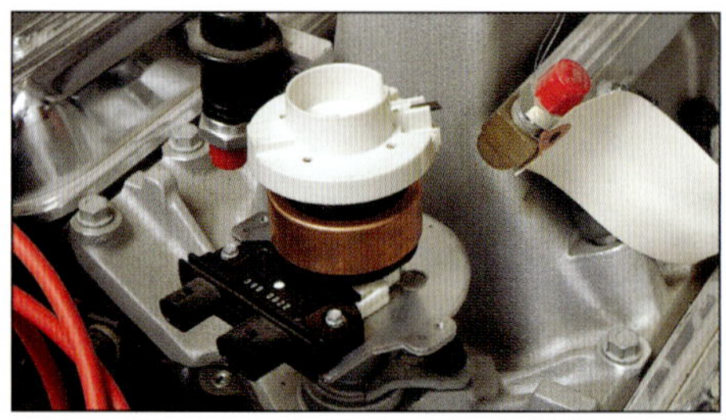

***Late-model injected Gen I engines received an electronically controlled, magnetic pulse distributor with a separately mounted coil, unlike previous HEI distributors, which mounted the coil in the cap. Connectors go to the coil and the ECU.***

is connected by a vacuum hose that is hooked up to a carburetor port. As engine vacuum goes up or down, or as the engine comes under a load, the amount of vacuum acting on the diaphragm changes ignition advance appropriately. The amount of distributor advance given by the vacuum canister is marked on the canister itself. The last two digits of the number is the amount of vacuum advance in crank degrees. These two advance systems, vacuum and mechanical, are separate and in addition to whatever amount of initial advance is put on the front balancer at the timing pointer when you set initial ignition timing.

Be aware that factory stock noncomputer distributors came with different mechanical advance rates and vacuum advance settings depending on what vehicle application the distributor was going into. This created different ignition advance curves for different engines in different vehicles. If you have a used distributor, which came out of a 2-barrel, small-block V-8 station wagon application, it may not have the correct advance curve for a high-performance small-block in a lighter car. The distributor drops right in and the car probably runs with it, but the incorrect ignition curve may prevent the engine from achieving its best power.

The point of this is that whatever application you intend for your engine, the ignition advance must be tuned for that application. In addition, the vacuum canister diaphragms do sometimes fail. This makes the engine feel like it lacks power when you step on the throttle. The canister can be tested by applying suction to the canister nipple and seeing if the arm on the other side of the diaphragm moves the advance plate. The mechanical advance weights can become worn or corrode, affecting the advance as well. The weights can rust or be covered with grime so that they can't move as they should. The springs can also break or the little plastic bushings that the weights pivot on can wear out and get very sloppy. Side play in the distributor shaft itself can develop when the shaft bearings wear out. If you are being driven crazy by a problem causing a lack of engine power or a low speed hesitation, don't overlook the possibility that the ignition advance systems may not be working correctly.

Some performance distributors have no provision for a vacuum advance. In this case, usually you can adjust the mechanical advance to provide the type of ignition advance curve and total ignition advance you need. On some race engines, the desired total ignition advance is determined and then locked into the distributor (no centrifugal or vacuum advance). Running locked-out timing will make it difficult to crank over due to the advanced timing setting, but on race engines a device can be used to retard total timing when the engine is first started. Once the engine fires up, the ignition is switched to full advance timing. If you are driving on the street or the engine is operated at part throttle, then you need some type of ignition advance curve.

## Stock HEI

High energy ignitions (HEI) were introduced on some vehicles in the 1974 model year. They were designed to upgrade from mechanical points to maintenance-free electronics. Surprisingly, the HEI distributor is still available from Chevy Performance as PN 93440806 and is one of the most-popular ways to fire your small-block. The distributor uses an electronic trigger that cannot wear and has an internal ignition module, a centrifugal and vacuum advance, and an integral coil. In short, all you need to do is connect 12 volts and hit the key.

In the mid-1980s, Chevrolet added more electronics to the HEI distributor. If you come across an HEI without a vacuum advance canister, the unit is made to work in tandem with more electronics on the vehicle (that used to control the carburetor). The tell-tale sign between the standard HEI and computer-controlled version is to look at the ignition module. Four-pin modules are the standard HEI with vacuum and centrifugal advance, while five- or seven-pin modules are electronic versions.

Chevy Performance offers a cast-aluminum HEI distributor as PN 93440806. For racing and performance applications, there is also a heavy-duty billet-aluminum HEI (PN 88961867) with a higher-output ignition module and coil.

## Understanding Ignition Advance

Spark advance is the number of crankshaft degrees that the spark occurs before the basic (static or initial) spark timing. It has a great effect on how smoothly and efficiently your engine runs. In order to obtain the maximum pressure on the piston at the optimum position in the power stroke, ignition is often initiated well before the piston reaches the top of the compression stroke. However, as engine speed increases, there is less real time for the ignition process to be completed. Fortunately, flame speed increases nearly proportionally with engine speed—primarily due to the increase in combustion-space turbulence. This means that, for most of the RPM range, the crank angle through which combustion takes place can remain relatively constant. It is fortunate that flame speed is linked to engine speed. If this relationship did not exist, it would be impossible for spark-ignition engines to operate at high speeds because there would be insufficient time for efficient combustion to take place.

The job of the various advance-control mechanisms, whether they are located in an electronic black box or controlled by various mechanical systems in a distributor, is to ensure that the spark is delivered to each cylinder at the correct time to gain maximum work (horsepower) from combustion. This should occur at all speeds from idle up to the rev limit. Timing advance is expressed as the number of crankshaft degrees BTDC that the spark is delivered to the plug. A spark triggered ATDC is said to be retarded. Simply stated, the purpose of spark advance is to harness optimum power from the combustion process regardless of engine speed and load.

### *Initial Advance*

Initial advance is the amount of fixed advance supplied to the engine during the startup period. When the distributor is installed into the engine block and tightened in place, initial timing is fixed. Within the distributor, the rotating breaker point cam or reluctor is mounted on the center shaft. By loosening the hold-down bracket and adjusting the position of the distributor housing in the block, it is possible to change the relative position between the breaker plate and the center shaft, changing the initial timing at which the spark occurs relative to the crankshaft. Once set, the distributor clamp is tightened, locking the housing (and initial timing) in place.

### *Mechanical Advance*

While flame propagation speed increases with engine speed, this relationship is not directly proportional below about 3,000 rpm, especially in low compression engines with low combustion chamber turbulence. From idle to 2,500 to 3,000 rpm, the combustion rate increases much more slowly, and the centrifugal (mechanical) advance mechanism compensates by advancing ignition timing as engine speed comes up from idle. However, as speed continues to climb, turbulence in the charge begins to speed flame propagation and reduce combustion time. This faster combustion rate offsets the need for further ignition advance.

To match these variations in combustion time, most centrifugal mechanisms rapidly advance ignition timing in the lower RPM ranges, but as the engine speed builds,

## Understanding Ignition Advance *(Continued)*

timing is held constant or advances very slightly. If engine speed and best centrifugal advance are plotted on a graph, the curve usually resembles a steep slope up to about 2,500 rpm, followed by a flat plateau at higher speeds. To accomplish this, most small-block distributors are equipped with bob weights and springs that move the breaker point cam or reluctor relative to the distributor center shaft, advancing the ignition point as engine speed increases.

### *Vacuum Advance*

The other major factor affecting ignition timing is the variation in combustion time as the density of the air/fuel mixture changes. Since mixture density is much lower when the throttle is partially closed, cylinder pressure, turbulence, and flame speed are reduced. As a result, more time, in the form of additional ignition advance, is needed to burn the mixture. Since charge density and flame speed are directly related to manifold vacuum, a vacuum-sensitive mechanism is commonly used to increase or decrease advance, independently of the centrifugal mechanism.

Virtually all small-block vacuum-advance mechanisms use a spring-loaded diaphragm connected to the contact breaker or magnetic pickup plate with a linkage arm. At high vacuum levels, the diaphragm is retracted against the spring. This moves the breaker plate in a direction opposite to that of the distributor center shaft, triggering the points or magnetic pickup sooner and advancing ignition timing. As the throttle is opened, vacuum decreases and the spring in the diaphragm assembly returns the breaker plate to its standard position, eliminating the additional timing advance that could otherwise cause ping or detonation at higher engine loads.

It is helpful to view the vacuum advance system as a load-sensitive ignition control. Since the vacuum advance is progressively activated as power demands are reduced (e.g., during cruise), this system is the single most important ignition factor affecting fuel economy during normal street driving. If fuel economy is at all important, equip the engine with a fully functional vacuum advance.

### *Total Advance*

Total advance at any RPM is the amount of timing lead supplied to the engine when all of the variable-advance systems have corrected spark timing. This includes the initial advance put in by basic adjustment of the distributor housing, centrifugal advance supplied by the springs and weights in the distributor, and vacuum advance supplied by the vacuum canister. ■

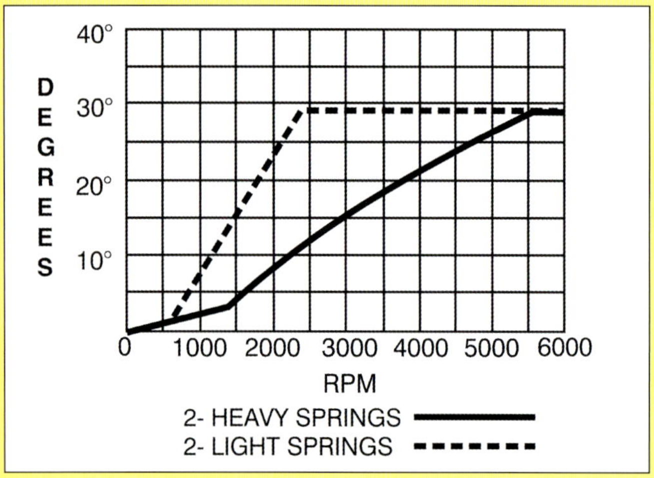


***This chart illustrates two different timing curves that can be achieved by simply changing the springs of the distributor. Note how long it takes through the RPM range for the heavy springs to allow the timing to advance. Conversely, the light springs let the timing ramp up quickly.***

It is very popular to install a stock HEI distributor with vacuum advance into an early vehicle that originally had a stock points distributor. This eliminates the need to replace worn out ignition points. If you do this, remember that the stock HEI needs a 12-volt power supply directly to the distributor. A 10-gauge wire is routed from a 12-volt power source, such as a switched circuit on the fuse block, to the HEI distributor. Do not use a ballast resistor or resistance wire in this HEI circuit. These resistor items are meant to reduce the voltage to a point-type distributor, which will reduce the output of an HEI.

Due to the internal coil, HEI distributors have a large, wide distributor cap that may not fit against the firewall of some vehicles. In this case, you need to use a distributor with a smaller, narrower cap. Keep this in mind, especially when doing engine swaps. If you swap a GM HEI distributor for your old stock point-type distributor, remember that you can generally open the plug gap to 0.045 inch. The HEI provides more power and can fire plugs with a larger gap. The stock noncomputer GM HEI can be updated and improved for high-performance and high-RPM use by using an upgraded module and coil from MSD Performance, Accel, or another aftermarket company. The stock unit lays down above 4,500 to 5,000 rpm and the MSD upgrade enables the HEI to work well up to 9,000 rpm.

Chevrolet also has used another electronic distributor, in the late 1980s and on, due to the introduction of more advanced fuel injection. This computer-controlled distributor (PN 1103952) has no advance weights, nor is there a vacuum advance. The ignition coil was moved out of the cap so an external coil was required. There is a simple, thin metal base plate that holds the module, magnetic pickup, and two wire harnesses with weather-tight female connectors. A different design small rotor is used with a small cap. This cap has male plug wire posts similar to HEI distributor caps and a male center post for the coil wire. Aftermarket ignition companies also offer a drop-in model of this distributor.

## Chevrolet Performance and the Aftermarket

If you are building a high-performance engine for the street or to race and you spin the engine above 5,000 rpm, it is recommended to step up your ignition game. The most common upgrade includes moving up to a multiple spark, capacitive discharge ignition (CDI). Chevy Performance used to offer a CDI as PN 10037378, which can still be found, or you could go to the aftermarket sources such as MSD, Mallory, or FAST.

These CDI are triggered by the distributor but will fire many times on each compression stroke of the engine. During lower RPM, there will be multiple sparks for about 20 degrees of crank rotation. As RPMs go higher, the ignition changes to a single spark on each compression stroke. This result is a more complete combustion process of the air/fuel mixture creating power, cleaner emissions, easier starting, and better fuel mileage.

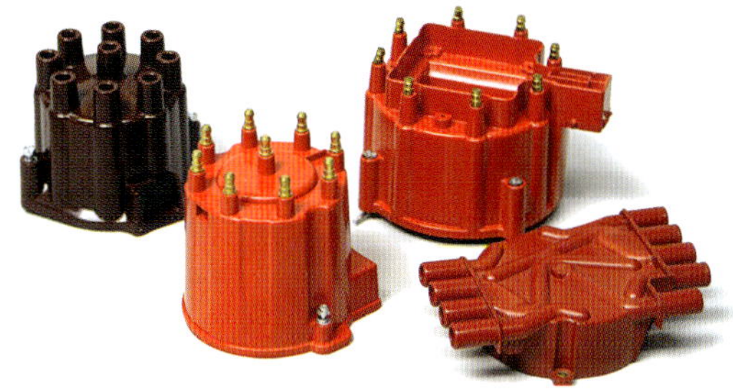

*These are examples of different distributor caps that have been used over the years. The cap at the back left fits single-point distributors. To its right is an HEI, which is much larger and has the ignition coil mounted in the top of the cap. The smaller cap at the front left is used on later-model EFI engines that use an external coil, and the flat-looking cap is used on most Vortech engines of the late 1990s.*

These ignition boxes work with just about any type of distributor to trigger the ignition system. The distributor becomes a switch that tells the ignition box when to turn on and off and routes the spark to the correct plug. Use one of the aftermarket electronic distributors that reliably provide spark to the RPM levels you need with more accurate timing. Point distributors can be modified to spin reliably above 7,000 rpm, but these days it's hardly worth the cost or effort. Electronic distributors with LED mechanisms or magnetic triggers work much more reliably at high RPM and there are no points to replace. It's recommended to upgrade the ignition coil when using a CDI as well. Chevy

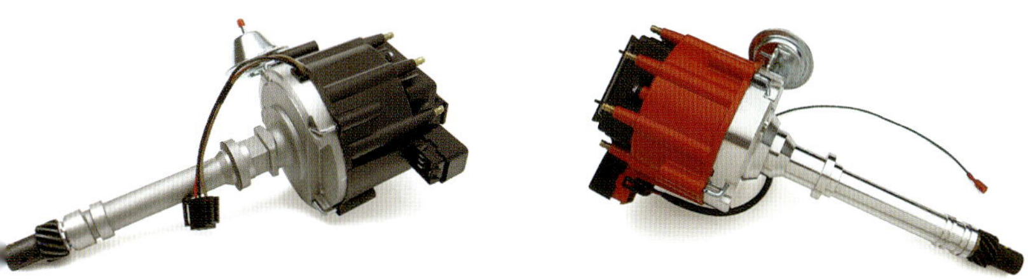

*Though an HEI distributor hasn't been installed in a new vehicle for more than three decades, Chevrolet Performance still offers new models. A cast-aluminum model is available for street use (PN 93440806), while a billet-aluminum version with a high-output ignition module is available for performance and racing use (PN 88961867). (Photos Courtesy Chevrolet Performance)*

*The HEI distributor (PN 1103436) is for noncomputer applications. It has vacuum and mechanical advances with a performance ignition curve. These distributors are very popular for their ease of installation and operation, though their girth and diameter may limit their use in tight engine compartments.*

*The GM internal coil HEI distributor was introduced in 1974 to 1975 as an advanced, electronic replacement to breaker points. These are examples of the two different modules used over the years. In the mid 1980s, General Motors incorporated computer-controlled timing in the HEI module. The noncomputer-controlled module is the most popular and is known as a four-pin module (top). The computer-controller version has seven pins, and the distributor is recognized by its lack of vacuum advance canister.*

*The Chevy Performance billet aluminum distributor (PN 10093387) uses a magnetic pickup to trigger the ignition. When using this distributor, a GM Heavy Duty CD Ignition is required (or an MSD 6A-Series Ignition Control). This distributor also features an easy-to-adjust mechanical advance assembly. (Photo Courtesy Chevrolet Performance)*

used to offer a coil (PN 10037380) to complement a CDI.

One note about the CDI box: They put out a very large amount of electrical energy. If you have ever been zapped by an ignition or plug wire on a point-style or stock HEI, just wait until you touch a leaky plug wire hooked up to the GM/MSD ignition. Be careful! Unlike a traditional ignition system, a CDI uses a capacitor to store voltage directly from the battery. When the distributor triggers the box, the voltage in almost instantly delivered to the coil where it is stepped up even further. Consider this, a standard ignition puts 10 to 12 volts into the primary side of the coil. With a CDI, more than 400 volts are blasted into the coil. Big difference!

Since CDI boxes provide much more ignition power than the stock HEI unit and over a much larger RPM range, spark plug gaps can be opened up from 0.045 inch to as much as 0.060 inch, if you have high-quality spark plug wires that keep the electrical energy in the wires and prevent leakage. A CDI can provide measurable increases in horsepower and torque because of its multiple-spark capability, larger possible plug gaps, and better flame travel in the combustion chamber. Also, because of these improved flame travel characteristics, you can retard the total timing advance on the engine 2- or 3-degrees and richen the carburetor slightly.

To complete an ignition upgrade, Chevrolet Performance offers a high-performance, billet-aluminum, magnetic pickup distributor as PN 10093387 with an adjustable-height hold-down collar. This distributor does not have a vacuum advance and uses a standard-size Chevy cap and rotor. It is important to note that they must be used with a CDI control. The cap and housing of this distributor is about the same size as a points distributor and will clear most induction systems. Smaller cap distributors are available from MSD if you have an induction system that requires more distributor clearance. If you cannot source one of these distributors, most aftermarket ignition companies offer a similar model.

If you are building a higher output engine leaning on the edge of a race-only combination, many CDI can be triggered by a crank trigger system. A crank trigger mounts to the vibration damper of the engine and incorporates a pickup and magnet combination to create a trigger signal. This system is very accurate and reduces ignition timing variables or fluctuations caused by timing chain slack, camshaft twist, or crank vibrations transmitted to the distributor shaft. A distributor is still used, but only to deliver the spark from the ignition coil to the appropriate plug wire. Since a crank trigger requires spacing the crank pulley out, these are typically not used on street engines, especially equipped with power steering or air-conditioning.

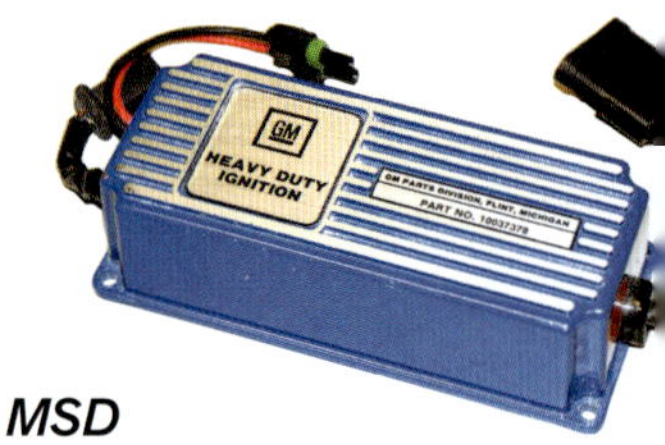


*GM used to offer this Heavy Duty Ignition, which was similar to an MSD CD ignition. Chevy Performance no longer offers them, but you'll see them at swap meets and in online auctions. They can be used with breaker points as well as with magnetic pickup distributors, such as PN 10093387 offered by Chevy Performance. (Photo Courtesy Chevrolet Performance)*

*Chevy still offers an electronic rev limiter (PN 10037379) that plugs directly into the CDI, which is now discontinued. The rev limit was easy to adjust with plug-in RPM modules (similar to the old MSD modules). (Photo Courtesy Chevrolet Performance)*

## Rev Limiters and Timing Controls

One of the benefits, mostly to racers or for serious street engines, is the ability to add RPM accessories and timing controllers. Rev limiters and timing controls are easily added to CDI controls. A rev limiter will pro-

## Advanced Ignition Electronics

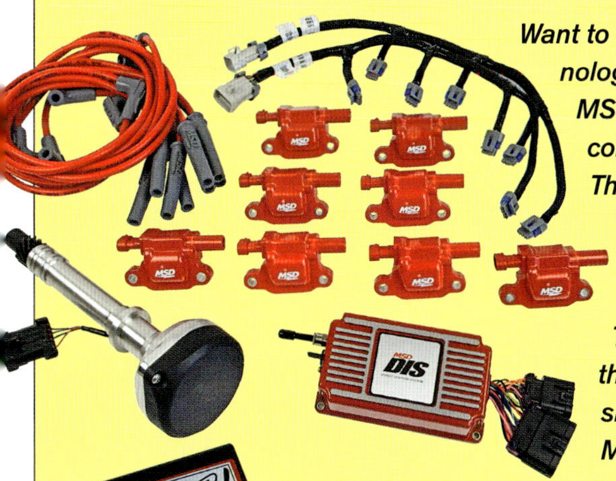

*Want to bring modern ignition technology to your Gen I small-block? MSD offers a complete retro-fit coil-per-cylinder ignition system. The key is a distributor plug that provides both a trigger signal and a cam synchronization signal to the control box. The eight coils are similar to the coils used on the Gen III small-block. (Photo Courtesy MSD)*

*MSD offers a distributor that provides an electronic version of advance weights and springs. The E-Curve Pro-Billet Distributor uses a digital controller to control the timing. Two rotary dials allow you to select from more than 100 different timing curves, including a vacuum advance. (Photo Courtesy MSD)*

*If your engine cranks hard and slow, the timing may be too advanced. MSD offers a Starter Saver that retards the timing 10 or 20 degrees during cranking only to help ease the pressure on the starter. (Photo Courtesy MSD)*

tect your engine from damage in the event of driveline failure or a missed gear. MSD offers a number of different rev limiters and in the case of aftermarket fuel injection systems, you can also program a fuel cutoff to serve as a rev limiter.

If one rev limit is good, how about a two or three rev limiter? A two-step or three-step rev limiter is generally used in drag racing and gives the racer the ability to set a different RPM limit for the burnout, for staging the car, and to use as overrev protection. All of these limiters can be easily tied in to line locks, trans-brake buttons, and other electronic gizmos you may decide to use.

Add-on timing control accessories can also be helpful in racing. As a bracket drag racer, you can set a timing retard to come on when you shift into high gear. The engine is under a heavy load in high gear and total ignition timing can be retarded a few degrees for more power. Another use for the retard box is with a nitrous race engine. With nitrous, the timing needs to be retarded depending on the amount of retard. Boxes with a single timing retard, or multiple retards for multi-stage nitrous systems are also available. For turbo and supercharged applications, there are also timing controls available that will retard the timing based on boost pressure.

Most performance ignition manufacturers offer a number of add-on accessories such as RPM-activated switches, shift lights, adjustable timing controls, and more. A lot of these components used to be adjusted with little plug-in modules that are commonly called chips. Ever hear a racer talk about "putting it up on the chip," well that means the rev limit module that was installed. However, in our modern age of computer controls, some higher-end racing systems can be programmed from a laptop or handheld tablet. MSD's PowerGrid programmable ignition allows racers to map a timing curve for each gear, manipulate the timing to each cylinder, and more. If you can imagine it, it can be done through the PowerGrid.

For racers running boost, high compression, or other huge power-producing engines, CDI are available in race-only models with different outputs. MSD offers a 7AL-2 and MSD 8 that produce extreme amounts of voltage and spark energy. In short, there's a CDI out there for nearly any kind of racing to fire your small-block.

One of the latest ignition innovations available through the aftermarket is a coil-per-cylinder ignition system. When the Gen III small-block was introduced, it was conspicuously lacking a distributor and fitted with eight individual coils. Today, you can install a complete distributorless ignition system onto your Gen I or II small-block. MSD's system incorporates a distributor plug, which is still driven from the cam gear and turns the oil pump. It has electronics in it that send a trigger signal to the ignition system to fire each coil at a specific time. The benefit is more accurate trigger signals and increased programming control over the ignition timing.

## Alternators

Many racers who use a high-powered ignition box choose to remove the alternators and recharge the battery between rounds using a portable generator and battery charger. Their feeling is that they recover some lost power because there is no parasitic loss from the drive belts to the alternator and it drops a few pounds off of the front end of the vehicle. The problem that can arise is that modern race ignitions, and other electron-sapping components, can take a fully charged battery down from 13.5 to 10 or 11 volts during a single pass down the track. This swing in output voltage will affect the operation of the ignition, fuel pump, ECU, and other components.

Consistency also suffers because the battery voltage is fluctuating and falling. Electric fuel pumps are affected by the drop in battery voltage, and total pump volume can decrease. Putting the alternator back on the car improves consistency and provides full battery voltage during an entire quarter-mile pass. This is especially important in the late rounds, when the turnaround time between elimination rounds gets shorter and there is not much time to charge a battery.

An alternative is to use a 16-volt battery system on a race engine, which essentially carries more reserve voltage. Battery voltage still falls without an alternator, but the voltage stays high enough to run your ignition and fuel pumps properly. Using a 16-volt system and an alternator can help you make those quick turnaround late elimination rounds when there is not much time to recharge a battery. Note that if you opt to run a 16-volt battery, you'll need a charger designed to function properly with the higher voltage battery.

Alternator technology has come a long way, and there's almost no reason not to have one installed on your race car. Powermaster Performance offers compact, lightweight alternators that will keep your race battery charged. Their 100-mm XS Denso unit weighs under 8 pounds, can be mounted low on your engine, and will provide more than 70 amps at higher RPM. Another helpful feature is that the output is actually adjustable, so if you decide to step up to a 16-volt battery, you just turn a potentiometer to increase the charging output.

Chevy Performance offers a 90-amp alternator for competition as PN 88958690. This unit is based on a common CS 121 housing and features a serpentine belt pulley. If you plan to run a V-belt pulley, you may consider a large, deep-groove pulley with a deep belt groove.

A deep V-belt groove will help keep the belt stay in place at higher RPM. The alternator speed is reduced, V-belts stay on, and the parasitic power loss is probably less than 1 hp with a fully charged battery. Even with an alternator, during a two-day race the alternator may not be run long enough to fully recharge the battery. If you have a number of other electronic gizmos (delay boxes, two-step rev limiter, electric fan, electric water pump, electric solenoid shifter, etc.), you still will have to recharge the battery between rounds with a portable generator and battery charger in addition to using the highest amperage alternator you can use.

As far as losing the weight, you can find somewhere else to reduce weight. You could go on a diet and lose 5 pounds and accomplish the same thing.

## Plug Wires

Spark plug wires are an integral component to the ignition system, as well as being important to the overall performance of your small-block. It is important that you realize that plug wires need to be considered as a maintenance item. They operate in a harsh environment with excessive heat, vibration, and voltages.

Another important aspect of plug wires is their ability to suppress electrical interference. As the electricity pulses through a spark plug wire, it causes electromagnetic interference (EMI), sometimes referred to as radio frequency interference (RFI). EMI can cause other electronics in the vehicle, such as the ignition or fuel injection ECU, to freeze up or function erratically. To combat these effects, you need to run a suppression or spiral wound wire, which Chevy Performance or a number of aftermarket companies offer.

***The alternator plays an important role in the performance of the ignition system and other vehicle electronics. Powermaster offers a number of high-output alternators, or if you're looking for something smaller, its Denso style 100-mm delivers good amperage in a compact and lightweight housing.***

PN 12361051 is a set of suppression wires designed specifically for the small-block. The wire features a conductor with only 600 ohms of resistance for effective suppression characteristics. The heavy-duty red wire is cut-to-fit with black 90-degree booths and terminals. A 10-inch coil wire is also supplied. To keep the wires secure, Chevy offers optional wire looms (PN 12496806, PN 12495502, or PN 12342049).

If you're looking for a different color or style spark plug wire, the aftermarket is ripe with choices from MSD, Taylor, Moroso, Accel, and more. You can choose a custom-fit set or a universal kit that allows you to cut each wire to length for more of a custom installation. There are also a lot of different plug boots and terminals to choose from.

## Spark Plugs

Different spark plug types have been used over the years. From 1955 to 1969, cast-iron heads used 3/4-inch reach, 13/16-inch hex, gasketed plugs. From 1970 to the present, production cast-iron heads used 3/8-inch reach, smaller 5/8-inch hex, tapered seat spark plugs. Cast-iron Bowtie Phase 2 heads use a 3/8-inch tapered, 5/8-inch hex plug. Aluminum Bowtie heads use a 3/4-inch reach, tapered or gasketed spark plug. Pay attention to what size and length spark plug is recommended by the cylinder head manufacturer.

Spark plugs used in aluminum heads should have their threads coated with anti-seize to help prevent corrosion and thread pullout on the heads.

If you are going to use heads with an angled spark plug entry, keep in mind that spark plug access can be a problem. Depending on the type of exhaust manifold or tube header you use, the exhaust may hit the plugs or prevent the use of a socket to remove or install the spark plugs. Later-model production exhaust manifolds used on Corvettes, Firebirds, Impala SS, Caprices, and Z28 Camaros, which were originally fitted with angle plug heads, provide the clearance you need and may fit in your vehicle engine compartment. Header manufacturers have different versions of their products to fit angle plug heads. Let them know what you are using when you order. There are some spark plugs on the market with shorter, smaller diameter porcelain sections, which are meant to give you a little more clearance room to install the plugs in angle plug heads.

Remember, if you build an engine using parts from different engines, you must determine what year your cylinder heads were made and use the spark plug type for that year. For example, a 327 block with a 1968 block casting date using cylinder heads cast in 1974 needs the spark plug type used in 1974 because Chevrolet changed to a 5/8-inch hex tapered seat plug in 1970.

Spark plug gaps vary with the type of ignition system you use. A single-point stock distributor and coil fire plug gaps of 0.035 inch. A vehicle using a stock HEI uses plug gaps of 0.045 inch. The Gen II engines with a front-mounted Opti-Spark ignition use spark plug gaps of 0.050 inch. CDIs can fire plugs with even larger gaps of up to 0.060 inch. Blower or nitrous engines may find that smaller plug gaps work better. You need to make sure that the rest of the ignition system, such as plug wires and distributor caps, can handle higher electrical power. Any weakness in any part of the ignition system allows leaks, because, like water, electrical current flow follows the path of least resistance.

*Spark plug size has changed over the years. Large 13/16-inch hex was used until 1970. Smaller 5/8-inch plugs were used after that year. Check the casting date of the heads you are planning to use to determine which plugs to use. It is possible to thread the wrong type of plug into the heads.*

## Distributor Drive Gears

If you change from a camshaft made from cast iron, like most factory non-roller cams, to a steel billet roller cam, you may need to change the distributor gear. Some cam manufacturers are making steel cams with a cast iron or alloy distributor drive gear that works with stock distributor gears. Check with your cam supplier.

Chevrolet offers a melonized distributor gear (PN 10456413), which is required on all of the crate engines and Chevy Performance camshafts.

*If you are using a steel roller camshaft in a racing engine, you may need to change the distributor drive gear to a bronze gear. Bronze gears will wear, so they are not recommended for use on street engines.*

## Small-Block Spark Plug Tech

Prior to 1970, all small-block Chevy cylinder heads were machined to accept 14-mm, 3/8-inch reach, flat-seat spark plugs with sealing washers (left). These plugs have 13/16-inch hex heads. In 1970, Chevrolet continued using 14-mm threads but switched to 5/8-inch reach, tapered-seat plugs. These later plugs all have 5/8-inch hex heads. Tapered-seat plugs are a better choice when indexing the plug electrodes with the piston domes. If galling becomes a problem with tapered seat plugs, use anti-seize compound on the threads.

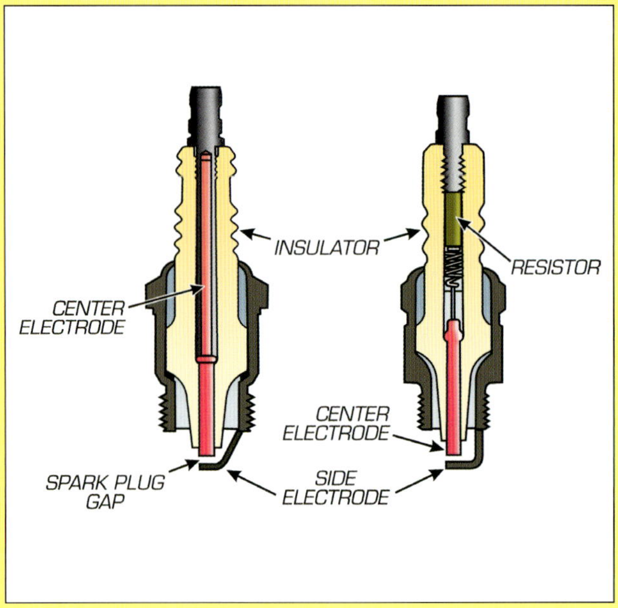


This cutaway gives you an idea that not all spark plugs are created equal, or at least not for every application. The center electrode must be well insulated and sealed to keep the voltage isolated so it must jump to the ground electrode. The plug on the right has a resistor built in to help reduce radio and other electronic interference.

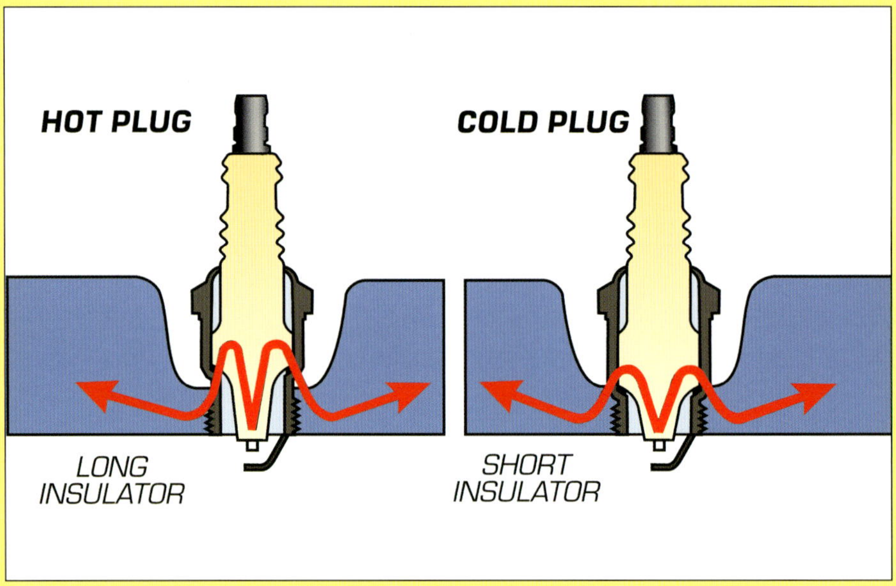


A colder spark plug (on the right) has a shorter insulator tip to promote quicker heat dissipation of the heat through the housing and to the cylinder head. The longer insulator helps the plug retain heat, which may help a high-mile or a poorly tuned, rich-running engine.

Projected-tip plugs were designed for applications where cylinder contamination from leaking valve guides and piston ring blowby require a hotter plug tip to prevent fouling. Most late-model engines are equipped with powerful HEI systems that reduce the need for projected tips. A good rule of thumb is to use the factory-recommended plug and heat range unless you have a definite fouling issue that requires a plug modification.

CHAPTER 9

# Exhaust, Cooling, and Engine Swaps

From 1955-on, small-blocks came with a variety of cast-iron exhaust manifolds, and in some late-models, with tubular stainless steel exhaust manifolds. These manifolds also had differing shapes, exit angles, exhaust dumps in different locations, and bolt bosses to help mount accessory brackets. Some of the manifold runners ran above the spark plugs and some had runners that ran below the spark plugs. A few extremely rare optional Z28 302 Camaro tube headers were available. These were shipped uninstalled in the trunk of the Camaro Z28s from the factory, then the dealer or owner installed them.

Chevrolet designed these differently shaped manifolds with the primary goal of moving the exhaust gases to the rest of the exhaust system while still fitting in the particular vehicle and mounting whatever accessory brackets were necessary at the time. Almost all small-block exhaust manifolds bolt onto a small-block head, but the manifolds may not physically fit inside a specific engine compartment. Frame crossmembers, steering boxes, firewalls, upper control A-arms, and steering links might get in the way if you use an exhaust manifold that was designed to be used in a different vehicle. Other manifolds may interchange and fit in the engine compartment. On some later-model passenger-side exhaust manifolds, the rear exhaust manifold bolt hole has been moved slightly to the rear to fit seven-hole cylinder heads.

The least-restrictive Gen I cast-iron factory manifolds were the large-diameter-outlet ($2^1/_2$ inches) Corvette ram's horn manifolds that had a straight down exhaust exit. These manifolds, originally developed in the mid-1960s, are not available from Chevrolet any more, but you can search them out under PN 3797901 LH and 3814970 RH. Both of these manifolds come with mounting bosses located on the side of the manifold, so you can mount a generator or an alternator on either side with a short water pump and the appropriate upper and lower mounting brackets.

PN 3846563 LH is another $2^1/_2$-inch-diameter-exit ram's horn, driver-side manifold, but it has a mounting boss on the front end of the manifold to accommodate a generator or alternator. Most production ram's

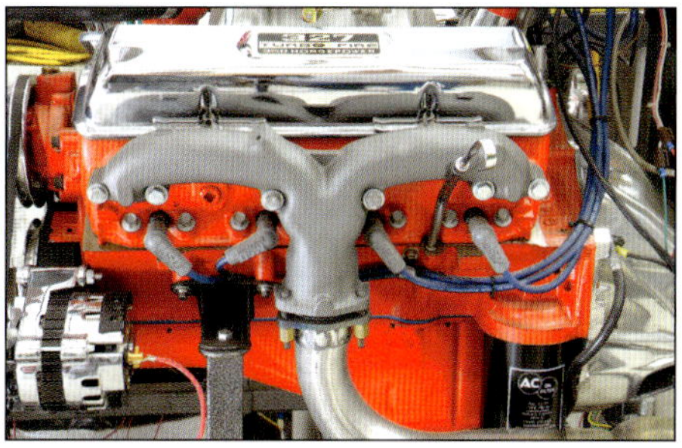

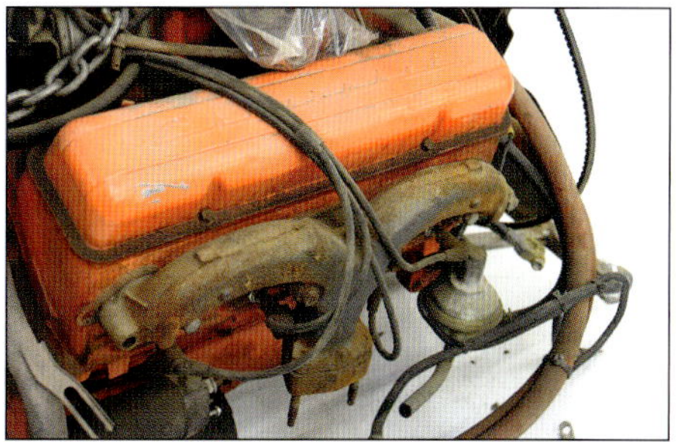

*These factory-style cast-iron exhaust manifolds are from an early 1960s engine and are commonly called a ram's horn design. Note that the spark plugs are under the runners and there is no provision for an alternator or accessory bracket. There were many modifications made over the years on small-block exhaust manifolds.*

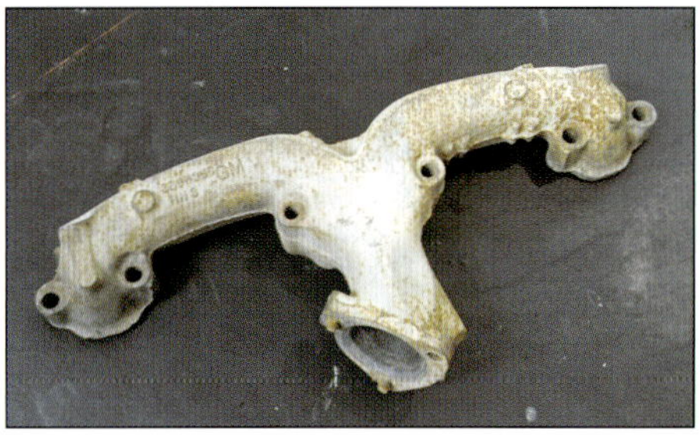

*This factory cast-iron exhaust manifold is designated for the passenger bank of the engine (note the "RH" cast into the manifold). This manifold (casting number 3896956) was used during 1967 and 1968 model years.*

*Shown is a production exhaust manifold found on Gen II LT1 350. Most, but not all, exhaust manifolds bolt up to any Gen I or II production head; however, the exhaust manifold may not fit in the engine compartment of a particular vehicle. This style of "log" manifold is favored for its rear exit and narrow profile but not for its performance.*

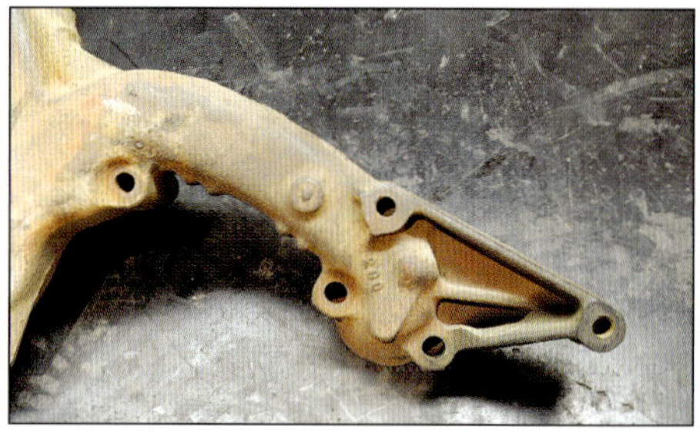

*This ram's horn cast exhaust manifold has a provision to mount the generator/alternator on the passenger side.*

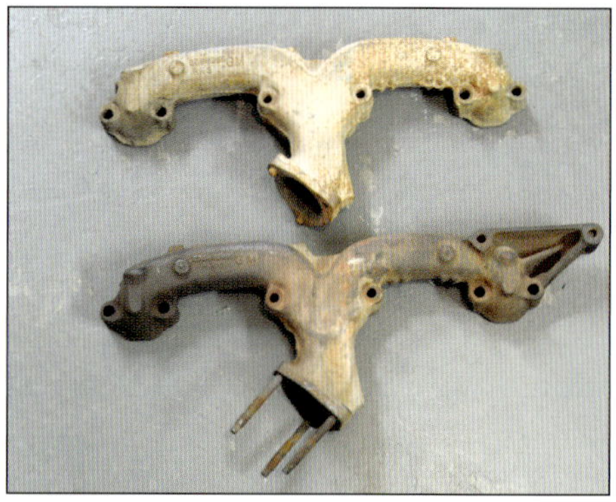

*Early ram's horn exhaust manifolds came with different bolt bosses to mount accessories. These two passenger-side examples also show the difference in outlet angles. Diameters varied in size with up to 2½ inches found on some high-powered Corvettes.*

horn exhausts had smaller-diameter exhaust outlets of 2 inches. Some production ram's horn manifolds had a straight, center dump exit, and others had an exit that was slightly angled toward the rear.

The 1986 to 1990 Corvettes used tubular stainless steel exhaust manifolds that had a center exhaust dump. These were listed as PN 10055734 RH and 14087511 LH and are readily available on forums and enthusiast sites. Make sure that these exhaust manifolds fit in your vehicle's engine compartment before you do an interchange. These manifolds do have A.I.R. fittings and tubes.

Chevy Performance offered a number of stainless steel Tri-Y tubular exhaust headers available for 1985 to 1992 Camaro and Firebird applications. The mandrel-bent primary tubes are $1^5/_8$ inches in diameter and have a 3-inch-diameter outlet. A.I.R. tubes and fittings are in place. These tube headers were designed to work with low-restriction exhaust systems, including the low-restriction catalytic converters, but they can be adapted to other applications. Depending on the vehicle and model year application, these small-block V-8 Tri-Y headers were offered under PN 12341404 through 12341408 and would need to be found at a swap meet or reseller.

If you are building a performance engine and you have significantly improved the induction side of the engine, you must also improve the exhaust side of the system. It does little good to put in a larger cam, better intake manifold, carburetor, and performance heads and leave on the restrictive cast-iron exhaust manifolds and stock exhaust pipe system. The increased air/fuel volumes flowing into the engine must also be able to flow out of the engine. The factory production cast-iron manifolds, especially the log type found on many small-block-equipped vehicles are quiet and long lasting, but they are restrictive. Adding a good, well-designed, low-restriction exhaust system frees up horsepower in a street-driven small-block.

Factory cast-iron exhaust manifolds bear cast-in part numbers and casting dates, which may be important if you're doing a numbers-matching restoration. The casting numbers are visible when the manifolds are in place. The casting dates, however, are generally on the side of the manifold that faces against the engine, and they can't be seen once mounted to the engine.

Be careful when buying used cast-iron exhaust manifolds if they are off an engine. Many of the exhaust manifolds crack with age and leak when you install them. The cracks may be under the heat shields and can't be seen. If the exhaust manifold is still installed on a running engine, listen for any cracks and leaks before you buy.

*The manifolds on this 1996 Impala SS (Gen II small-bock) have been swapped out for a set of headers. The aftermarket must incorporate factory A.I.R. connections to meet strict emission standards.*

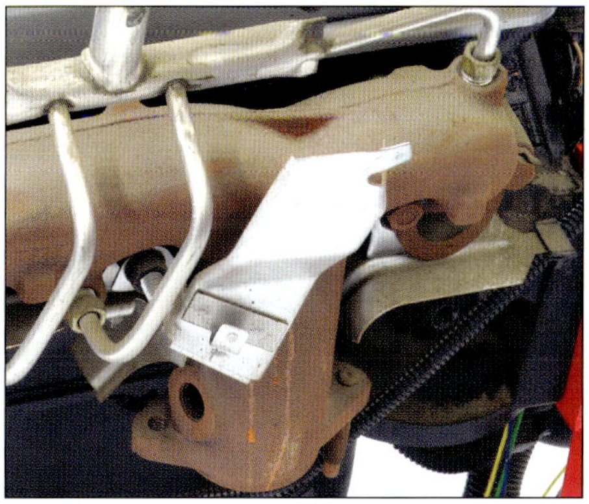

*Spark plug heat shields were installed on a variety of OEM applications. These should always be retained to help protect the plug wires from the extreme exhaust temperatures.*

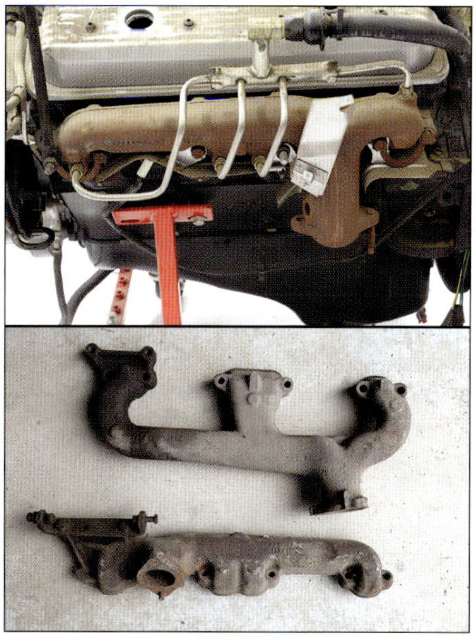

*Cast-iron exhaust manifolds have come in many shapes over the years. Some have provisions for A.I.R. fittings and some do not. Some have heat shields and some do not. Note the various positions used for the exit dump.*

*More and more race associations are requiring mufflers on race cars in order to keep racetrack neighbors happy. This drives the performance muffler makers to provide better systems with lower noise levels while still providing exceptional flow without restriction. Magnaflow produces stainless steel exhaust kits for a variety of applications. Note the single inlet with dual outlets.*

Chevrolet used cast-iron and a few stainless steel exhaust manifolds on all small-block engines, and you can interchange these between Gen I, Gen II, and Vortec production engines. Depending on the make and model year, however, changes have been made in the runner shape, outlet angles, and the number of exhaust bolt holes of these manifolds in order to fit various vehicle chassis and engine compartments. All Gen I and II small-block cast-iron exhaust manifolds physically bolt up to any production Gen I or II small-block head, but the manifolds from one vehicle style may not fit in a different vehicle. In addition, air injection tubes were added to the exhaust manifolds of later models to help lower emissions.

To avoid the spark plug access problems sometimes created when using angle plug heads, use the production exhaust manifolds or tube headers that were designed to provide enough clearance with those heads. If you run into a clearance issue, you can also try a spark plug with a shorter, small-diameter porcelain section.

With the stock factory exhaust manifolds, try to use a dual exhaust system of at least 2-inch pipe on a stock engine and 2½ to 3-inches on a performance street engine with tube headers. A crossover pipe that connects the two tailpipe assemblies helps the system breathe and may lower the decibel level of the exhaust. The stock exhaust manifolds and some factory catalytic converters and mufflers can be restrictive, so anything you can do to reduce restrictions in the system helps.

Low-restriction catalytic converters that are street-legal and pass 50-state emissions requirements are also available from aftermarket sources, as are low-restriction mufflers. Now, I said low-restriction, not loud. Just because a muffler is loud does not mean it is a low-restriction muffler. In fact, many airflow tests have shown that some of the loudest mufflers are also some of the most restrictive. Many aftermarket companies have spent the time developing low-restriction street exhaust systems. Some of these muffler systems approach or equal the power levels of open exhaust headers, yet they are much quieter. If you are racing in a restricted class or at a track that requires mufflers, some power can be gained by selecting a good, low-restriction muffler and exhaust system.

*Flowmaster is known for its low-restriction, high-flow mufflers. The power levels in many of the modern muffler designs are equaling, and in some cases surpassing, the power found with open exhausts.*

*"Shorty" tube headers are available from several aftermarket companies. This example is from Edelbrock. These are required in tight engine compartments or cars with low clearances.*

*This small-block-powered 1964 Chevelle features Hooker metallic ceramic-coated Super Competition tube headers. The coating reduces underhood temperatures and will keep the headers looking good for years to come.*

## Tube Exhaust Headers

Aftermarket tube exhaust headers are available for straight or angle plug head applications. They're also available in different lengths and diameters. If you are considering using them, remember that they are noisier than cast-iron manifolds, and they don't last as long, unless they are made with rust-resistant materials or coatings. However, a good tube header increases your gas mileage and produces more power because the engine breathes better. You can order air injection tube fittings for the headers that you choose. Also, many header makers now offer special coatings that preserve the finish, make them more heat and rust resistant, and help them make slightly more power.

Most stock or mildly modified small-block engines can use a street header with a tube diameter of 1⅝ inches and about 32-inch-long primary tubes, with a collector diameter of 3 inches and about 6 to 8 inches long. Race engines can use larger diameter tubes and collectors, depending on many variables. Smaller, longer primary tubes generally result in more low- and medium-RPM power. Larger diameter primary tubes with large-diameter short collectors, tend to produce more power at a high, narrow RPM band and less power at low and medium RPM.

Tube headers come in many tube lengths, tube diameters, and collector sizes. Street headers are compromises by header makers. They are designed to work with a number of possible engine parts and installation challenges yet still produce more power than a stock cast-iron manifold. Race headers are specifically designed for a particular engine parts combination and vehicle to produce as much power as possible.

Hooker Headers have been in the performance exhaust business for many years. Call them, and let them help you make the correct choice for your particular application and vehicle, whether your system uses mufflers or open exhaust.

When you switch from cast-iron manifolds to tube headers, you can usually jet up from the stock carb settings and perhaps use slightly less ignition advance. However, some engine combinations may benefit from different tuning decisions. Check the spark plug color or your elapsed times and miles per hour; they let you know what the engine wants.

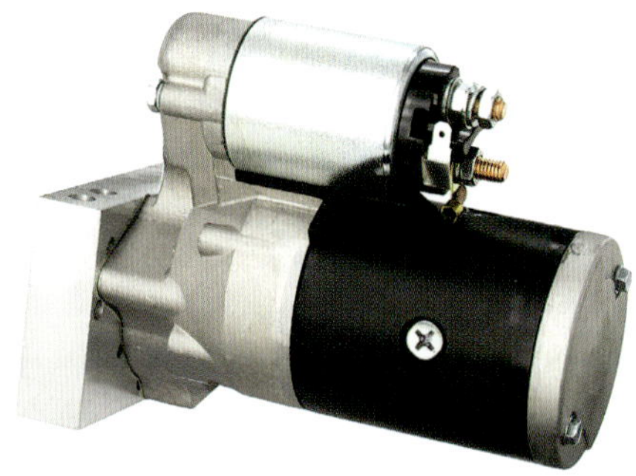

*Unless you're going for a numbers-matching restoration, it's best to go with a gear reduction mini-starter. PN 12361146 is a high-torque unit that weighs less than 11 pounds and delivers more torque than the full-size units from the old days. (Photo Courtesy Chevrolet Performance)*

## Starter Shield

If you install a set of tube exhaust headers and then have a problem starting the car when the engine is at operating temperature, try installing a starter heat shield. Header tubes passing near the starter in some vehicles radiate enough heat to cause starter solenoid problems. The starter heat shield solves the hot soak solenoid blues.

Another option to help avoid any cranking issues is to move to a

## Horsepower and Torque

Here are two old standby, often quoted, equations for calculating horsepower and torque. There is a problem with using them, however. Each equation requires that you know either horsepower or torque before you use them. You need a dyno run before you can accurately use the equation. There is a solution, but let's look at the equations first.

HP = (RPM x Torque) / 5,252
Torque = (5,252 x HP) / RPM

See what I mean? You want to know the horsepower and torque of an engine, but since you don't know the horsepower and torque, how can you plug in the required amounts to use the equations? If you had the actual dyno figures for horsepower and torque, you wouldn't need these two equations. By the way, the number 5,252 is a constant in these equations. Because of a constant in the math, torque and horsepower are always equal at 5,252 rpm. When you look at a dyno output graph, the line for torque and the other line for horsepower always cross at 5,252 rpm and are equal at that point.

So what do we do now? Well, try this if you can't afford dyno rental prices. Weigh your vehicle, with you in it, at the nearest truck scales. They usually only charge a few bucks for the privilege. Then take your vehicle to the nearest drag strip. Make a number of runs without changing anything so that you get a pretty good idea of what the average elapsed time (ET) and miles per hour (MPH) are. Then try the following formula:

HP = Weight x 0.4 x (quarter-mile mph / 282)

An example would look like this:

HP = 3,200 pounds x 0.4 x (110 mph / 282)
HP = 3,200 x 0.4 x 0.3900709
HP = 499.29072

You can flip this equation around to find quarter-mile mph, now that you know HP and vehicle weight.

Quarter-mile mph = (HP / Weight) x 282 / 0.4
Quarter-mile mph = (499 / 3,200) x 282 / 0.4
Quarter-mile mph = 0.1559375 x 282 / 0.4
Quarter-mile mph = 43.974375 / 0.4
Quarter-mile mph = 109.93593 mph

You can round that off to 110 mph.

Now you can solve for 1/4-mile ET.

Quarter-mile ET = (Weight / HP) x 5.825 x 0.3333
Quarter-mile ET = (3,200 / 499) x 5.825 x 0.3333
Quarter-mile ET = 6.4128256 x 5.825 x 0.3333
Quarter-mile ET = 37.354709 x 0.3333
Quarter-mile ET = 12.450324

You can round that off to 12.45 ET.

Now, the use of these three equations does not take into account the variables found at a drag strip, such as track surface, weather, driver's reaction, etc., but they can get you in the ballpark without having to take your engine to the nearest dyno facility.

You can solve that torque equation now that you know horsepower.

Torque = (5,252 x HP) / RPM
Torque = (5,252 x 499) / 6,500
Torque = 262,0748 / 6,500
Torque = 403.192 ft-lbs at 6,500 rpm ■

gear reduction starter, such as Chevrolet Performance's PN 12361146. A gear reduction starter is lighter and smaller than a traditional starter, plus it creates much higher torque. This is accomplished through the use of a gearset in the starter that typically produces a 4:1 ratio. In the end, the starters use a higher speed motor to produce higher torque, which is important when cranking over performance engines. Also, with their smaller package, gear reduction starters are not as affected by the excessive heat of exhaust manifolds or headers.

### Water Pumps and Brackets

Short or tall water pumps mount and interchange between Gen I engines. Tall cast-iron (PN 12685965),

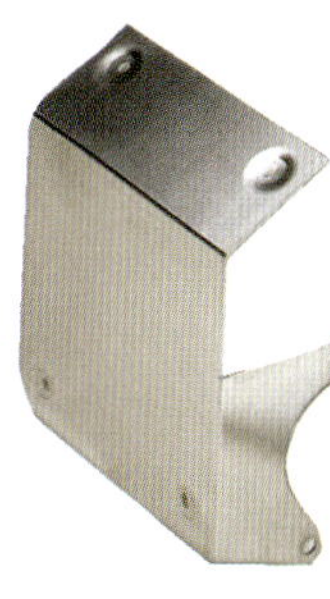

***Starters are squeezed between the engine block and the exhaust manifolds—a tough environment for an electrical component. Moroso offers a couple different heat shields that block the heat from the starter motor to ensure operation.***

***Two types of Gen I water pump heights have been used over the years: short and long. Each requires that you use accessory brackets and pulleys to match your type of pump. If you need room at the front of your engine compartment, the short pump should be used.***

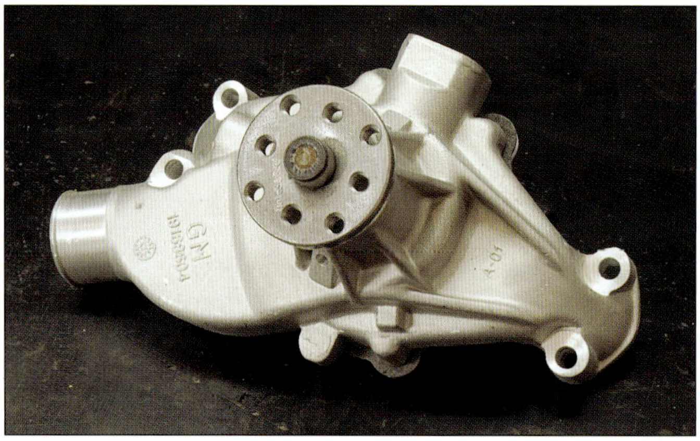

***This Chevy aluminum heavy-duty small-block water pump is the short style (PN 19168604). It removes some weight from the front of a vehicle and has a dual-bolt pattern to mount the fan.***

short cast-iron (PN 10048921, obsolete), and short aluminum (PN 19168604) water pumps are available from Chevrolet Performance. In 1969, most Gen I engines were switched from a short water pump to the tall pump (Corvettes kept the short water pumps until 1982, and the 1975 to 1980 V-8 Monza also used a short pump). Tall and short-leg cast-iron versions can be used to fit various vehicles.

Depending on which length you use, you must use the accessory brackets and pulleys that fit a short or a tall pump. Spacer kits are available from aftermarket suppliers to convert a short water pump into a tall water pump application.

If you are using a late-model serpentine belt system, you must mount a reverse-rotation water pump and its associated brackets and pulleys. Chevy Performance offers a replacement pump (PN 89060527), which is cast iron and set up for counterclockwise rotation.

If you are going to use a long water pump, you need cylinder heads that have the accessory mounting holes in the ends of the heads in order to mount the accessory brackets that are used with long water pumps. Short water pump applications, such as those used on 1974 to 1982 Corvettes, can use alternator bracket PN 14015539 (cast-iron) or PN 14015510 (aluminum).

Gen II engines use a water pump that works with reverse-flow coolant engines. On these engines, coolant is circulated into the front of the block and then sent directly to the heads. From there, the coolant flows from the front of the heads to the rear of the block, then forward in the block and out. Gen II water pumps are driven by a gear and shaft that are connected to the cam timing gear. These pumps are not interchangeable to Gen I engines.

If you are trying to find a set of V-belt or serpentine belt brackets and pulleys and you have enough room, you also can use the assemblies found on 90-degree V-6 engines. Many of these have the same setup as a Gen I small-block V-8. The 90-degree 4.3-liter V-6 engines are commonly called three-quarter small-blocks. These are basically 350s with two of the middle cylinders removed (number-3 and number-6). The front and rear faces of the block are the same as the front and rear of the Gen I small-block V-8.

Many parts on the 90-degree V-6 engines are interchangeable with the Gen I small-block V-8s,

***This Gen II water pump is shaft-driven off of the cam gear. It is unique to the Gen II engines and is not interchangeable to other small-block engine families. Note the position of the thermostat housing on the pump as well.***

including accessory brackets, pulleys, water pumps, timing chains, gears and timing covers, valvetrain parts, pistons and rings, camshaft bearings and main cap bearings, dampers, flywheels, and flexplates. The 90-degree V-6 engines were produced from 1978 through the late 1990s and they have been made in 200 (bore 3.5/stroke 3.48 inches), 229 (bore 3.74/stroke 3.48 inches),

## Transmissions

Transmission choices depend once again on what your intentions are. There are some interesting choices for the street, which work with the Chevy small-block. The now venerable Muncie 4-speeds are available, but they are getting harder to find outside of specialty shops. The last ones were factory installed in 1974. Late-model small-block vehicles could be ordered with 4- or 5-speed manual transmissions. Plus, the aftermarket is ripe with overdrive manual transmissions.

Depending on the torque output of your engine and the type of vehicle use you intend, you have a number of choices of gear ratios, including overdrive on some. If you are seriously racing a vehicle with a manual transmission, it is hard to beat the Liberty, Jerico, or Lenco 4- and 5-speed transmissions for strength, ease of maintenance, and the number of possible gear ratios available.

Automatic transmissions such as the 2-speed Powerglide, 3-speed Turbo 350, and 400s can be used on the street and, if raced, can be upgraded for additional strength. Racing with a 2-speed Powerglide should be limited to vehicles less than 2,800 pounds with driver, while the 3-speed autos help launch a heavier car with an additional low-gear ratio. The Chevrolet auto trannie cases had different engine-mounting bolt hole patterns than those fitted to Buick, Oldsmobile, or Pontiac (BOP) engines; however, a number of companies make easy-to-use adapter plates that allow you to use a BOP bolt pattern T-400, for instance, with a Chevy V-8.

Later-model 4-speed overdrive transmissions such as the 200-4R, 700-R4, or electronic models such as the 4L60E or 4L80E have been used by engine swappers who want the low first gear found in these transmissions for performance while still retaining the overdrive final gear for decent mileage when on the highway.

Before selecting a trans, you need to make an honest appraisal of how much power your engine is making to ensure the trans will be reliable and have the strength to hold up. A stock small-block may work with an upgraded and strengthened 700-R4, but if you have a large-torque, high-power engine, a 4L80E series overdrive automatic may be a better starting place.

The "E" transmissions are computer controlled and will require a trans control to function. Chevy Performance offers several versions of its popular electronic transmissions including the 4L60E, 70E, and 85E, as well as the control ECU. There are also adapters to convert the electronic speed sensors to a mechanical speedometer. ■

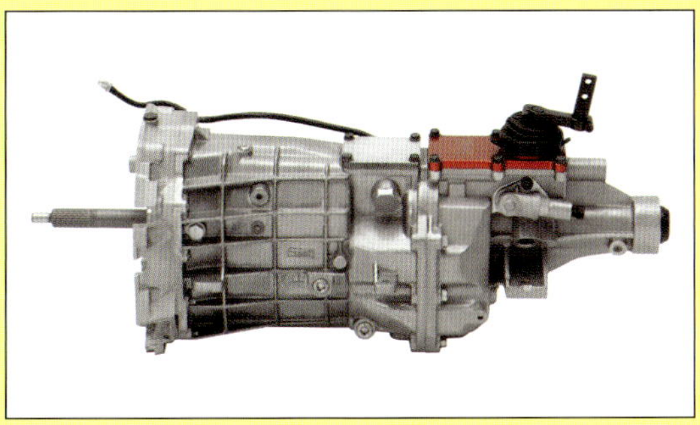

*When it comes to transmissions, you just can't beat the low-RPM cruising speed of an overdrive. Chevy Performance offers several 4-speed automatic transmissions that are electronically controlled as well as a T56 Super Magnum 6-speed manual trans (PN 19352208). (Photo Courtesy Chevrolet Performance)*

*Accessory brackets can be a challenge when a small-block is being transplanted in a different car. There are a variety of kits available to mount the alternator, power steering pump, or air compressor. Make sure tall valve covers or headers don't present a problem with your installation.*

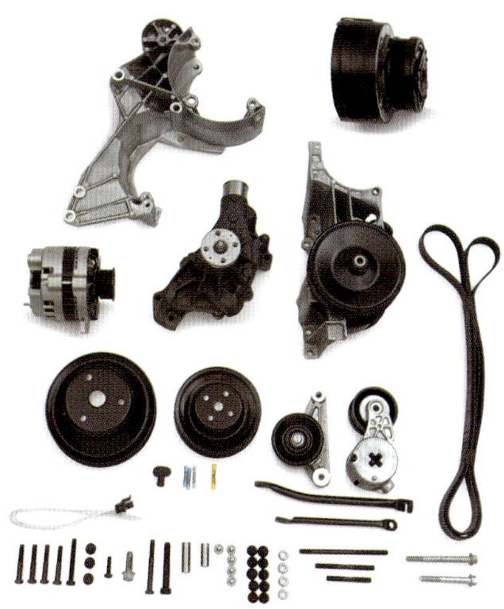

*Chevy Performance now makes it easier to get your accessories all dialed in and aligned properly with a complete kit. Two are available: PN 19369258 provides an air-conditioning compressor, while PN 19369257 only has the power steering and alternator brackets. Both are serpentine systems and are supplied with a long water pump, hardware, and a new belt. (Photo Courtesy Chevrolet Performance)*

and 262 (4.3 liters, bore 4.0/stroke 3.48) cubic-inch displacements.

If you are restoring a correct numbers-matching classic, use the proper water pump, brackets, and pulleys for that vehicle. The water pumps have casting numbers and casting dates that were found on particular vehicle types. If you are doing an engine swap, choose a long or short water pump and the accessory brackets that match them. If space between the radiator and the fan is narrow, you can use the early style short water pump and related brackets and pulleys to gain a few inches of clearance.

*Moroso offers a 5-inch-diameter deep-groove alternator pulley, which helps keep the V-belt on a high-RPM small-block. The larger diameter slows the alternator speed, so keep that in mind if you have an engine that idles high and has an overdrive transmission, as the charging system may not be up to snuff. (Photo Courtesy Moroso)*

## Deep Pulleys

High-RPM engines work better with deep-groove pulleys on the crank, water pump, and alternator. These help prevent V-belts from flying off at higher RPM. Chevrolet used to offer a 6⁵/₈-inch diameter deep two-groove crank pulley for use with short-leg water pumps as PN 3858533. The corresponding two-groove, 7¹/₄-diameter, short-leg water pump/fan pulley was PN 3770245. There was also a deep, wide-groove alternator drive pulley (PN 3829387) that was 3⁵/₈-inch diameter. If you cannot find these obsolete part numbers, the aftermarket sources will get you dialed in with deep-groove performance pulleys.

*Different pulleys are available from aftermarket suppliers than underdrive accessories. Make sure the accessories turn over fast enough to keep the engine cool or sufficiently charge the battery. Deep-groove pulleys help keep V-belts on at high engine RPM. Make sure to match the pulley styles to the type of water pump you are using, whether it is a short or tall pump, V-type, or serpentine belts. This engine is using a dual-serpentine system to drive the blower with a second belt for the water pump, power steering, and alternator.*

## Underdrive Pulleys

With the advent of serpentine belt systems and reverse rotation water pumps, many aftermarket manufacturers are offering underdrive pulleys that free up a few horsepower on late-model engines. The pulleys work, but make sure that the water pump still turns over quickly enough to cool your engine adequately. Likewise, if you have a lot of electrical power accessories, such as a high-power stereo system, the alternator needs enough alternator RPM speed to keep the battery charged.

## Thermostats

All engines should use a thermostat. The thermostat not only controls the coolant temperature but also places a designed restriction on how fast the coolant flows through the engine. Without a thermostat, the coolant can flow so quickly through the engine that there is not enough time for the fluid to pick up engine heat and the engine may never warm up to operating temperatures. Chevrolet has used 160-, 180-, and 195-degree Fahrenheit thermostats. If water temperatures reach above 230 degrees, serious engine damage can be done. An engine that runs too cool does not boil off water vapor in the crankcase and won't produce all of the power it is capable of. Oil flow may also be sluggish in a cold engine.

Small-block Chevy and big-block Chevy thermostats are interchangeable. Many late-model computer-controlled engines can benefit from a 160-degree or 180-degree thermostat, if you have changed parts and improved performance. The lower coolant temperature can help avoid detonation.

## Water Temperature Senders

The water temperature sender in early engines was mounted in the intake manifold, and early cylinder heads did not have a mounting boss and hole for the sender. Later model designs mounted the sender in the driver-side cylinder head.

If you can, use a water temperature gauge instead of an idiot light. The gauge gives you advance warning of any problem. However, an idiot light only lets you know about problems when it's too late.

## Radiators, Fans, and Fan Shrouds

Depending on the application, Chevrolet used different-size radiators to match cooling requirements, and the radiator frame supports usually had different sets of bolt holes to accommodate whatever engine and radiator were installed. Generally, when a small-block with air-conditioning, heavy-duty cooling, high-performance engine, or towing package was ordered, the vehicle received a larger radiator with more cores and greater fin area. A larger fan with more blades was often added.

*Muscle car and street rod enthusiasts are expecting late-model drivability and technology from their 40-year-old street machines. This 1956 Corvette, built in the late 1990s, was fit with an LT4 small-block and retains the factory fuel injection and accessories. (If it was built today, there would likely be a Gen III Chevy in its place.)*

If you install a small-block in a vehicle that originally had a 6-cylinder or 4-cylinder radiator and fan, keep these larger radiator requirements in mind. Also, keep the fan shroud; it makes a big difference in cooling.

Make sure that the radiator itself is clean inside and out. Most local radiator shops can rod out a used radiator or add cores or larger tanks to restore its full cooling abilities. Aftermarket suppliers can provide a new, correct radiator for your application or an upgraded aluminum radiator for most applications.

Keep road debris from building up on the front of the radiator. Also, using plain water in a radiator is looking for trouble. At least a 50-50 mix of antifreeze and water inhibits the formation of rust and corrosion, raises the boiling point of the coolant, and protects the engine during cold months.

Chevrolet often used a clutch fan in small-block applications. The clutch disengages the fan at higher RPM, so that the parasitic horsepower losses from the fan are reduced. Some of these clutch fans are temperature controlled. It's a nice feature, and if one fits in your street application, it will be advantageous.

There is sometimes a temptation to get rid of the fan shroud. It may be difficult to get on and off, or it may be cracked or broken. If it is missing or damaged, replace it. The fan shroud makes the radiator and fan much more efficient. The engine runs cooler with a shroud in place, because cool outside air is pulled directly through the radiator. Also, nothing freaks me out more than working around a running engine that has fan blades spinning out in the open with no shroud to help keep someone from getting their arms or hands torn off.

*With a few well-chosen performance parts, a stock small-block really wakes up. One horsepower per cubic inch is easy, still very reliable, and durable.*

*For aesthetics, you can pick and choose from different valve covers, air cleaner covers, and more things to match the style of your vehicle. This well-dressed small-block has a vintage hot rod look to match the shoebox it powers.*

Today's electric fan technology has really come a long way with very efficient fans. You need to ensure that your charging system is up to supporting the current demands of an electric fan, but there are also benefits. Generally, you can control the activation temperature point of the fan through a sensor or even a controller. If you're in a pinch for space, an electric fan (or fans) may be the best bet.

## Emissions

You thought I was going to skip this part, didn't you? Well, I can't and neither should you. If you live in a state, a region of a state, or a municipality that requires that your street-driven vehicle be able to pass an emissions test, then your vehicle must pass the test in order to be registered and driven—period. Don't bother trying to get around it; it's not worth it. If your vehicle needs an air pump or catalytic converter to pass inspection, leave them on. If the emissions test includes a visual inspection of the factory-installed engine and related emissions equipment, for that vehicle year, you can fail the test if the parts are not there. You can fail the visual test even though the tailpipe emissions may be within the accepted norms.

Depending on whatever regulations you must live by, you may be able to replace a smaller 4- or 6-cylinder engine with a small-block V-8, if a small-block V-8 was offered in that same vehicle and model year as a factory-installed engine. If so, related small-block emissions equipment are available from Chevrolet for that model year.

Aftermarket suppliers are doing their very best to supply performance parts that meet stringent 50-state-legal emissions requirements, and these parts can be interchanged with factory-installed parts. Cylinder heads, intake manifolds, camshafts, tube headers, free-flowing catalytic converters, mufflers and exhaust pipes, and fuel injection systems that improve performance and have been certified to pass 50-state emissions requirements can all be purchased. Check with your local and state emissions authority before making your parts purchasing decisions for a street-driven, emission-regulated vehicle.

## Engine Swaps

Two of the great advantages to using a Gen I small-block Chevy in an engine swap are its compact size and the parts cost. Dollar for dollar, the Chevy delivers more power for less money than any other brand of engine. More parts are available, both from Chevrolet Performance and the aftermarket, than those made by or for the other guys. This includes swap kits that allow you to use a small-block Chevy in practically anything you set your mind to. Engine mounts, transmission adapters, transmission mounts, exhaust manifolds, or tube headers to fit your vehicle, chrome parts, you name it, it's being made by someone. Small-block kits are made to put small-block V-8s in Vegas, Mustangs, Porsches, Mercedes, Jaguars, airplanes, any street rod,

4WD Toyota SUVs, Corvairs, road racers, boats, Jeeps, even motorcycles, and three wheel trikes, just to name a few. If it needs an engine, chances are someone somewhere has swapped a small-block Chevy in it.

Of course, if you have a Chevy vehicle with a 4- or 6-cylinder engine or a big-block, most of the time a small-block conversion can be accomplished. It may take some scrounging for parts or a little fab work here and there, but it's possible. The transmission bellhousing bolt pattern used with straight 6-cylinder engines and on 90-degree V-6s is the same as that used on small-block and big-block engines. If your project has a straight-6, the existing transmission bolts right up to a small-block V-8. If not, there are many transmission adapters available to connect the two.

## Engine Break-In

When you have your new engine installed and you are ready to start it for the very first time: Stop! Resist the temptation to fire it up. Instead, one more time, check to see if you are really ready to start the engine.

Is everything hooked up?

Did you or your helpers actually tighten all the bolts down or are some of the bolts just finger-tight?

Is there actually oil in the engine? Is the oil filter on? Is the oil pressure takeoff fitting on the engine?

Insert an engine oil priming tool into the distributor hole. If you don't have one, you can make one from an old points distributor (just take off the mechanical advance weights and plate and the point plate, leaving the top end of the shaft. Then grind off the teeth on the drive gear on the bottom of the shaft.) When you have inserted this in the engine, use a 1/2-hp electric drill to turn the priming tool in a clockwise rotation. Keep turning the tool until you see oil coming out of all of the rocker arm oil feed holes. You may have to turn the engine over slightly, maybe one-half to one full revolution, to expose all of the oil passages in the engine. When oil runs out of all of the rocker arms' feed holes, you know that the air that was in the oil passages has been forced out. Always oil prime an engine before it is started for the first time. Now, you can install the distributor that you intend to use. Add a can of GM Engine Oil Supplement (EOS) (PN 88862587, 1 quart). The EOS is an excellent oil supplement that helps cam and engine parts break in.

- Is there coolant in the radiator? Are all the hoses clamped in place?
- Are all of the vacuum lines hooked up? Are all of the vacuum ports on the carb or on the intake manifold that you are not going to use plugged?
- Are the accessory belts on and are they tight?
- Are the fuel lines hooked up to the fuel pump and the carb? Are they tight? Are the exhaust pipes hooked up?
- Did someone put in the engine mount through bolts and tighten the nuts down? Was the torque converter bolted to the flexplate?
- Is the distributor rotor in the correct firing position or is it 180 degrees off? Are the spark plug wires attached to the plugs and distributor in the correct clockwise firing order (Gen I and II = 1-8-4-3-6-5-7-2)? Do you have a timing light already attached and ready to set the timing?
- Do you have extra water, oil, transmission fluid, and a fire extinguisher close at hand if you need them?
- Do you have a ratchet and the correct socket handy to make a final adjustment on the rocker arms?
- Is someone watching the oil pressure gauge to make sure that there is oil pressure when the engine fires?
- Is the ignition hooked up? How about the throttle linkage? Is the throttle linkage return spring hooked up? Starter wires? Is there enough gas in the tank to run the engine for 20 minutes? Is the transmission in park or neutral?
- Is everybody safe?

Yes? You're ready? Hit the key. Sounds great! Nice job! But wait, there's more to do. Turn the idle up on the carb, so the engine is idling at 2,000 to 2,500 rpm. Did the oil pressure come up? Is the engine running smoothly? If not, find out why.

Check for air, vacuum, water, fuel, or oil leaks. Any weird noises?

Oil pressure still okay? How about the water? Do you need to add some more? Does the automatic transmission need more fluid? What's the water temperature?

Everything still okay? If so, run the engine at high idle for 20 minutes. Don't let the engine idle fall below 2,000 rpm. This ensures that the cam and lifters have enough oil splashed on them to prevent cam lobe failure and properly break in the cam.

After 20 minutes, adjust the idle screw back down to the normal idle RPM. Adjust the idle mixture screws on the carb. Then set the dwell on a points distributor, if that is what you are using, and set the timing. Adjust the lash on the rocker arms while they are hot. You can retorque the head bolts if you need to. Put the valve covers on. Make another check for leaks. Everything still cool? Change the oil and oil filter and top off the fluids.

Okay. Let's take your Chevy for a ride!

A.B.S. Products
591 W. Apollo St.
Brea, CA 92821
714-671-0728
abs-products.com

Accel Performance Products
P.O. Box 10360
Bowling Green, KY
42102-7360
866-464-6553
accel-ignition.com

AirBorn Coatings
108 Rush St.
Mount Holley, NC 28120
800-986-4646
jetcoat.com

ATI
6718 Whitestone Rd.
Gwynn Oak, MD 21207
410-298-4343
atiracing.com

Automotive Racing Products (ARP)
1863 Eastman Ave.
Ventura, CA 93003
805-339-2200
arp-bolts.com

The Blower Shop
880 W. Amity Rd.
Boise, ID 83705
208-985-7650
theblowershop.com

Brodix Cylinder Heads
301 Maple
Mena, AR 71953
479-394-1075
brodix.com

Callies Performance Products
P.O. Box 926
Fostoria, OH 44830
419-435-2711
callies.com

Chevrolet Performance
chevroletperformance.com

Cloyes Gear and Products Inc.
7800 Bal Rd.
Ft. Smith, AR 72908
479-646-1662 ext. 228
cloyes.com

Comp Cams
3406 Democrat Rd.
Memphis, TN 38118
800-999-0853
compcams.com

Crane Cams
8649 Hacks Cross Rd.
Olive Branch, MS 38654
866-388-5120
cranecams.com

Crower Cams
6180 Business Center Court
San Diego, CA 92154-5604
619-661-6477
crower.com

Dart Machinery
353 Oliver St.
Troy, MI 48084
248-362-1188
dartheads.com

Eagle Specialty Products (E.S.P.)
8530 Aaron Lane
Southaven, MS 38671
662-796-7373
eaglerod.com

Earl's Performance Products
P.O. Box 10360
Bowling Green, KY
42102-7360
866-464-6553
holley.com

Edelbrock Corporation
2700 California St.
Torrance, CA 90503
310-781-222
edelbrock.com

Elgin Industries
1100 Jansen Farm Dr.
Elgin, IL 60123
800-323-6764
elginind.com

FAST (Fuel Air Spark Technology)
3406 Democrat Rd.
Memphis, TN 38118
877-334-8355
fuelairspark.com

Federal-Mogul Corporation
27300 West 11 Mile Rd.
Southfield, MI 48034
248-354-7700
federalmogul.com

Fel-Pro Corporation
7450 N. McCormick Blvd.
Skokie, IL 60076
847-674-7700
fel-pro.com

Ferrea Racing Components
2600 NW 55th Ct., Ste. 238
Ft. Lauderdale, FL 33309
954-733-2505
ferrea.com

Fluidampr
180 Zoar Valley Rd.
Springville, NY 14141
716-592-1000
fluidampr.com

Goodson Shop Supplies
156 Galewski Dr.
Winona, MN 55987
800-533-8010
goodson.com

Hedman Performance Group
12438 Putnam St.
Whittier, CA 90602
562-921-0404
tdperformance.com

Hilborn Fuel Injection
22892 Glenwood Dr.
Aliso Viejo, CA 92656
949-360-0909
hilborninjection.com

Holley Performance Products
P.O. Box 10360
Bowling Green, KY
42102-7360
866-464-6553
holley.com

Hooker Headers
P.O. Box 10360
Bowling Green, KY
42102-7360
866-464-6553
holley.com

JE Pistons
10800 Valley View St.
Cypress, CA 90630
714-898-9763
jepistons.com

Jesel
1985 Cedar Bridge Ave., Ste. 2
Lakewood, New Jersey 08701
732-901-1800
jesel.com

K&N Engineering
P.O. Box 1329
Riverside, CA 92502
800-858-3333
knfilters.com

Lunati
8649 Hacks Cross Rd.
Olive Branch, MS 38654
662-892-1500
lunatipower.com

Manley Performance
1960 Swathmore Ave.
Lakewood, NJ 08701
800-526-1362
manleyperformance.com

Moroso Performance Products
80 Carter Dr.
Guilford, CT 06437
203-453-6571
moroso.com

MSD Performance
P.O. Box 10360
Bowling Green, KY
42102-7360
866-464-6553
msdignition.com

Nitrous Oxide Systems (NOS)
P.O. Box 10360
Bowling Green, KY
42102-7360
866-464-6553
nosnitrous.com

Oliver Racing Parts
5339 M66
North Charlevoix, MI 49720
231-237-4515
oliverracingparts.com

Performance Distributors
2699 Barris Dr.
Memphis, TN 38182
901-396-5782
performancedistributors.com

Powermaster Performance
1833 Downs Dr.
West Chicago, IL 60185
630-957-4219
powermasterperformance.com

Precision Turbo & Engine
616A South Main Street
Hebron, IN 46341
855-996-7832
precisionturbo.net

Ross Racing Pistons
625 S. Douglas St.
El Segundo, CA 90245
800-392-7677
rosspistons.com

Summit Racing Equipment
1200 Southeast Ave.
Tallmadge, OH 44278-3161
800-230-3030
summitracing.com

Total Seal
22642 North 15th Ave.
Phoenix, AZ 85027
800-874-2753
totalseal.com

Turbonetics
14399 Princeton Ave.
Moorpark, CA 93021
805-581-0333
turboneticsinc.com

Vortech Engineering
1650 Pacific Ave.
Oxnard, CA 93033
805-247-0226
vortechsuperchargers.com

Wiseco Performance Products
7201 Industrial Park Blvd.
Mentor, Ohio 44060-5396
800-321-1364
wiseco.com

World Products
19654 Eighth St. E
P.O. Box 1608
Sonoma, CA 95467
707-996-5201
worldproducts.com